ASSESSMENT DEBATES

edited by
Tim Horton
at The
Open University

HODDER AND STOUGHTON
LONDON   SYDNEY   AUCKLAND   TORONTO
in association with The Open University

This reader forms part of the Open University course E271 *Curriculum and Learning*. For further information on the course, write to School of Education (E271), The Open University, Walton Hall, Milton Keynes M17 6AA.

This reader is one part of an Open University integrated teaching system and the selection is therefore related to other material available to students. It is designed to evoke the critical understanding of students. Opinions expressed in it are not necessarily those of the course team or of the University.

The E271 course team is against the use of sexist language and gender stereotyping. We have tried to avoid the use of sexist language in this reader but some examples may remain from the original articles, and for this we apologise.

British Library Cataloguing in Publication Data

Assessment debates. – (Curriculum and learning).
   1. Great Britain. Education. Assessment
   I. Horton, Tim   II. Open University   III. Series
   379.154

   ISBN 0-340-54008-7

First published 1990

Typeset by Butler & Tanner Ltd, Frome and London
Printed for the educational publishing division of Hodder and Stoughton Ltd, Mill Road, Dunton Green, Sevenoaks, Kent by Clays Ltd, St Ives plc.

CONTENTS

ACKNOWLEDGMENTS

The Publishers would like to thank the following for permission to reproduce material in this volume:

Centre for Language in Primary Education for the extracts from 'Reading Tests' by Barry Stierer from M. Barrs and E. Laycock (eds) *Testing Reading* and *The Primary Language Record* by Barrs, Ellis, Hester and Thomas; Falmer Press for 'School Examinations – Some Sociological Issues' by Jan Eggleston from P. Broadfoot (ed) *Selection, Certification and Control* and 'An achievement-led college' by Jenny Shackleton from J. Burke (ed) *Competency-based Education and Training* (1989); C. Gipps, S. Steadman, T. Blackeston and B. Stierer for the extracts from *Testing Children: Standardised Testing in Local Education Authorities and Schools*; HMSO for the extracts from *National Curriculum Task Group on Assessment and Training: A Report* and from *Records of Achievement: Report of the National Evaluation of Pilot Schemes* by P. Broadfoot, M. James, S. McMeeking, D. Nuttall and B. Stierer; Nafferton Books for 'TGAT: A conflict of purpose' by Patricia Murphy from *Curriculum* Vol 9, No. 3, Winter 1988; National Union of Teachers for 'Testing Teachers? A Critical Look at the Schools Council Project "Extending Beginning Reading"' by Barry Stierer from *Primary Education Review*, No. 13, Spring 1982; Open University Press for 'The Need for Change' from Murphy and Torrance (eds) *The Changing Face of Educational Assessment* and 'Negotiation and Dialogue in Student Assessment and Teacher Appraisal' by Mary James from H. Simons and J. Elliott (eds) *Rethinking Appraisal and Assessment* and 'Assessment in NVQs: Disentangling Validity from Reliability in NVQs' by John Burke and Gilbert Jessup; Scottish Academic Press Ltd for the extract from *Assessment: A Changing Practice* by Sally Brown; Ward Lock Educational for 'What is reading: Which model?' by Elizabeth Goodacre from M. St J. Raggett, C. Tutt and P. Ragget (eds) *Assessment and Teaching in Reading*.

Every effort has been made to trace and acknowledge ownership of copyright. The publishers will be glad to make suitable arrangements with any copyright holders whom it has not been possible to contact.

INTRODUCTION

Testing in schools and colleges has never been a fad. In one form or another, the assessment of pupils and students has been a constant part of life in educational institutions.

A quarter of a century ago the vogue in literature in assessment was for new insights into the procedures that surround testing, say – eleven-plus and university entrance. The reappraisal of approaches towards assessment in the late 1960s and 1970s was however as much concerned with *purposes* as *techniques*. The initial divide was between assessment for selection against assessment for curriculum appraisal, but, as the contributors in the first part of this book make clear, the actual, as well as potential reasons, for conducting assessment broadened too. In the United Kingdom, the movement towards greater central government engagement with curriculum and the form establishment of a national curriculum in England and Wales led to attempts to fuse separate traditions in assessment. Several contributors indicate a sense of unease about the use of date collected for a specific purpose but used for another.

In parts two, three and four of the book, there are close examinations of three arenas for assessment. One is well established, that is reading, but here much contemporary research data is brought to bear on familiar topics. The other two debates – records and profiles and tertiary education, involving vocational qualification are marked out by altogether more contemporary movements. The contributors to these studies are primarily taken up by the *practice* of assessment and from this vantage point add to our understanding of why assessment is carried out.

part one
CONTEMPORARY ASSESSMENT ISSUES

INTRODUCTION

The Education Reform Act (1988) overhauled not only curriculum control in England and Wales, but also introduced a 'new language' to school-level assessment. The changes seem often to be overwhelming for teachers who might take only a little comfort in the fact that other countries have also embarked on substantial reform in education and training. Sally Brown, until 1990 Director of the Scottish Council for Research in Education, traces the broadening notion of 'assessment' but implies that concerns for validity and reliability are timeless. The current 'multiple-purpose' concept of assessment is that the 'range of qualities assessed' should be increased as well as the 'contexts in which that assessment takes place'. Murphy and Torrance in Chapter 1.2 cite Macintosh and Hale in describing six purposes of assessment: diagnosis, evaluation, guidance, grading, selection and prediction. They argue generally for more informal assessment processes in schools.

One crucial issue features in the first of two articles from the main report of the Task Group on Assessment and Testing (TGAT). Progression was sought in several Schools Council working documents, but no attempt had been made to utilise the assessment system to this end. The concept in TGAT was to provide statements for all students that not only indicate performance relative to peers, but indicate the next stages or activities for study within *programmes of study*. Chapter 1.4 makes it clear that the TGAT report entails a good degree of compromise with organisational realities of schools. This leads towards the use of the same data for both formative and summative purposes – an exercise called into question by Patricia Murphy in Chapter 1.5. She suggests: 'The lack of relationship between a subject-based cognitive description of knowledge and the process by which pupils' understanding develops and is deployed, is a central inconsistency within TGAT's proposals.'

Robert Wood seeks a position that is seemingly more radical. He argues that it may be desirable to differentiate educational from psychological measurement and to 'ignore psychology altogether'. He examines how McIntyre and Brown, after Ryle, assert the importance of 'mastery' not only as a sound educational objective, but as an achievement altogether more capable of measurement than the knowledge of principles and concepts.

In Chapter 1.7, John Eggleston quotes Patricia Broadfoot's paraphrase of Karl Marx: 'assessment has become the opium of the people'. Following

Durkheim, Eggleston considers the particular role of examinations as instruments of social control. In order to explore the issue he considers 'who' and 'what' should be examined – and what value to place on the process. His analysis – historical as well as contemporary – suggests that users of the examination system are 'remarkably conservative – unwilling to devote time or effort to improve qualifications'. Altogether, examinations provide a means for legitimating social status.

1.1 ASSESSMENT: A CHANGING PRACTICE

SALLY BROWN

A SCENARIO FOR CHANGE

Change can be unsettling, sometimes overwhelming, but it can also be motivating and bring about real progress. In the field of assessment, a great deal of talk over the last decade has been about change and substantial attempts have been made to introduce new practices. Different practices usually reflect different ideological commitments, and one of the most salient features of the movement has been the recognition that assessment, as part of education, must be about promoting learning and opportunities, rather than about sorting people into social roles for society.

There are, of course, those who say that there has been no basic change in assessment practices, and indeed there is evidence of resistance from groups with vested interests in holding on to the past. This tendency to try to hang on to the traditional and tested methods at a time when a new philosophy and practice of assessment is being introduced has resulted, in some circumstances, in confusion and impossible demands on practitioners. However, it is important to emphasise that much valuable and ordered progress has been made in this field. Ideas about assessment are discussed and debated among policy-makers, practitioners and researchers more, and more openly, than in the past, and this has led to greater understanding of its role in, and effect on, the education of young people. [...]

THE TRADITIONAL VIEW OF ASSESSMENT

It is not so long ago that the notion of 'assessment' in schools and colleges carried with it, in the United Kingdom at least, a vision of tests or examinations, certificates and grades or lists of marks. All of these were regarded as very important and as providing objective, reliable and precise measures of achievement. The use to which such measures were put was primarily one of the *selection* of young people for such things as further study, training courses, apprenticeships or careers. This system had the great advantage of administrative simplicity: it made comparisons among individuals (norm-referencing), and everyone knew that a grade B performance was better than a grade C and a mark of 49 was less than 51. It appeared to provide an effective means of sorting out those at the 'top', the 'middle' and the 'bottom', and of directing them towards an appropriate niche in society.

The assessment itself usually was carried out in a formal atmosphere and under strictly controlled conditions. Not all of it was undertaken under the auspices of national examination boards, but schools and colleges tended to try to replicate the boards' strict examination conditions: a large hall with an invigilator, no 'cheating', examination 'papers', a fixed allocation of time for responding in writing to the questions and the whole exercise undertaken at the end of something (a course, a term, a year or a school career). Teachers in 'non-academic' areas of the school curriculum without formal examinations tended to assert that they had no assessment. In some subjects, however, it was acknowledged that skills other than those which can be manifest in written answers may be important, and efforts were made to include practical examinations in, for example, home economics, music and science. Where examination boards took such initiatives, teachers were sometimes asked to administer the practical tests, but in strict accordance with instructions prepared by the board.

There were, of course, a wide range of activities going on in which teachers were trying to find out, often in classrooms and by informal means, what pupils had learned or could do. Employers too were making judgements about what apprentices had achieved. All of this we would now include within the concept of assessment, but that has been the case only in recent years.

Over the last two decades the ideas underlying the traditional concept of assessment increasingly have been questioned, and the last ten years have seen some dramatic changes in practice. [...]

QUESTIONING PAST PRACTICE

The questioning of past assessment practice has been of several different kinds. Some of it has been concerned with technical matters and has asked: Are grades and marks reliable? Would another marker, or the same marker on another day, make the same judgement about the performance of a young person? Are the assessments valid? Do they assess all they claim to assess? Are they fair? Do they give recognition for achievement or are they more concerned with sorting people out? Perhaps the most searching questions, however, are about the purposes of assessment. Should the focus be on selection, or can it play a more constructive and educational role? If so, is the traditional form of marks and grades appropriate and adequate? And finally, there is debate about who has control of making and reporting the assessments, and of deciding which young people will have access to the benefits which any system of assessment might offer.

There has always been concern about whether tests and examinations are reliable, valid and fair. A substantial body of work of high technical quality has been undertaken, particularly in North America, which has ensured that much is now known about the conditions under which a group of items constitute a reliable test: that is, one which will give the same assessment of the performance of an individual no matter who marks it, and regardless of whether the individual takes the test this week or next. Objective tests with each item having one right answer are most likely to fill the bill; assessment instruments which have heterogeneous items, and subjective marking procedures (e.g. essays), are much less likely to do so. Indeed, measures of reliability on examination essay marking have sometimes produced results which are alarming, especially when it is remembered that the future career of a young person can depend on the outcome of an argument between two examiners about a grade. To avoid this problem, one approach has been to restrict examination questions to objectively marked items. But this may well distort the set of achievements which are assessed; some things which it is intended young people should learn or be able to do are not amenable to objective testing. The capability to create a literary idea, to understand a complex theory or to generate an imaginative artifact, may not be assessable by such means as answering a multiple choice question, or completing a single answer calculation.

A narrowing down of what is assessed to that which can be accurately measured may engineer some improvement in the reliability of a test, but it is likely to endanger its validity. One may ask what use is a grade or mark which is highly reliable but does not reflect the full range of achievements for which the course or set of experiences is aiming? Where such a grade or mark is used for selecting young people, what confidence can there be in its capability to predict that they will be successful in any subsequent course or career?

At a more general level, traditional tests are seen as having substantial limitations in the extent of their sampling of the variety of competences which it is intended young people should acquire. At one level, it is clear that a three-hour examination is an inadequate means of assessing, say, the learning from a two-year course. There are, furthermore, some kinds of performance which, in principle, cannot be assessed by traditional examinations, particularly where these are restricted to written tests. The validity of marks and grades as measures of performance in any given area, therefore, has been constrained by the form the assessments have taken. In particular, the assessment of practical skills, personal development, attitudes and performance in contexts other than conventional classrooms and laboratories has been neglected.

The matter of the fairness of assessments has been a continuing and agonising concern. Because the main aim of traditional assessments has been to spread out the performance of candidates (so that selection procedures could be carried out more efficiently), great emphasis was placed on choosing test items so as to maximise discrimination between the performance of the high achievers and those of the low achievers. This resulted in the omission of those items which everyone would get right, and so the lowest achievers were denied the opportunity to show what they were able to do. In some parts of the world this has been further exacerbated by the development of 'standardised tests'. Standardised tests are designed to spread out the performances and make no pretence to match the curriculum to which any given individual has been exposed. They are general tests within a broad area which discriminate well among the whole population of young people. High discrimination, however, is most effectively achieved by reducing the specific content of items; the greatest discrimination is to be found in those tests which closely resemble content-free IQ tests. As soon as a move is made in that direction, the validity of the test as a measure of *educational achievement* must be in doubt. A valid test of such achievement must clearly reflect all the qualities of which it claims to be a measure, and those qualities will be identified with the substance of the curriculum which has been followed.

Many of the characteristics of assessment in the past have resulted from the dominant purpose towards which it has been directed, i.e. selection. In recent years the question has been raised of whether there are not other, and more important, functions for it to fulfil. Since it is part of the educational process should it not have a more constructive role to play in teaching and learning? Should the very considerable efforts which are put into making assessments not be able to produce more, and more useful, information for teachers, students and others? If other functions are to be fulfilled by assessment, then it is unlikely that the traditional form of grades or marks will be adequate. An important limitation of that form is that while it enables comparisons to be made among the performances of individuals (norm-referenced assessment), it provides no information about *what* has been achieved. Any kind of function for assessment which aims to provide information which will help young people to learn, or teachers to teach, will require an evaluative description of what has been achieved (criterion-referenced assessment).

The question of who should carry out the assessment of young people has not been a matter for debate in the past. Most frequently it has been assumed that the teacher will be the assessor, although examination for certification (probably seen as the most important manifestation of assessment) has generally been the province of professional examiners. There are obvious constraints on the ability of a professional examiner, who under normal conditions would not see the candidate, to carry out a comprehensive assessment of that young person's capabilities in those areas where he or she has had the opportunity to learn. It has been suggested that the teacher will always be in a better position than the examiner to assess, but would that hold when the young people are out of school on, say, work experience or residential courses? The way in which educational aims have changed over the last few years, so that experiences of this kind are now commonplace in the school or college curriculum, clearly has implications for who should be the assessor. Furthermore, the fact that assessments may be carried out by a variety of people, with a range of perspectives, draws attention to the question of whether it is important to have a single measure of achievement for a young person in a given area, or whether it is more rational to accept that different people assess individuals differently, and that such differences should not be concealed within some compromise overall mark or grade.

The notion of young people themselves being involved in self- or peer-assessment has not been a facet of past practice. More recently the question of whether such involvement would be of value in helping to consolidate learning and to increase self-awareness is frequently mooted. For some aspects of personal and social development, which are currently receiving substantial emphasis in curriculum planning, it might seem that the young people are in the best position to make the judgements which assessment of such qualities calls for.

This debate on the possible inadequacy of the range of qualities assessed by traditional measures and the restrictions on who should carry out those assessments, has been accompanied by concern about the proportion of young people leaving formal education without any record of what they have achieved. The established (and academic) certificate courses were not designed for the whole population and, in any case, were unsuited to the educational aims for many young people. Educational 'qualifications', however, have become more and more important. If the curriculum is to develop in various ways to prepare everyone more effectively for their future in work and in society generally, then surely, it has been argued, *all* should have the opportunity to work for a certificate which recognises what has been achieved? And if everyone has the chance to earn a certificate, surely such recognition will have a motivating effect on learning and, perhaps, reduce the alienation from education characteristic of many of the low achievers?

The doubts and dissatisfactions with the traditional concept of assessment have resulted in more than academic debate. There have been substantial changes in practice, and the experience gained has led to greater understanding of the potential and the problems associated with assessment. Assessment now commands a much wider conceptualisation than in the past, and tends to be seen as an important and necessary ingredient of effective teaching and learning. [. . .]

INNOVATIVE THEMES IN ASSESSMENT PRACTICE

The first theme concentrates on the way in which the concept of 'assessment' has progressed from the traditional notion of 'testing' for selection purposes. Assessment is now seen as *a much broader concept and fulfilling multiple purposes.* It is considered to be closely integrated with the 'curriculum' (a concept which is itself conceived in very much broader terms than in the past) and its purposes include fostering learning, improving teaching, providing valid information about what has been done or achieved, and enabling pupils and others to make sensible and rational choices about courses, careers and other activities. Evaluation of pupils for various selection purposes will continue, but there have been major efforts to ensure that we progress from the simplistic notion that young people can be put in some kind of rank order by grades (frequently based on the results of a single examination). Assessment, therefore, now has several functions including the diagnosis of causes of young people's success or failure, the motivation of them to learn, the provision of valid and meaningful accounts of what has been achieved, and the evaluation of courses and of teaching. We are much more cautious these days about making claims for how effectively assessment in one context can predict the success of young people in other contexts at later dates. The emphasis has shifted away from assessment for summative purposes: that is a report at the end of a course or period of study which purports to predict future performance. Much more stress is laid on assessment for formative purposes: that is the use of the information gathered to improve the current educational process.

This multiple-purpose concept of assessment, which is closely linked to the totality of the curriculum, leads directly to the second theme. This theme is concerned with the considerable *increase in the range of qualities assessed and contexts in which that assessment takes place.* Stringent boundaries put on many assessment systems in the past are breaking down. No longer is it necessary for the qualities assessed to be 'academic' and strictly amenable to measurement. Assessment of personal, social and attitudinal characteristics is frequently under consideration, and what counts as 'achievement' within even traditional subject areas has expanded considerably. In addition, the contexts in which assessment takes place are much more diverse than in the past. No longer are examination halls the places which one immediately associates with assessment; long-overdue recognition is being given to the fact that most, and the most valuable, assessment is carried out on the site where the learning takes place. Changes in the curriculum have brought about acceptance that the place of learning is no longer always the school or college. The rise of work experience and community activities, for example, have opened up the issue of assessment for school pupils in the context of the workplace.

The third theme is directed to the rise of *descriptive assessment*. Much of this has manifested itself in the form of concern for criterion-referenced approaches which replace or complement traditional norm-referenced systems. The aim has been to provide descriptions of what has (or has not) been achieved rather than to rely on pupils' marks or grades, which have little meaning other than as a comparison with the marks and grades of others. Descriptions of this kind are seen as having the potential to help us understand what, and why, children are or are not learning, and to facilitate improved learning. Such descriptions may also be able to ameliorate the disadvantages of the competitive traditional system and to promote more cooperative attitudes to learning. Perhaps the most persuasive argument, however, has related to the anticipated value of the descriptive information to teachers and young people in making rational decisions about such things as courses to be followed, curricula to be reformed, work to be done, remediation to be carried out, and so on.

A fourth theme is concerned with the *devolution of responsibilities for assessment* to, for example, schools, teachers, work experience employers and young people themselves. Teachers have always carried out most of the assessment to which pupils and students are subjected, but traditionally the assessment which 'matters' (i.e. national certification) has been firmly in the hands of external examination boards. The recognition that at all levels internal assessment by educational institutions is of crucial importance is changing all that; but things are going further in some quarters. The concern with the assessment of a wider range of things some of which, like work experience, happen outside the classroom has led to the involvement of others, such as employers, in the assessment process. Furthermore, many of the arguments about the value of assessments to pupils themselves have suggested that the benefits will be greatest if the young people can be persuaded to undertake self-assessment.

A fifth and final theme focuses on assessment for certification. Much of the public debate and changes in government policy in the 1980s have supported the view that *certification should be available to a much greater proportion of the population of young people* than has been the case in the past. The nature of certification is also undergoing reform. [...]

The innovations identified in these five themes are by no means restricted to assessment developments in the United Kingdom. Apart from the fifth theme, which reflects the substantially greater obsession with certification in this country compared with most others, there is a considerable and worldwide literature concerned with similar matters. [...]

1.2 THE NEED FOR CHANGE

ROGER MURPHY AND HARRY TORRANCE

INTRODUCTION

It is our central argument that assessment should play a critical part in any educational process. Wherever learning takes place, or it is intended that it should take place, then it is reasonable for the learner, the teacher and other interested parties to be curious about what has happened both in terms of the learning process and in terms of any anticipated or unanticipated outcomes. We would argue that good education, by definition, encompasses good assessment. However we would wish to dissociate ourselves immediately from much of what has gone on previously under the guise of 'good' educational assessment. In many cases assessment, in our view, has hindered the cause of education, and in fact has often been a major stumbling block standing in the way of curriculum innovation, improved teaching methods and changed attitudes among teachers and learners. Assessment has been viewed for far too long as a formal process, which normally involves the administration of formal tests and examinations through procedures that are totally divorced from the educational process and setting to which they are supposed to relate.

We are not alone in wishing to criticise approaches, such as testing, as the only way to carry out assessment, although our position is not as extreme as say Holt (1969), who wrote about the 'tyranny of testing' from a stance of unbridled opposition:

> Let me not mince words. Almost all educators feel that testing is a necessary part of education. I wholly disagree – I do not think that testing is necessary, or useful, or even excusable. At best, testing does more harm than good; at worst, it hinders, distorts, and corrupts the learning process. Testers say that testing techniques are being continually improved and can eventually

be perfected. Maybe so – but no imaginable improvement in testing would overcome my objections to it. Our chief concern should not be to improve testing, but to find ways to eliminate it (Holt, 1969, p. 51).

Holt goes unswervingly to the heart of the matter in his own inimical style:

> we teachers say that we test children to find out what they have learned, so that we can better know how to help them to learn more. This is about ninety-five per cent untrue. There are two main reasons why we test children: the first is to threaten them into doing what we want done, and the second is to give us a basis for handing out the rewards and penalties on which the educational system – like all coercive systems – must operate. The threat of a test makes students do this assignment. The outcome of a test enables us to reward those who seem to do it best. The economy of the school, like that of most societies, operates on greed and fear. Tests arouse the fear and satisfy the greed (Holt, 1969, p. 52).

The crucial role that assessment plays in operationalising the educational goals of teachers and those others involved in planning and monitoring any educational system is difficult to refute. However, we would see the same argument applying to the ambitions and hopes of the learner – that is, if the learner is given good assessment information about his or her progress and successful, and unsuccessful, learning strategies, then this will be of assistance, even if in any individual case the desired end may be a different one from that intended by those planning the programme. Thus to argue that assessment plays a crucial part in successful education does not necessarily close down the discussion of what successful education is, or the role of the learner in retaining responsibilities for his or her learning objectives or strategies.

Clearly some assessment systems go a long way towards defining both educational goals and the route that is to be prescribed for all learners who set off on the road towards those goals. Thus assessment can be seen as the carrot and stick for unwilling donkeys in any setting where one regards the education on offer as being foisted on unwilling learners. Hargreaves (1988) has raised this particular issue in relation to any unquestioning enthusiasm for new assessment initiatives that appear to increase pupil motivation, which may leave aside a critical scrutiny of the type of education experience such initiatives promote:

> What is absent, however, is any discussion of the relationship between the new patterns of assessment and the *content or focus* of the curriculum. There is virtually no discussion within the new assessment initiatives of the social purposes of the curriculum or of the essential knowledge and experiences to which all pupils are entitled. The profound implication of this is that in records of achievement, we have a system designed to enhance pupil motivation but without any broadly-based political or professional discussion and agreement about what pupils are being motivated *towards*;

about what sorts of things we are committing young people *to*, and whether these have any education or social legitimacy... Under circumstances such as these, the enhancement of pupil motivation shifts from being an *educational* process of positive disposition to learning worthwhile knowledge; to a *socio-political*, state-managed process of accommodation to the realities of economic crisis, of adjustment to diminishing prospects of employment and economic reward and to an educational experience that, for many pupils, can no longer promise social and economic benefits in adulthood. Motivation, that is, becomes transformed from a process of educational encouragement, to a strategy of social crisis management (Hargreaves, 1988: original emphasis).

The force of Hargreaves' argument, as we see it, is that assessment is not necessarily bad, but every assessment initiative should be viewed with suspicion until it becomes clear what curricular or socio-political aims are embedded within it.

This is a position with which we are entirely in sympathy as we regard it as the most serious deficiency in the assessment literature of the past 40 years or so, where often the discussion has focused entirely upon the technical qualities, or deficiencies, of various assessment methods, without paying any attention at all to the much more serious educational questions which subsume them. Certainly reliability, validity and comparability are all important constituents of any assessment procedure, but by themselves they are totally worthless, unless the assessments that are being carried out are supporting and promoting a worthwhile educational process. Our emphasis is as much on the *impact* of assessment on educational processes and experiences, as it is on the *technical attributes* of recent assessment initiatives.

The change in emphasis in the discussion of educational assessment issues has also been reflected in a change of attitudes towards public examinations, such as CSE, GCE and the recently introduced GCSE. [...]

Central to that analysis is the theme of the stranglehold on the curriculum that the examination boards have held through their published syllabuses. The old adage 'we tend to assess what we can easily assess' provides an apt description of what has traditionally happened within the GCE examination-led system. The plea from the Boards, that their syllabus aims are not intended to encompass all teaching aims, has hardly prevented a narrow concentration on a restricted range of cognitive, academic areas of achievement in both assessment and teaching (Hargreaves, 1982).

This issue of allowing narrow thinking about assessment to lead to a narrow view of educational achievement is critical in any analysis of what has happened in British secondary schools during the last 20 or 30 years. It is probably not surprising that this was the first issue addressed by the Hargreaves Committee in their inquiry into underachievement in Inner London Education Authority (ILEA) secondary schools (ILEA, 1984). They rejected the view that any realistic estimate of overall achievement could be obtained from the results of public examinations. They then went on to outline four separate, but equally important, aspects of achievement only one of which is, in their view, adequately assessed by the current 16+ public examinations. Clearly their concern to direct attention towards a more holistic view of educational achievement, to include the application of knowledge, social and personal skills, and motivation and commitment, requires a major shift in emphasis. Change would also be needed in terms of the development of new assessment systems so as to ensure that such aspects of achievement are accorded equivalent status. The Hargreaves Committee has attempted to do just this through their proposed system of units and unit credits, which bears many of the characteristics of other modularised curriculum and assessment systems that are being developed simultaneously in other parts of the country.

As soon as one attempts to break away from a traditional view of educational achievement, one is confronted with the need to make a similar break with traditional views of assessment. In the same way that, for years, intelligence tests restricted the view of human intelligence, prominent assessment methods (as used in public examinations) have tended to distort concepts of educational achievement. Indeed, one can go even further in claiming a strong link between the two movements. Much of the development work, in the area of educational assessment, conducted by the public examination boards, has been influenced by psychometric concepts and ideas borrowed directly from the same psychologists who promoted the development of intelligence tests in the early part of this century (Wood, 1982). The traditional presentation of results in the form of single letter (or number) grades, and the aggregation of such grades, by many users, to give an overall estimate of an individual's achievements (and potential), reflects much of the former thinking of psychologists such as Burt and Spearman who believed in a basic (largely inherited) single trait of mental ability that could be used to explain most, if not all, human behaviour (cf. Norton 1979; Torrance 1986a; Vernon 1957).

Many of the developments that we will be considering in this book fall outside that paradigm, and the challenge for those who are centrally involved in changing the face of educational assessment is how far they can go in terms of creating an alternative paradigm that gains widespread professional and public acceptance. The psychometric approach has already been exposed as having major limitations as a basis for thinking about and analysing educational assessments (Wood, 1982) and even major exponents of a basic single measure approach to assessment and evaluation are now calling for a broadening of the enterprise (Tyler, 1986). The Hargreaves Report has provided an added dimension to the new face of educational assessment by questioning a widely held concept of what educational achievement is. They have also introduced a new agenda for educational assessment to cope with, by extending the range of aspects of educational achievement that need to be covered.

At the time of writing we are in the midst of a full-blown national debate which has been fuelled by the National Curriculum proposals, about the nature of the school curriculum. How narrow or broad it should be, and what areas should be core areas or optional areas are key questions in this debate.

This dilemma is mirrored in the parallel debate about assessment and testing. The view that assessment should concentrate on basic skills and core areas of the curriculum is widely held. Those that argue for this limited view of the assessment of educational achievement argue that other areas can be taught but are not so important to assess. Those, like the members of the Hargreaves Committee, who have argued for assessments that can encompass a much broader notion of achievement, regard a flexible approach as being essential if all areas of a broad curriculum are to be taken seriously and valued, and not squeezed out by the force of demands 'to increase standards' (i.e. through improving scores on narrow achievement tests related to the core areas).

We [...] wish to argue that the debate about whether or not, or how far, to change educational assessment is at the heart of the debate about the nature and purpose of education in schools. Choosing between alternative approaches to assessment usually means choosing between different curriculum emphases, and each assessment method that could be used will undoubtedly have implications for teaching and learning strategies, study skills, and the extent to which pupils need to utilise skills drawn from outside the particular curriculum topic being assessed.

THE VARIOUS PURPOSES OF ASSESSMENT

Having stated in the previous section that assessment has a critical part to play in any educational process, we would also accept that the role is likely to vary quite a bit between different situations. Macintosh and Hale (1976) have provided a much quoted breakdown of six possible purposes of assessment: (i) diagnosis, (ii) evaluation, (iii) guidance, (iv) grading, (v) selection and (vi) prediction.

This is helpful in pointing to the wide range of functions that educational assessment can perform, although more and more in the current debate one might be inclined to add motivation to their list as a seventh purpose. The desire to increase pupil motivation for learning is widespread, and motivation is in itself probably the most novel part of the Hargreaves Report's four-part definition of educational achievement referred to in the previous section. Leaving that issue aside for the moment, it is instructive to reflect on the extent to which Macintosh and Hale's six purposes of assessment are reflected both in the standard assessment procedures in use in British schools, and in the many new assessment initiatives that are being developed.

David Hargreaves' (1982) position on this issue is instructive. He sees the selection function of assessment as a dominant influence on comprehensive schools, both in terms of the way in which the curriculum is defined and in terms of the images of success and failure that are associated with that curriculum. Thus the Hargreaves Report (ILEA, 1984) seeks to break away from the mould of the narrow academic curriculum geared to the selection requirements of higher education and the needs of a society obsessed with selecting an elite minority through the process of schooling. The main planks upon which their strategy is based are a re-definition of educational achievement, and an entirely new approach to assessing achievement through a school-based assessment of a curriculum based upon units and unit credits. Their analysis of the narrow selection function performed by the academic curriculum is illustrated by a quote from Wilby, the education correspondent of *The Independent*:

> The trouble with our comprehensives is not that their academic standards are too low but that they are too high. Academic standards still have a virtual stranglehold on English education – and they are the enemy of genuine educational standards. Our secondary education is organized to select those few who will go to university and, ultimately, the even tinier minority who will approach the frontiers of theoretical knowledge. For their sake, all our children are being put through an over-blown, over-academic syllabus, in which the dominant experience, for the majority, is one of failure, not of achievement (Wilby, 1979).

It is clear from this quote that once again our apparently straightforward discussion of the various purposes that assessment can perform has taken us quickly into the political battlefield of the control of the school curriculum, the definition of what kinds of achievement are regarded as superior, and the purposes of school education within a developed industrial society. It is not difficult to find examples around the world of re-enactments of parts of this battle as the 'political right' have argued with the 'political left' about the need to focus on 'basic standards' within the teaching of the school curriculum. In many cases this debate has also involved associated proposals to introduce national testing programmes, which concentrate specifically on 'basic skills' in core areas. [. . .]

There is no doubt at all that the public view of assessment in schools has been dominated by both the selection function [. . .] and the accountability demands. [. . .] Clearly, both of these functions are necessary, and are certainly important enough to warrant improvements in the often inadequate way in which they are carried out. What is also necessary, however, is the need to ensure that these particular purposes, or functions of educational assessment, are not allowed to dominate both the entire school curriculum and the complete range of assessment procedures that are associated with it.

Unfortunately, in the past, selection, along with grading and prediction, has tended to dominate thinking and practice in relation to educational assessment. Lip service is often paid to Macintosh and Hale's (1976) other three purposes of assessment, but in reality diagnosis, evaluation and guidance have a very small part to play in most assessment schemes. This is in spite of the fact that most educationalists acknowledge that these are the more important and educationally beneficial characteristics of the assessment of any particular course or educational experience.

Most traditional assessment systems are organised in such a way that they militate against this type of formative use. The assessment procedures are frequently carried out towards the end of a course or unit of work, are veiled in secrecy, and the results, when they are given to the pupils or students, are usually coded in a language of grades which gives them little constructive insight into the nature of their performance. The idea that a student might diagnose particular learning difficulties from a single letter (or number) grade which covers two or in some cases many more years of study, is in itself laughable. Furthermore, the widespread practice of not returning examination scripts or test papers to students, and not revealing marking procedures, or entering into any kind of post-assessment discussion of the work of individuals, are all features of an approach to assessment which emphasises the 'rites of entry' selection function and destroys most if not all educational benefits which could be derived from it. [...]

REFERENCES

Hargreaves, A. (1988), *The crisis in motivation and assessment*, Hargreaves, A. and Reynolds, D. (eds.) Educational Policy Initiatives, London, Falmer Press.

Hargreaves, D. (1962), *The Challenge for the Comprehensive School*, London, Routledge and Kegan Paul.

Holt, J. (1969), *The Underachieving School*, London, Pitman.

Inner London Education Authority (1984), The Hargreaves Report, *Improving Secondary Schools*, London, ILEA.

MacIntosh, H. G. and Hale, D. E. (1976) *Assessment and the Secondary School Teacher*, London, Routledge and Kegan Paul.

Norton, B. (1979) Charles Spearman and the general factor of intelligence, *Journal of the History of the Behavioural Sciences* 16 (15), 142–54.

Torrance, H. (1986a) Assessment and examinations: social context and educational practice, Ph.D. Thesis, Norwich, Centre for Applied Research in Education.

Tyler, R. (1986) Changing concepts of educational evaluation, *International Journal of Educational Research* 10 (1), monograph.

Vernon, P. (ed.) (1957) *Secondary School Selection*, London, Methuen.

Wilby, P. (1979) Towards a comprehensive curriculum, Pluckrose, H. and Wilby, P. (eds), *The Conditions of English Schooling*, Harmondsworth, Penguin.

Wood, R. (1982). Educational and psychological measurement: further efforts at differentiation. *Educational Analysis* 4 (3), 119–34.

1.3 | PROGRESSION

(Extract from NATIONAL CURRICULUM – TASK GROUP ON ASSESSMENT AND TESTING: A REPORT)

We regard it as one of our priorities to ensure that criteria and scales used should relate to expected routes of development, giving continuity to each pupil's assessment at different ages, and thereby giving a detailed picture of each pupil's progress.

AGES OF ASSESSMENT AND REPORTING

92. To provide a clear basis for subsequent discussion, we first consider the ages at which national assessment and reporting should take place. For national purposes we believe that the balance of advantage lies with reporting towards the end of the school year in which a cohort of pupils becomes 7, 11, 14 or 16. With very few exceptions, the ages of 7 and 11 come either at the end of or, in middle school systems, at least two years into a phase of schooling. By those ages children should therefore feel settled in that phase, and the teachers should know them well. It is important that 7 year olds who have not made a satisfactory beginning in learning to read, write and calculate should be identified and helped to make progress. Where there is transfer, whether after 7 or after 11, the process of reporting should allow useful information to be passed to the next school. The age of 14 is desirable because it is commonly the time when decisions are taken about the courses children should subsequently follow; and 16 allows a summative assessment to be made for those children moving out of the school system, whether to work or to further education or training.

We recommend that the ages for national assessment should be 7, 11, 14 and 16, with reporting occurring near the end of the school year in which each cohort reaches the age involved.

PROGRESSION

93. Given a framework of reporting at those four ages, we go on to assume progress to be defined in terms of the national curriculum, and the stages of progress to be marked by levels of achievement as derived from that curriculum. It is not necessary to presume that the progression defined indicates some inescapable order in the way children learn, or some sequence of difficulty inherent in the material to be learnt. Both of those factors may apply, but the sequence of learning may also be the result of choices for whatever reason, which those formulating and operating the curriculum may recommend in the light of teaching experience.

94. The consultative document on the national curriculum, published in July 1987, proposed that 'the main purpose of assessment will be to show what a pupil has learnt and mastered ...' (paragraph 28); that 'attainment targets will be set' for the core subjects, establishing what children should normally be expected to know, understand and be able to do at around the ages of 7, 11, 14 and 16, so enabling the progress of each child to be measured against established national standards (paragraph 23). The subject working groups should, among other things, take account of the need for continuity and progression throughout compulsory schooling (Annex A, 3.1.c).

95. [...] In the following paragraphs we consider how information about the pupil's stage of learning can best be conveyed.

COMMUNICATING INFORMATION ABOUT STAGES OF LEARNING

96. Most straightforwardly, one could simply describe what a pupil understands, knows and can do in terms similar to those that will be used by the subject working groups to define attainment targets. We believe that it would be right for much of the communication between teachers and parents to take that form at the reporting ages and between them. However, two considerations make it advantageous also to convert the descriptions into a marking scale. One is to convey some sense of where a child is in the process of learning; the other is to make easier the analysis of results from groups of

children. The last is of interest to parents who wish to know where their child stands in relation to others of about the same age and also, at various levels of aggregation, to teachers, heads, LEAs, the Government and the wider community [...]

97. Commonly used systems of scaling pupils' achievements divide those of about the same age into five or six groups. In England and Wales, some schools use a five-point scale: A to E, for example. In the Federal German Republic a six-point scale is common, and the numbers 1 to 6 are used. Generally the scaling is based on assessment, including the results of tests, which judge a pupil's performance against that of others in the group, or some comparable group: that is, the judgements are norm-referenced. Furthermore, the reference groups are usually of pupils of the same age group. Commonly, in the five-point system the scaling is so arranged that small proportions of pupils are likely to be in grades A and E, larger proportions in B and D, and perhaps half of the children in C. These proportions may vary when the groups being assessed are untypical of the general population. It is, of course, possible deliberately to arrange for the proportions to be different, and a five-point scale could be adjusted, for example, to divide the pupils so that very few are judged to be 1 or 5 and the rest are spread evenly between 2, 3 and 4.

98. Levels of achievement could therefore be translated into a five- or six-point scale at each of the reporting ages. This could have the attraction of apparent uniformity across all ages. However, age-specific grading has drawbacks. Pupils are more likely than not to remain in the same grade or level, plus or minus one, at each reporting age. A child might be assessed to be on level 1 at one reporting age, on level 2 at the next and back to level 1 at the third, despite, in absolute terms, having made progress. Even if the child remains on the same level from age to age, he or she will be given no sense of having made the progress which must in fact have been made. Furthermore, even though level 3 at 7 years of age would indicate that a child had achieved specific competences, those same competences would merit a different level number for a slower child, only 1 or 2, at the next reporting age. There would be no simple relation between the level numbers and performance.

99. More generally, the combination of a norm-referenced system with age-specific scaling would not be consistent with the proposals in the National Curriculum consultative document. The overall national purpose is to work for achievement of the attainment targets of the curriculum. Assessment, whether for feedback to pupils or overall reporting and monitoring, should therefore be related to this attainment, i.e. it should be criterion-referenced. Given this, it follows that different pupils may satisfy a given criterion at different ages: to tie the criteria to particular ages only would risk either limiting the very able, or giving the least able no reward, or both.

100. In view of these disadvantages of age-specific scaling, we consider that the scaling system should be directly related to the development of pupils' competences as described by the attainment targets of the national curriculum.

That is to say, scales should be used that indicate where a pupil has reached in a profile component. We shall use the word level to define one of a sequence of points on a scale to be used in describing the progress of attainment in the profile component. The sequence of levels represents the stages of progression. 101. A pupil assessed as achieving a given level, say level 2, will have satisfied the criteria for level 2 and will be working towards the criteria for level 3. Progress is marked by achievement of successive levels over time. For the purposes of national assessment, a broad indication of progress is required. We propose that the criteria defining successive levels be so chosen that a pupil could reasonably be expected to progress by one level in two years of work in that profile component. Over the age range 7–16 this would imply a need for five or six levels. At both ends of the age range, however, some will be unable to progress as fast as others, and some will be able to make quicker progress. This leads us to recommend that a total range of ten levels will need to be defined: fuller justification of this number will be given below.

We recommend that each of the subject working groups defines a sequence of levels in each of its profile components, related to broad criteria for progression in that component. For a profile component which applies over the full age range 7 to 16, there should be ten such levels, with corresponding reduction for profile components which will apply over a smaller span of school years.

PROGRESSION THROUGH THE LEVELS

102. The implications of this proposal may be seen from Figure 1. The details of the representation in this diagram will be explained in three steps below, considering respectively age 7, age 16 (with GCSE) and then intervening ages.

AGE 7

103. The first step in the explanation applies to age 7. The range of levels likely to be achieved by the youngest children will be narrower than the range likely to be achieved by the oldest. For reasons that are outlined in this report, we believe this to be advantageous, and we recommend that, for reporting purposes, the levels for the 7 year olds should be confined to levels 1, 2 and 3. These levels should, for this age group of children, be regarded as mainly diagnostic in the sense that level 1 identifies those children who may need more help in their learning than can be provided from ordinary classroom resources; those in level 3 have made such advances that they also need

additional help if they are to maintain their speedier progress. We recognise that assessment at levels 1 and 3 will be more common in some aspects of learning than others; for example, there are likely to be more children in level 1 for literacy and mathematics than for some other aspects of learning.

We recommend that levels 1 to 3 be used for national assessments at age 7.

AGE 16

104. To develop the second step of the explanation of Figure 1, we note that at the other end of the age range, there has in the past been a variety of attempts to derive written criteria from GCE and CSE grades. That experience suggests that no more than four sets of levels can be identified in relation to the GCSE population.

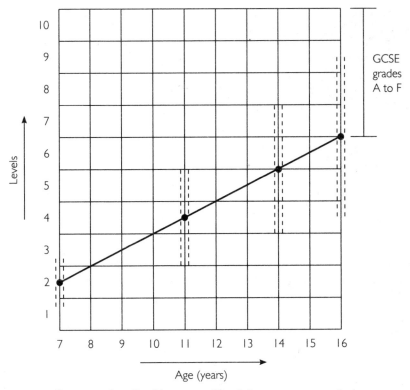

Figure 1   *Sequence of pupil achievement of levels between ages 7 and 16*

The bold line gives the expected results for pupils at the ages specified. The dotted lines represent a rough speculation about the limits within which about 80 per cent of the pupils may be found to lie.

105. We are conscious of the tendency for new assessment systems to overlay rather than to replace existing schemes, resulting in a growing burden on the

schools. It would be unfortunate to have two independent systems in operation for the 16 year old age group. On the other hand, problems of comparability are not readily solved and a premature attempt to link the national assessment system with GCSE could lead to a top-down approach which placed undue constraints on the design of the national curriculum at earlier ages. It is our expectation that the phasing of the introduction of national assessment will work towards GCSE rather than away from it.

We recommend that the formal relationship between national assessment and GCSE should be limited, in the first instance, to this one reference point: the boundary between levels 6 and 7 should correspond to the grade F/G boundary for GCSE.

106. The four levels from 7 to 10 could, following this recommendation, bear some relationship to upper GCSE grades, but we believe it would not be helpful at this stage to attempt to specify equivalences between the two systems while they operate in different ways. These upper levels should be set by criteria which specify attainment targets appropriate to the GCSE population at age 16, although again this relationship cannot be precise.

We recommend that as they develop the upper four levels of their profile components, the subject working groups adopt present practices for determining GCSE grades at A/B, C/D, mid-E, and F/G as a starting point.

107. It has been suggested by some that GCSE should be revised and extended to provide appropriate targets for the entire age group. We feel this would be unwise on three grounds. GCSE is a major educational innovation which has led to considerable upheaval in the secondary school system: teachers need a period of stability to come to terms with these changes. Secondly, if the national assessment system meets its objectives, a larger proportion of the age group will be served by the existing GCSE system. There is value in setting up a dialogue between the GCSE system and the curricular approaches characteristic of earlier years of education and the time scale allows for this. Finally, in a system of progression, extension of GCSE in the short term is unnecessary, since the levels designed for the middle range of 14 year olds will present appropriate challenges for pupils who at age 16 have not yet progressed into the GCSE grade range.

We recommend that GCSE be retained in its present form until the national assessment system is initiated at earlier ages.

AGES 11 AND 14

108. To develop the third step in the explanation, we return to the assumption that a level should be roughly equivalent to two years of educational progress in a profile component. The average expectation for 14 year olds will therefore be the level 5/6 boundary. On similar grounds the average expectation for an age 11 pupil will be level 4. In mathematics, the widely recognised seven-year gap in attainment between the most advanced and the slowest pupils at age 11 would imply that levels 3, 4 and 5 should be characteristic of profile components in that subject for the age group but that there will be a few pupils who have already progressed to level 6, the highest level of report for junior school pupils. In general, however, level 6, which should give an indication of how levels might be interpreted in relation to GCSE, should be achieved by some pupils at 14. Level 6 at age 14 is indicative of a pupil who is on target for a GCSE grade. At earlier ages, however, not all of the requisite knowledge and experience may be in place. Furthermore, GCSE grades involve combinations of profile components, and some components may be encountered only late in the curricular experience of the pupil.

109. In reviewing the above argument, it should be emphasised that the basis is the definition, by subject working groups, of a sequence of levels so tied to criteria that two years' learning represents one level of progress. The spread that may be found at any one age, given such a system, remains to be discovered, but the above speculations have some basis in practical experience. For instance, a growing body of evidence indicates that in English and mathematics there is a very broad range of achievement in any year group, sufficiently broad to ensure that there will be overlapping achievements at ages 7 and 11, 11 and 14, 14 and 16. Thus a curriculum target designed for one age group may be quite appropriate for some pupils in an adjacent age group. The need for differentiation at any particular age, coupled with the overlap of achievements between reporting ages, supports our proposal for a single sequence of levels across the age range for national assessments. Indeed in our view the differentiation of attainment targets at a particular age arises naturally from the notion of age progression upon which the reporting scales of national assessment are based. In a criterion-referenced system there should be no distinction between the definition of the sequence of levels of a profile component to reflect progress between ages, and its use to differentiate progression at a particular age. Only one set of criteria is required. The levels defined by the National Curriculum attainment targets will provide differentiated challenges at each age according to the needs of the individual pupil. All pupils should then have an expectation of making progress in every profile component: progress which will be indicated by the achievement of new targets.

DIFFERENTIATION

110. This leads naturally to a discussion of differentiation. As we shall argue in a later section, we think that for the youngest age tests should be devised that, from the children's point of view, are similar in form to their normal school work, should be based on familiar material, and should allow children to exhibit different levels of knowledge, understanding, and skills in their responses. So as to take account of the varying maturity of pupils and the burden of testing on the class teachers, considerable restraint in the number of assessment tasks will also have to be exercised at the 7 and at the 11 year old stage, and this is further discussed in this report.

111. At the later reporting ages it may not always be possible to rely on differentiation by outcome in this way, and the tests devised may themselves have to be sequenced according to the targets being tested, though within the same profile component.

112. Given the view that the differences in performance at any one age must be appraised by the same criteria as progress between ages, it follows that any pupil who has made remarkably fast or remarkably slow progress may well be assessed by the methods used for normal pupils at much older or much younger ages respectively. Thus it would not be impossible for a pupil at age 7 to be capable of level 4 in some components. With this strategy, which is easy to implement because of the cross-age sequence of levels, there would be no need, for the purposes of reporting within the national assessment system, for pupils to take tests or other assessments at earlier or later stages than those specified.

> We recommend that assessment and reporting for the national assessment system be at the same ages for all pupils, and that differentiation be based on the use of the single sequence of levels set up to cover progression over the full age range.

IMPROVEMENT OVER TIME

113. The normal distributions across levels at each stage will indicate that the attainment targets corresponding to those levels constitute the range of targets appropriate to that age. But as curriculum and teaching are adapted to the new system, improvement in these distributions may be expected: these can be recorded and investigated in our scheme because it is criterion-referenced and not tied to limited expectations at particular ages. Nevertheless, for the reporting and subsequent analysis to be effective, it is important that virtually all pupils be assessed at the same age. It would be possible in any

analysis to take account of the fact that (say) 2 per cent of pupils at age 14 achieved level 9 in a particular profile component (and the means for them to exhibit this would be available); it would not be possible to feed into analysis the fact that they were allowed to attempt assessments for level 7 at age 12 and, having succeeded, were excused at age 14.

114. For reporting at a particular age, it will be possible to say of pupils in a particular class, or school, or LEA, what proportions were in each of the levels of the sequence. As recommended above, that set of proportions would constitute the form of report for each profile component.

SPECIAL NEEDS

115. In considering the guidance appropriate for individual pupils, the teacher should be giving particular attention to cases of special need. For example, any children who do not move into a higher level between reporting ages should certainly have been identified as needing extra help, as may some who move through the level system slowly. There may be particular difficulties with pupils who might not be able to undertake the normal assessment tasks. All children who are assessed in the agreed profile components should take part in the nationally prescribed tests unless the headteacher certifies that a child with special educational needs is, by reason of those needs, unable to participate in the test. Some children may be able to take tests in an adapted form or with special help – which should be taken into account in determining the results. Children who are statemented will be exempt if their statements exclude their participation in the relevant aspect of the national curriculum.

CONTINUING ASSESSMENT BETWEEN REPORTING AGES

116. While most of the above discussion has concentrated on assessment and testing at the four specified ages, it will be necessary to set this programme in the context of the frequent assessment of pupils' work that teachers make, and will continue to make. This work is far more extensive than that of the national assessments, covering progress over all of the periods intervening between 7, 11, 14 and 16. The system of levels tied to criteria which we propose should provide a valuable framework for relating this work to the attainment targets of the National Curriculum. A training programme should

be arranged to help teachers to become more effective in the frequent assessments that they make, and to help relate these to the criteria embodied in the national tests and assessments. This need was envisaged in paragraph 74 of the consultation document on the national curriculum.

> We recommend that support items, procedures and training be provided to help teachers relate their own assessments to the targets and assessment criteria of the national curriculum.

117. Teachers will also need a varied set of diagnostic tests to help explore special difficulties shown up in the national and other assessments.

> We recommend that a review be made of the materials available to schools for detailed diagnostic investigation of pupils' learning problems, and that the need for extra help with production or advice about such materials should be considered.

ASSESSMENT OF NEW PROFILE COMPONENTS

118. Most of the foregoing discussion has been set out on the assumption that it is about profile components that are applicable across the full age range from 7 to 16. We recognise, however, that it may be necessary, in some aspects of the curriculum, to introduce new profile components as the children progress, and that these new components may be suitable only for children who have already acquired certain levels of knowledge and understanding. It is for the subject working groups to recommend whether and about what this should be so. The initial level for these wholly 'new' profile elements should be level 1. A modern foreign language is a special case, since under the National Curriculum this would not normally start being taught until the secondary school stage; the reporting system for *all* profile components in a foreign language will need to begin at level 1. We regard this clear divorce of level number from age to be advantageous rather than otherwise, since it will emphasise the criterion-referenced nature of the assessment.

Number of Profile Components
Assessed at Primary Stage

119. While it follows from the above that the number of profile components to be assessed at 7 and 11 will be less than at 14 and 16, there is still a potentially serious problem because of the size of the burden that could too easily be placed on teachers in the primary phase. If the subject working groups were to work independently in making recommendations for primary pupils, then a single class teacher of 7 or 11 year olds could have to assess pupils in at least 20 and possibly 30 or more profile components. Furthermore, some components of foundation subjects would be inappropriate, in their fully differentiated form, at least at age 7.

120. One solution would be to limit assessment in the primary phase to the three core subjects. This could have the effect of narrowing the primary curriculum to an undesirable extent, even if it were only adopted for age 7.

121. There is a different approach to this problem which could be more fruitful. As recommended earlier, subject working groups should pay particular attention to profile components which might overlap, or be identical, between different subjects because they represent important cross-curricular areas of knowledge, understanding and skill. We expect that some profile components will have a wide range of applicability across the subjects of the curriculum, so as to encourage pupils, teachers and parents to recognise common and overlapping aspects in the work being reported. In addition some profile components which should be separately identified in separate subjects in the secondary phase could well be combined up to age 11 because the aspects which differentiate them are not relevant at younger ages. Thus profile components at older ages might evolve by differentiation from a smaller number at younger ages. Figure 2 illustrates this approach.

122. While this approach reduces the numbers of profile components at 7 and 11, it does not neglect the emergence of subject identification at age 11, indeed it allows the context in which assessments and tests are set to become increasingly identified with curriculum subjects as pupils mature. One most important advantage of the scheme represented by Figure 2 is that it stresses the need for continuity in assessment, and therefore in curriculum planning, across the whole age range from 5 to 16. Thus, work at age 11 should both have a planned relationship to the work suitable for 7 year olds and also provide a suitable basis for more highly differentiated work in the next phase. The information provided from national assessment at 11 would then be relevant to the interests of all secondary subject teachers in appraising the starting points for work with pupils after age 11.

123. It is not possible for us to develop this theme beyond the very general form sketched in Figure 2. The underlying issue is a curricular one and it is for the subject working groups to collaborate with one another in their recommendations for 7 and 11.

Primary Age 7	Single profile with few basic elements
Primary Age 11	More elements perhaps grouped in broad subject areas
Secondary Age 14	Full profiles for each subject, over the foundation subjects
	carried through, to 16, mainly as GCSE profile elements

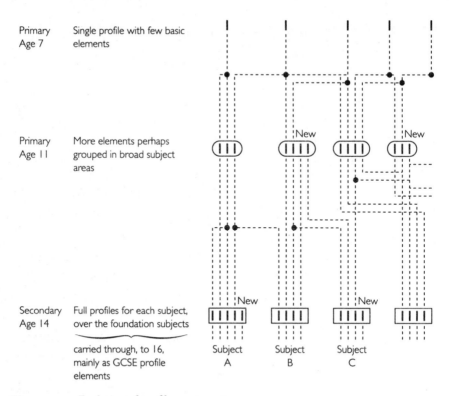

Figure 2 *Evolution of profile components*

We therefore recommend that a working group be established, with some shared membership between the subject working groups, to coordinate their proposals for assessment, including testing, at the primary stages, in the light of a comprehensive view of the primary curriculum and of the need to limit the assessment burden on teachers.

124. In summary, progression would be identified through the reporting system on the basis of identifying changes in what the children know. Many of those changes would be denoted by the changes of level within a profile component. Some components would be subdivided as learning progresses, and the level numbering would continue. Some might be wholly new and the level system would commence from level 1. New components and some subdivisions of components may be for use only with children who have reached pre-defined levels or, in the case of a modern foreign language, the appropriate age. At the first reporting age, some profile components would be general and not specific to subjects, but would form the basis for a growing number of subject components which would be developed from them at later ages. Thus progression would be firmly emphasised across the transition from primary to secondary work.

|1.4| Purposes and Principles

(Extract from National Curriculum – Task Group on Assessment and Testing: A Report)

Purposes

23. The terms of reference and the letter of guidance from the Secretary of State require that information derived from assessments (including tests) shall be capable of serving several purposes:

1 *formative*, so that the positive achievements of a pupil may be recognised and discussed and the appropriate next steps may be planned;
2 *diagnostic*, through which learning difficulties may be scrutinised and classified so that appropriate remedial help and guidance can be provided;
3 *summative*, for the recording of the overall achievement of a pupil in a systematic way;
4 *evaluative*, by means of which some aspects of the work of a school, an LEA or other discrete part of the educational service can be assessed and/or reported upon.

24. Our attention has also been drawn to the effects all forms of assessment have on teaching and learning. We are required to propose a national assessment system which enhances teaching and learning without any increase in 'the calls on teachers' and pupils' time for activities which do not directly promote learning'. We judge that it would be impossible to keep the burdens on teachers and pupils within reasonable bounds if different batteries of assessments and tests had to be created to serve each separate purpose. We must therefore reflect the priority given in our brief to the need 'to show what a pupil has learned and mastered'.

SERVING SEVERAL PURPOSES

25. Some purposes may, however, be served by combining in various ways the findings of assessments designed primarily for a different purpose. It is possible to build up a comprehensive picture of the overall achievements of a pupil by aggregating, in a structured way, the separate results of a set of assessments designed to serve formative purposes. However, if assessments were designed only for summative purposes, then formative information could not be obtained, since the summative assessments occur at the end of a phase of learning and make no attempt at throwing light on the educational history of the pupil. It is realistic to envisage, for the purpose of evaluation, ways of aggregating the information on individual pupils into accounts of the success of a school, or LEA, in facilitating the learning and achievements of those for whom it is responsible; again, the reverse process is an impossibility.

FORMATIVE AND SUMMATIVE

26. We judge therefore that an assessment system designed for formative purposes can meet all the needs of national assessment at ages before 16. At age 16 the focus shifts from formative to summative. The GCSE is a terminal examination in the sense that it comes at the end of the compulsory period of education and thus cannot avoid summative judgements. Similar considerations would apply to other forms of assessment at that stage. Summative judgements or aggregations may be made at ages other than 16, but only at 16 does it seem appropriate for assessment components to be designed specifically for summative purposes.

FORMATIVE AND DIAGNOSTIC

27. We do not see the boundary between the formative and diagnostic purposes as being sharp or clear. If an assessment designed in formative terms is well matched to the pupil, it is likely to provide some information which will help in the diagnosis of strengths and weaknesses. Some assessments of this kind will be of value as indicators of learning problems which require further investigation. Further diagnostic investigations would, however, often involve the use of highly specialised tests of relevance to only a limited set of circumstances and pupils. It follows that the results of such tests should not be included in aggregated results for groups of pupils. Furthermore, a detailed diagnostic report on every pupil would lead to an excess of information and hence be counter-productive. The formative information about pupils will be passed on to their next teacher; if diagnostic reports are confined to problems

outside the normal range, these will be highlighted and made more salient to the receiving teacher.

> We recommend that the basis of the national assessment system be essentially formative, but designed also to indicate where there is need for more detailed diagnostic assessment. At age 16, however, it should incorporate assessment with summative functions.

OVERALL RESULTS FOR A PUPIL

28. The complete range of formative and diagnostic purposes will be served only if the results for each pupil are aggregated in various ways: for example, across cognate elements in part of a subject or field of study or across the whole of that subject or field. There may also be value in comparisons which place the performances of the pupil in the contexts of his or her earlier achievements and the achievements of the class as a whole. Out of these aggregations and comparisons can come judgements to be presented to the pupil and/or parent so that they are involved in making decisions about the pupil's future educational programme. Such judgements raise questions of the confidentiality of information about individuals. We see confidentiality as crucial if assessment is to serve a positive role.

> We recommend that all assessment information about an individual be treated as confidential and thus confined to those who need to know in order to help that pupil.

EVALUATION

29. The other purposes listed in paragraph 23 can be fulfilled by shifting the focus from individual to class, or to a group of classes in a school, or to the school, or to a group of schools within an LEA. The same processing procedures of aggregation and comparison, together with an analysis of the spread of the results around the average, can be applied to yield information of value to a range of audiences. National assessment designed to have formative/diagnostic functions and to serve as a foundation for all the purposes will give results which have a common basis in the progress of the pupils in relation to national targets.

> We recommend however that for summative and evaluative purposes results should be aggregated across classes or schools so that no individual performances can be separated out. [. . .]

PROFILE COMPONENTS IN THE ASSESSMENT FRAMEWORK

31. The basic unit of information in any assessment system is the response of an individual pupil to a particular demand or task: for example, a written response to a test item, an observed action in a practical task, or a sequence of actions assessed by a teacher's rating. To base an interpretation upon only one unit of information is neither sufficient nor desirable. Any particular unit of information will depend heavily on the context in which the information is gathered. Before any such response can be interpreted with any certainty, it must be compared with the responses of the same pupil to other tasks and perhaps with the responses of other pupils to the same tasks. The standard method of making these comparisons is by aggregating the responses.

FEEDING FORWARD

32. The formative and summative purposes of assessment, concerned with the immediate needs and achievements of the pupil, necessarily involve aggregations of the responses to a range of tasks by individual pupils. As we have already said, the formative purpose is fundamental to the national assessment system. In order to serve that purpose effectively, the results must both feed back to the pupil and feed forward to the next teacher or institution. The emphasis on the formative function serves to underline the 'feed forward' aspect. This is enhanced by the choice of reporting ages, which carries with it the implications that the teachers responsible for making the assessments will not be those responsible for acting upon them.

33. This feed forward role is diminished if the assessment of a pupil's progress in a subject is designed to produce only a single overall score. For example, in developing graded assessments in science, the London Group chose to assess and report separately on three components – skills (mainly practical), knowledge and understanding, and exploration (project) work. The results in these three components form a profile which represents the pupil's attainment in science. Similarly, many schemes for English recognise the need to attend separately to writing, oracy, reading comprehension, and listening: again, results on these four would give a profile. Information of value to pupils, parents and others would be lost if (say) a teacher were to add the results of writing to those of oracy, and to ignore those separate results when discussing pupils' future work. If subject attainments are presented as a profile of separately determined scores, then receiving teachers will be better able to use the information to share their teaching strategies.

We recommend that, to realise the formative purpose of the national assessment system, pupil results in a subject should be presented as an attainment profile of the kind discussed above.

PROFILE COMPONENTS

34. The profile will thus be composed of a set of profile components. These components should be broadly based so as to be informative to the teachers of a range of subjects being studied by the pupil. In addition, each reporting age may herald the introduction of new subject areas. For these in particular, teachers will want a report on subjects already studied which goes beyond subject-specific knowledge and skills to the general skills, knowledge and understanding upon which they can build. Including in a subject profile those components which have applicability beyond that subject will serve to emphasise the underlying unity of a subject-based curriculum.

35. Defining the profile components will be the responsibility of the relevant subject working groups. We envisage that each component will comprise a cluster of attainment targets which have some homogeneity in relation to the skills, knowledge and understanding which the subject promotes. But their internal consistency should not be the only determining factor. To demand high correlation between scores on all of the attainment targets within each profile component might lead either to an unmanageable number of profile components, or (worse) to the omission on statistical grounds of educationally important targets. There is a balance to be struck. On the one hand, a large number of components would daunt teachers and confuse parents. On the other, a small number would mean that each component might be too heterogeneous to be meaningful.

We recommend that an individual subject should report a small number (preferably no more than four and never more than six) of profile components reflecting the variety of knowledge, skills and understanding to which the subject gives rise. Wherever possible, one or more components should have more general application across the curriculum: for these a single common specification should be adopted in each of the subjects concerned.

36. Each profile component ought to be assessed separately and separately moderated. This has implications for the amount of assessment and moderation overall. [...]

FEEDING BACK

37. While the above argument for profile components rests on the feed forward aspect, profiles also provide feedback. The successes of the graded assessment movement point to the educational value of detailed feedback to pupils. Attainment targets, shared by teachers and pupils, appropriate to the current stage of the pupil's achievement and pointing the way forward to further progress, appear to play an important part in raising standards of achievement. Thus formative assessment must be in terms to which pupils can respond and which clearly indicate what has been and what remains to be achieved. The profile components should give meaningful information for this purpose and help to convey and draw upon the diversity of performance that a pupil may exhibit in any one subject.

AGGREGATION FOR EVALUATION

38. These arrangements should serve the evaluative purposes of national assessment equally well. Aggregating pupil performances to the level of the class, the school, the LEA, or the age group should help to monitor the delivery of the national curriculum. These aggregates can be based on any unit of analysis. Aggregates of performances in test items, standard assessments, attainment targets, profile components, whole subjects or larger curriculum segments all have their evaluative uses.

39. To sum up so far, we envisage that the outcomes of the national assessment system will be presented as the attainments in a set of profile components, some cross-curricular, some subject specific. The profile will become the main vehicle of communication in helping both pupils and teachers to evaluate their work. [. . .]

1.5 | TGAT: A Conflict of Purpose

PATRICIA MURPHY

INTRODUCTION

The proposals for a national curriculum and an associated national assessment system were published as a consultation paper, *The National Curriculum 5–16* (1987). In the responses to the paper (Haviland, 1988) several fundamental characteristics of the proposals were consistently challenged. Of particular interest here were the question marks raised about the validity of the proposals' assumptions about children's learning, and the nature of their knowledge and understanding. Such questions, if pursued to their logical end-point, confront one of the proposed major outcomes of the new system, i.e. a model of national assessment wherein formative and summative elements co-exist, and which therefore fulfils a multi-purpose role.

Many responses highlighted the lack of justification for expressing the curriculum in terms of narrow subjects and recommended a broader and more flexible approach to the curriculum. At issue is the whole question of how knowledge is constructed and abstracted and how such abstracted knowledge is acquired and used by pupils. It was further noted that a subject-based assessment system would impose additional constraints on the teacher in the classroom and limit the learning opportunities available to pupils. Such constraints were regarded as in direct conflict with the findings of recent research about children's learning.

Other responses focused on the lack of research justification for age-related attainment targets or for any model of learning which assumed linear, regular progression which the proposals implied. These responses drew attention to the complex nature of pupils' understanding and cast doubt on the feasibility of producing target statements which encapsulate progress or, as the proposals state, what pupils have 'learnt and mastered'.

The Task Group on Assessment and Testing (TGAT) was briefed to advise on a 'coherent system of assessment including testing' which would: cover the whole period of compulsory schooling; be applicable to the school system as a whole but be capable of accommodating appropriate variations between subjects. The assessments to be addressed were described in the group's brief as *diagnostic* or *formative* for planning pupils' curriculum, and *summative* for reporting pupils' achievements and evaluating the performance of schools. The *main* purposes identified were those of *reporting* and *planning*, thus both a formative and summative system was to be established. Any initiative to change assessment practice in schools must reflect a view of the nature and purpose of education, therefore in scrutinising the TGAT recommendations one must perforce consider the type of education experience they promote [...]

[My] paper focuses on aspects of the resulting compromise and raises the following issues for debate:

1 whether, given the underlying tenets of the government's proposal and the group's acceptance of them, the TGAT recommendations compound the overriding intent of the proposals to produce a summative rather than a formative model of assessment for reporting and evaluative purposes;

2 that in the attempt to reconcile the political and educational factors and the very real practical constraints on the system the recommendations are internally contradictory;

3 the nature of the contradictions is such that the aim to inform and guide pupils' learning in schools cannot be achieved and indeed will be mis-informed (Denvir, Brown and Eve, 1987).

THE ASSESSMENT MODEL – FORMATIVE AND/OR SUMMATIVE?

We will look at some of the recommendations in detail now and at what current research and assessment has to say about them. Early on in the report the group state 'that it is impossible to keep the burdens on teachers and pupils within reasonable bounds if different batteries of assessments and tests had to be created to serve each separate purpose. We must therefore reflect the priority given in our brief to the need to show what a pupil has learned and mastered'. They continue 'some purposes may be served by *combining* in various ways the findings of assessments designed primarily for a different purpose'. However, assessment practice over the years has indicated quite clearly that an assessment can usually only be designed for a specific purpose and thus its use for others is inappropriate. The experience of the Assessment of Performance Unit surveys, (DES – Science in schools. Age 13: Review

Report 1988; Science in schools. Age 11, 13 and 15: A Technical Review Report 1988) demonstrate that to provide general population performance scores requires, at least, different assessment *methods* and *tasks* to those necessary to judge an individual's understanding on any one aspect of the curriculum. The latter requires far greater coverage of issues. Nor can the assessment of an individual's understanding reflect the arbitrary boundaries drawn up to distinguish between artificial subject constructs.

TGAT further recommend that what forms the baseline prior to any aggregation for reporting purposes should be the 'separate results of a set of assessments designed to serve *formative* purposes'. They state categorically that the reverse process of extrapolating from summative data to formative data is not possible. A view substantiated by informed opinion. The recommendations, however, then continue to suggest that the formative results can be aggregated for summative purposes 'across cognate elements in part of a subject or a field of study or across the whole of that subject'. It follows from this that what is to be assessed must of necessity 'fit' a subject-based definition of an aggregate. These aggregates will then determine the nature of the tasks to be used in the assessment. Thus the summative needs appear to dominate in contrast with the earlier statement.

In their recommendations TGAT attempt to balance the demands for validity, reliability and feasibility that the assessment system must reflect to be acceptable to the profession and the users and consumers of compulsory education. The TGAT model constructed as it is within subject boundaries represents the traditional view of the curriculum hitherto enshrined in typical secondary schools. This perspective determines how educational achievement is defined and portrayed and hence education per se (Murphy and Torrance, 1988). Many may agree with TGAT that a subject-based profile of assessment is a perfectly adequate way of describing pupils' eventual achievements in school. Particularly if a broader view of subject achievement such as those outlined in some GCSE syllabuses is endorsed. However, this approach to enhancing the validity of assessment is disputed by current assessment research on, for example, records of achievement. Such research would challenge the narrow, cognitive subject-based definition of educational achievement both for summative and formative assessment purposes.

Yet the real dilemma for TGAT is not that there are alternative views held on educational achievement but rather that they themselves claim that the strength of the model rests on the quality of the formative elements. The formative elements of the assessment have to allow teachers to plan an individual's curriculum and to inform them and others of what the pupil has learnt and mastered. The question to be posed is 'what does a subject-based view of knowledge say about what it means to know or to learn?' The latter has to be the criterion against which pupils' attainment is assessed for formative purposes. The lack of relationship between a subject-based cognitive description of knowledge and the process by which pupils' understanding develops and is deployed is a central inconsistency within TGAT's proposals.

In a response made by the Scottish Council for Research in Education

(SCRE, 1988) it is stated that 'a system designed to ascribe pupils to some level of attainment on a national scale will not serve for diagnostic purposes – even if this is interpreted in the weak sense, of mapping out the individual pupil's strengths and weaknesses'. This requirement being, at least, what is needed for planning purposes. Denvir (1988) explains after extensive research into diagnostic assessment and the feasibility of defining and assessing attainment targets in mathematics 'at first glance the information collected for summative assessment for one stage would appear identical to that of formative assessment for the next. However, summative assessment seeks, for each student, to classify knowledge into what is "known" and what is "not known" whereas formative assessment attempts to focus on precisely the "grey areas in between" that summative assessment sets out to avoid.'

What the statements indicate is not that formative assessment collects *additional* information to that needed for summative purposes but rather *different* information.

In formative assessment the concern is not with what is known but how it is known and not with what is not known in terms of what is not achieved but rather the barriers which produce that lack of achievement. TGAT recommend no independent assessment of attitudes yet one must ask how in a subject-based assessment model are the cognitive and affective interactions which determine pupils' responses to tasks to be catered for? In particular, given present research, how does a traditional view of cognitive learning of subjects take into account alternative learning styles, developed by pupils under the influence of gender, culture and class? The different learning styles that children enter school with determine how they make sense of the world; the problems they perceive; the solutions they value; and the manner in which they choose to express themselves. Formative assessment is concerned with the totality of pupils' knowledge: the personal; the tacit and the explicit; and how their knowledge is integrated and accessed.

STRIKING A BALANCE – VALIDITY, RELIABILITY AND FEASIBILITY

TGAT is clearly aware of many of the dilemmas raised here about the validity of the model. For example they, to an extent, recognise the problem of the 'underlying unity of a subject-based curriculum' and suggest that pupils' achievements are recorded as a subject profile but with at least one element per subject representing 'general skills and knowledge'. The difficulty of how to access pupils' knowledge given individual and group differences in experience and world views is noted in the statement that 'any unit of information depends heavily on the context in which the information is gathered'. The group indicate that this can be tackled by *aggregation* of responses to a range of tasks. However the group have then to consider how to enhance the *reliability* and *feasibility* of the system. For example they want to minimise the amount of information collected but maximise the confidence in its interpretation. To meet these demands they advise limiting the number of profile elements to no more than 4–6 for any one subject. They also caution that the elements must be homogeneous in order to provide reliable data on a manageable scale. To further ensure the reliability of the data the group recommend that pupils' responses are elicited in a 'standard manner' using formal assessment procedures. However to maintain validity the standardised tasks are to cover a range of presentation modes, operation modes and response modes. All of which are known to contribute to the heterogeneity in pupils' responses. [...] It appears to be the case that the demands TGAT attempt to meet are technically in conflict. Aside from this the group themselves describe an extensive data collection in which detailed analysis of pupils' errors are to reveal much of pupils' learning difficulties for formative purposes. Clearly such error analyses are viewed as essential for informing decisions about the planning of pupils' curriculum. This position contradicts the group's recommendation that narrow, tightly defined data must be aimed for to enhance comparability and confidence for reporting and evaluative purposes. The group also urge that 'observed responses must be shown to be typical'. Again this raises a question. How is 'typical' defined given the previous statement that any unit of information is dependent on the context in which it is gathered? It is necessary to resolve both the internal confusions and the alternative perspectives on how validity and reliability can be reconciled prior to operationalising the model TGAT recommended.

PROFILE ASSESSMENT – SOME FORMATIVE AND SUMMATIVE TENSIONS

The use of a profile for recording pupils' achievement is seen as an important tool for maintaining the validity and reliability of the proposed assessment system. The *choice* of profile elements is not uncontentious. After a decade of research in science education and assessment, on a national scale, we find that the APU Science profile does not match the Science working group's, which in turn does not match that of the Grade Related Criteria working groups in science. Indeed between the physics, biology and chemistry GRC groups there were considerable differences of opinion. The various profiles described reflect major differences in educational philosophy and in epistemological and psychological perspectives. The choice of profile elements is therefore a national fixture which many may well consider invalid.

A profile element only exists in terms of the tasks that are deemed to 'fit' the element. Again the research into criterion-referencing (Gipps, 1988) has shown the lack of consensus that exists about the criteria to be used to judge pupils' educational achievement. The difficulty is in describing criteria at different levels in meaningful language so that the distinctions between both the criteria and the levels within them are clear and unambiguous. Importantly if one alters the tasks, either the range or the nature of them, one alters what it means to be successful or otherwise. Thus one person's definition of a criterion, translated into tasks, could be much more difficult than another's. It is therefore possible to manipulate the standards against which schools and pupils are assessed. Given the grave importance of setting such standards we must ask how a lack of consensus within the education community and outside is to be reconciled? How for example will moderators interpret the demands within the tasks set by teachers to ensure that equivalent tasks are set which reflect a similar level of difficulty and educational perspective? Furthermore how is this to be done when research such as that of the APU Science group is only just beginning to expose the complexity of task demands? Nor is it just the task that is problematic but most importantly the manner of scoring it.

It has already been pointed out that what to aggregate is contentious. The cut-offs between profile elements are artificial constructs. They serve only as devices to facilitate communication. Such artificial constructs in no way reflect learning or knowledge structures. The need to aggregate is for enhancing comparability so once again the summative requirement for reliability is at the expense of the formative need for validity. TGAT in recognising the practical constraints on the system intend to limit the number of tasks used. This compromise along with aggregation of responses will nevertheless, it is suggested, enable a high level of confidence in the results. [. . .] The requirements of domain sampling and of generalisability theory on the contrary indicate that statistical confidence in the data will not be achieved.

DEFINING AN ELEMENT

Another key to the relationship between validity and reliability lies in the report's recommendations for homogeneity within profile elements. This is an essential pre-requisite if a few tasks are to be aggregated to produce reliable scores for summative assessment. Again this can be interpreted as the summative purposes dominating the formative needs. What does homogeneity mean? It helps here to look at other assessment experience. The APU Science project have tightly defined task descriptions within profile elements. The tasks are externally validated by experts who judge their degree of 'fit'. Hence the tasks used in the surveys are considered to be homogeneous. Pupils' responses to them are not. It is the *responses* which need to be homogeneous if we are to be able to relax the requirement to have many tasks in order to determine performance levels with any confidence. The APU has also researched the nature of the heterogeneity of pupils' responses. The research exposes two issues. First, that what is demanded in tasks, albeit labelled for example as science and within one criterion element of that subject, actually requires understanding of numerous demands which span other profile elements and other subjects.

Failure to respond to a task, or to achieve success on it, can therefore arise for many disparate reasons other than the criterion stated. In science it includes the obvious dependency of achievement on mathematical and linguistic skills. The more narrowly defined the profile element then generally the fewer interactive features present and the more likely that pupils' responses will be homogeneous. Consequently the fewer profile elements that a subject is constrained to be represented by the greater likelihood for heterogeneity of response. This is assuming that for the sake of validity and for formative purposes all the significant learning demands of a subject are covered in the profile.

The APU Science assessment framework, like the TGAT model, is an assessment model for populations of pupils in primary and secondary schools. In this framework there are nine profile elements. Within one of these elements there is a small sub-group of tasks, defined as 'reading off from line graphs'. Such narrowly defined profile elements are definitely contra-indicated in the TGAT report. Yet even in responding to such tasks the range of pupils' performance is considerable. Why? Well, one can fail to read off from a graph because one does not have a concept of number, of scale, of the variable represented, the units used or indeed the algorithm itself. For younger pupils or lower achievers the density of text to be read prior to understanding what to do with the graph can be the insurmountable barrier. Given a group of tasks involving graphs it then follows that the same pupil can succeed or fail on various ones depending on those issues described. This is a common finding of the APU science surveys and there are numerous examples of it throughout the APU review reports. How do we then label pupils' achievements – under graphing skills? How do we judge mastery if failure is associated with something quite other than graphing skills?

Reporting of pupils' results by profile elements tends not to allow reporting of the type needed for formative purposes. Quite simply this is because the elements represent arbitrary divides and what one needs to know are the interactions between profile elements and their effect on pupils' responses. There is the further need to understand whether pupils can deploy the prerequisite skills from other subject areas.

For example the APU project in one in-depth research study moved away from judging population levels of performance to considering individuals' performance. The purpose of the studies was defined in only a weakly formative sense and yet it was essential in order to develop appropriate instruments for this study to generate questions which fell between the profile elements in the framework. To further strengthen the formative interpretation of the data, cross subject probes would have been necessary. Particularly to determine ways in which pupils assign meaning to words both in tasks and in their responses to them.

This in-depth study also focused on what might be called a general skill or knowledge profile – 'Measurement'. Such a profile element, it is suggested, is to be included in each subject working group's proposals. By definition an overarching profile element will cover several subject profile elements and their interstices (Murphy, P., 1988). This means that these profile elements will be even more heterogeneous than others if they are to fulfil the role recommended in the report. Again one must ask how such a profile element can be accommodated in a model demanding easily manageable, homogeneous and non-extensive data? Such an element could not be assessed reliably or validly by the use of a small number of tasks.

DEFINING THE ASSESSMENT TASKS

The natural multi-dimensionality of tasks is not an assessment artifact but rather an expression of the nature of learning activities. Hence even if the number of profile elements are restricted and the types of tasks within those elements further limited, homogeneity of pupils' responses will not be achieved. One would only achieve this by severely controlling the parameters of tasks. This has not been an exercise that has met with a great deal of success in assessment research. More importantly such tasks have limited validity and give few indications of what pupils have learnt and mastered. They could not fulfil a formative purpose. It would seem from the TGAT recommendations that reliability, albeit a technical chimera, is to be aimed for first and foremost for the purpose of reporting. Of course to be in line with the initial recommendation for a formative based system one would go for validity before reliability. The educational need is for accurate and insightful indications of what pupils' learning difficulties and successes are for formative purposes rather than many uninterpretable responses which combine to form a score that one can have confidence in but no understanding of. It is possible to build on real insights and the present system, at the level of teachers, does indeed lack explicit examples of these. Thus validity before reliability is an educationally sound compromise. However, it could in no way serve to compare pupils or schools. The question still remains whether the compromise represented in the TGAT model to serve the purpose of reporting can be achieved either reliably or validly.

The report does strive to consider formative assessment but one has to ask to what extent the implications of such a process of assessment are understood. Some of the tasks given in Appendix D of the report span profile elements and subjects and are of the type to provide formative insights. Given such tasks how could pupils' performance be scored prior to aggregation? The multi-dimensional nature of the tasks are such that pupils could achieve the same score for a gamut of achievements. The scores even if appropriately assigned to alternative profile criteria or to alternative subjects will result in a picture of achievement which has no coherence for reporting purposes. What is much more likely to happen, given the requirements to place pupils in a narrow range of subject levels, is that part-scores on tasks will be assigned to one or two criteria and consequently the same level will be achieved by pupils for very different performances. This is a problem that will resonate throughout the whole assessment. Aggregation is not a solution to any assessment purpose if what is to be aggregated remains problematic to score due to its multi-dimensional nature.

Finally, the second issue that has to be examined with respect to heterogeneity in pupils' responses is the affective and cognitive interdependence of pupils' understanding. The group recommend the use of a range of tasks covering different modes of presentation, response and operation. This is to deal with the complex nature of children's understanding and to enhance the validity and formative utility of the data. However, the solution to this complexity is not as simple as the report implies. The tasks described while perhaps fitting the same criterion actually measure *different achievements*. Many of these differences reflect the influences of gender, class and culture. As a consequence of these influences failure on tasks may well not indicate a lack of achievement but rather alternative world views. [...] Two problems need to be looked at here. First, that the assessment model and the tasks must not represent a dominant gender, culture or class perspective which of course it will. Second, that achievements of children and their potential are not to be seen as fitting a single norm-referenced continuum, and progress along any one dimension of achievement is not viewed as occurring in regular stages for anybody. The evidence does not exist to support such a view, indeed much of what exists contradicts it.

The diversity among adults is widely recognised. The same diversity in school pupils is frequently homogenised by imposing one perspective of achievement which reflects one set of values. In this way a population can be labelled as good, average and below average. For formative assessments the range of tasks described by TGAT are indeed needed to allow pupils the chance to demonstrate what they have achieved. However, the implications of recent research are that only certain tasks will suit certain groups of pupils hence the recommendation to aggregate the range of responses is too simple a solution. We know too little of the way in which a population of novices acquire expert knowledge for simple solutions to exist. Aggregation must reflect what is *achievement* for the novice and not be weighted and thus valued on the basis of abstracted 'expert' constructions of what is valuable knowledge. Of course the two hopefully can be articulated in such a way as to be related but the former must drive the aggregation for formative purposes. What assessment research is exposing is that a pupil's alternative problems and strategies lie at the heart of an individual's expression of his or her achievements and are not necessarily scorable. Scoring, by its ordinal and cardinal nature, assumes too simplistic a perspective for dealing with achievements in qualitatively different dimensions.

The problems of the ever present compromise between supposed criterion-referenced tasks and norm-referenced scoring and aggregation is widely recognised in assessment. TGAT again are aware of this yet their attempts at compromise raise further conflicts in the proposed model. For example they recommend that pupils' progress be marked by levels of achievement but that the levels are not to indicate some 'inescapable order in the way children learn' or a 'sequence of difficulty in the material to be learnt'. They elaborate this point by suggesting that the levels are not age-related but then go on to suggest about one level of progress in a two-year span. They also talk of 'average expectations' of particular aged pupils. The overlap they do allow for is between 7 and 11 year olds, 11 and 14 year olds and 14 and 16 year olds. However, the practical implications of for example the testing at age seven would make it very difficult to allow for this overlap. Moreover the overlap in no way reflects the degree of overlap identified in research studies. It raises the question whether the practical arrangements for testing at each age allow the levels of achievement to be anything other than age related?

Although the report indicates no sequence or order of difficulty in the levels it does include the statement that progress will be along a 'short scale in a profile component'. This statement if enacted would impose grave limitations on present understanding of the nature of pupils' success. What is at issue here is to do with the truism that the 'more you understand the less you know' or the more profound your ignorance. The U-shaped learning curve is not a new phenomenon. Its occurrence in a range of curriculum areas is, however, being increasingly documented. In science the work of the Children's Learning in Science project shows that as pupils understand more concepts then their responses to any one concept question are commonly at a lower level than previously or of younger pupils or those with less breadth of conceptual understanding. This is because the competing theories available to the pupils makes both the questions and the answer less certain.

APU Science research has shown that as children move from an everyday problem-solving approach to a more scientific approach they take account of an increasing number of complex issues. In attempting to integrate these issues into an overall strategy pupils' ultimate strategies are often less adequate because the problem they address is more difficult (Murphy, P., 1988 note). In both these cases pupils' apparent lack of success is representative of considerable progress and achievement. A system based on a hierarchy of levels cannot accommodate learning of this kind yet learning is like this. A simple hierarchical viewpoint would accord these pupils lower scores for higher personal achievements. To finish then we can pose a final question. Does the model recommended by TGAT in fact remove the 'heart' of formative assessment rather than represent it?

REFERENCES

Denvir, B., Brown, M. and Eve, P. (1987) Attainment targets and assessment in the primary phase: report of the mathematics feasibility study. London: DES.

DES (1987) *The National Curriculum 5–16: A Consultation Document.* London: DES.

DES (1988) Science in Schools. Age 11, 13 and 15: A Technical Review Report. London.

DES (1988) Science in Schools. Age 13: Review Report. London.

Gipps, C. (1988) Testing at 7 and 11: the national proposals, paper for the Nuffield Seminar 18/3/88.

Haviland, J. (1988) *Take care, Mr Baker!* London: Fourth Estate.

Murphy, P. (1988) Insights into pupils' responses to practical investigations from the APU *Physics Education,* 23 November.

Murphy, R. and Torrance, H. (1988) *The Changing Face of Educational Assessment.* Milton Keynes: Open University Press.

SCRE (1988) A response from the staff of the Scottish Council for Research in Education to the Government's proposals for Curriculum and Assessment.

THE AGENDA FOR EDUCATIONAL
1.6 MEASUREMENT

ROBERT WOOD

It is no longer necessary to plead for a distinction to be made between educational and psychological measurement but much remains to be done to elaborate and substantiate that distinction. To argue, as some of us have done, that educational measurement has for too long been under the sway of psychometrics is one thing, to establish what educational measurement is, or rather should be, is quite another.

The term itself tends to encourage people to equate 'measurement in education' with 'educational measurement'. What is needed is a striking word to signal a fresh enterprise. At one time I thought Carver's (1974) 'edumetrics' might do the job but it is an ugly word which does not seem to have stuck. What C. P. Scott is supposed to have said about television comes to mind: 'No good will come of this device. The word is half Greek and half Latin.'

Education has always been vulnerable to psychometric incursions and influence, although less so now than before. Lacking a distinctive and self-confident view about the purpose of testing in schools and about what kinds of tests were suitable and unsuitable, it has, rather like a client state, looked on helplessly as psychometric doctrines and practices have been installed and put to work. Which is not to say that there have not been, at all times, as in all client states, individuals in education ready and eager to embrace psychometric assumptions and beliefs about how children differ, and to suppress curiosity about the children themselves[1]. I should add that the classroom has been, for psychometricians, an excellent source of cheap available data.

But education and differential psychology do not have the same aims. Education is not, as far as I know, a permanent research endeavour, although in certain circumstances and at different times it can be made to yield research data (although not the sort that psychometricians took so freely). Educators, by and large, have to take children and students as they find them. This was the message which emerged from the 'Heredity and IQ' debate precipitated by Jensen (1969), an affair which symbolises education's growing determination to fend off gratuitous psychometric thinking. At the end of it all even someone like Bereiter, in an article characterised by Jensen as 'an exceptionally intelligent and penetrating analysis', was obliged to state that, with respect to social and racial differences, knowledge of a possible genetic basis is relevant neither to the classroom teacher nor to the educational policy makers.[2] Amen to that.

SOME HISTORY

That educational and psychological measurement have long been differentiated in *name* is not in doubt; as early as 1918 Ayres was able to write a *history* of educational measurement: there was Monroe's book in 1923 and the founding of the journal *Educational and Psychological Measurement* in 1941. But was educational measurement ever seen as anything other than the application of psychological measurement in an educational setting? The universal answer up to about 1950 would appear to have been 'no'. Nunnally (1975) revealed more than he knew when he wrote, 'Is there an important place for traditional measures of aptitude and achievement in modern education? In 1950 most persons who were prominent either in psychometric research or in education would immediately have answered "yes" but now there is a lively controversy about the matter.'

It is possible Nunnally took too sanguine a view. Consider *Educational and Psychological Measurement*, admittedly a journal which in all respects has changed little over the years. If you read the inside front cover you will see that it is, as it always was, concerned first and foremost with studies of individual differences, that is to say, with psychometrics or psychological measurement. Other categories of paper are mentioned but you will search in vain for a definition or description of educational measurement, even one as partial as Carver's (1974) 'measurement of intra-individual differences'. In important respects, the psychometric hegemony persists, or do I read too much into the fact that Robert Thorndike's new book (1982) about educational measurement is called *Applied Psychometrics*?

It could have been different. Levine (1976) draws a picture of 'professional test constructors' consistently overriding the requirement of classroom usefulness – 'test constructors wanted to construct tests with good measurement properties amenable to statistical analysis' – so fitting the educational foot to the psychometric shoe. There was an opportunity in the 1930s when Hawkes *et al.* (1936) pointed out that achievement could have been measured in absolute units, in relation to some absolute standard, or even in relation to some passing grade, but these same people managed to argue themselves out of this idea and the chance was lost.

Nunnally's choice of 1950 as a watershed year is significant because by then a group of American educators had already been working for two years on what turned out to be the *Taxonomy of Educational Objectives*, Vol. 1 (Bloom *et al.*, 1956). That ambitious and singular endeavour had little to say about measurement as such (although it did mention promising ideas like the Tab test, a primitive forerunner of the tailored test) but it was immensely successful – and subsequent denigration has done nothing to diminish this – in dramatising (and often stimulating) a felt need among educators for an approach to measurement which would be reflective of and responsive to what is peculiar to education, in particular the cycle of planning, instruction, learning, achievement and measurement. The mistake Bloom and his colleagues made, as we can see with hindsight, was to formulate educational objectives in ad hoc and naive psychological language. That this formulation exposed a flank which critics, especially philosophers, savaged is of less concern than that the *Taxonomy* gave the impression that educational measurement was still concerned with psychological constructs, indeed more so than ever. The consequence was that lay people, who had hitherto talked about content or just material to be learned, having perhaps been weaned away from faculty psychology not so long before, now wedded themselves to a new orthodoxy whose categories they did not understand, naïve though these were, and which, in the course of time, they came to reify.

But none of this held up the emergence of educational measurement. By the time criticism of the *Taxonomy* had become commonplace and its unfortunate side-effects had taken hold, a crucial event for educational measurement had long since taken place. This was the publication of Glaser's (1963) seminal paper in which he introduced the notions of criterion referencing and criterion-referenced testing (CRT) and differentiated them sharply from norm-referenced testing, emphasis on which, he thought, had been brought about by the preoccupation of test theory with aptitude and with selection and prediction problems. It is true, as Glaser acknowledged, that others had made this distinction previously[3] but it was Glaser's paper which caught the imagination. It can be said to mark the point at which educational measurement began to detach itself from classical psychometrics.

Since then there has been much embellishment, but little invention. Criterion-referenced testing (CRT) remains the embodiment of educational measurement; notions like mastery testing (although not mastery learning) and minimum competency testing are only developed versions of the original conception, given a particular twist. There is an irony here. The original conception was borrowed from psychology, to some minds a rather dubious branch of psychology which education ought to have resisted.[4]

The odd thing is – and here is another irony – that a paradigm of learning which in the psychological context is not readily associated with a benign, caring disposition towards the individual is, when translated to the educational context, and by dint of a heavily emphasised contrast with norm-referenced testing, and the evils thereof, turned into an instrument of educational equity or even deliverance for the individual. The persistent tendency to disparage the norm-referenced test reached ludicrous proportions when two educators,

English not American (Guy and Chambers, 1973 and 1974), wrote a bizarre article denouncing norm-referenced examinations as a violation of students' civil rights because they are made to show their ignorance. I wonder what they would say now as minimum competency tests, constructed on the most impeccable CRT principles, are being hauled regularly through the US courts by individuals who claim that their civil rights are being violated because the state is withholding learning certificates or diplomas granted as a result of these tests. Evidently there is a less benign aspect to CRT. The point is, of course, that the concept of referencing is ultimately irrelevant.[5] Powerful though it may be in mobilising emotion, it is subordinate to that of function; that is to say, measures can be used for selection, screening or monitoring whatever the referencing assigned to them (Wood, 1976). We might object that referencing determines test construction policy which in turn rules out certain functions but the fact remains that CRT results can be put to purposes generally associated with norm-referenced testing. The effect is the same, as witness the example above.

PAYING ATTENTION TO WHERE THE DATA CAME FROM

Attempts to differentiate educational from psychological measurement have generally been made in terms of the function or purpose of measurement, and the consequences for the individual of the act of measurement. Further differentiation can, and ought, to be made in terms of the data the two kinds of measurement produce, and the methods of analysis which are appropriate for treating each. Evidently one major difference is that achievement data arise as a direct result of instruction and are therefore crucially affected by teaching and teachers. Any model for analysing such data which neglects to incorporate some sort of teaching effect (never mind other effects which are responsible for variation, like interactions) is simply not credible, yet how often are models built expressly for treating psychological data, sometimes of a most specialised kind, taken over and offered as plausible descriptions of how achievement occurs? The experience with the Rasch model (actually only one of his models and a rather thin psychological model at that) over the past decade is instructive (see Goldstein, 1979, for fuller strictures). For the same reason, and because achievement data are 'dirty' compared to aptitude data, which plays havoc with given notions about dimensionality and traits, it is likely to be a waste of time applying the well-worn psychometric apparatus – reliability, validity, internal consistency, homogeneity, etc. But people go on doing it. No doubt the cause lies in the absence of theory to explain or elucidate achievement, which induces desperation and panic. But it is not clear how enlightenment will come from applying inappropriate models to data.

AN EXTREME PROPOSAL

A radical move would be to ignore psychology altogether and that is what McIntyre and Brown (1978) did. Until they came along no one was prepared to argue that educational achievement has nothing to do with psychology and, by extension, that educational measurement has nothing to do with psychometrics. This is such a bold forthright solution that one has to admire it, but it is also so provocative that it cannot be allowed to pass, especially as they go on to call for educational measurement to be abandoned.

Educational objectives, state McIntyre and Brown, have nothing to do with the psychology of thinking:

> When we talk about educational attainment, then we are concerned with whether or not intentions that various kinds of knowledge and ability should be mastered have been realised. Neither questions about patterns of variation among people nor questions about processes of learning and thinking are relevant to such judgments, there is indeed no way in which psychology would seem to be logically relevant to such judgments.

They continue, 'Furthermore we would stress that it is on an understanding of the processes of thinking involved in these subjects that educational objectives depend, since the criteria which inform educational objectives are intrinsic to the subjects, not to the psychology of thinking' (p. 42).

Taking the last statement first, it presents no difficulty because it is tautologous, the consequence follows from the way educational objectives are defined. And does the definition have to be so heavily subject-bound? How would a cross-disciplinary ability like problem-solving be treated? Perhaps it would not be allowed as an objective. All the same, one knows what they are getting at. The application of Piaget's scheme to 'O' level science courses (for example, Shayer *et al.*, 1975) may have elucidated why students fail but they still failed, which means that educational objectives have not yet been realised. One cannot quarrel with this, given the terms of the argument, but, of course, it is precisely the uncurious character of this conceptualisation of attainment which Shayer and others reacted against. The point about their work is that it can, and does, lead to improvements in the way mastery is ascertained, as well as to increased understanding of how a subject should be taught. Ascertainment of mastery is crucial to the McIntyre–Brown formulation. In the first quotation they are clearly right, logically at any rate, about variation being irrelevant, and this process I have dealt with. It is the first sentence from 'intentions' onwards which catches the eye. Allowing that 'knowledge' and 'abilities' must be classed as mental predicates, to use Gilbert Ryle's term, if not psychological constructs, the question arises, 'Can you check whether such predicates/constructs have been mastered without invoking psychological categories?'

This question would have appealed to Ryle. As a matter of fact, the McIntyre–Brown method of argument is distinctly reminiscent of the no-nonsense treatment of psychology meted out in Chapter 2 of *The Concept of Mind* (Ryle, 1949). Compare the second quotation above with this from Ryle.

> The competent critic of prose style, experimental technique or embroidery, must at least know how to write, experiment or sew. Whether or not he has also learned psychology matters about as much as whether he has learned any chemistry, neurology or economics.

Like Ryle, McIntyre and Brown want no truck with the 'ghost in the machine', preferring instead to deal with 'intentions'; tricky philosophical ground, one would have thought, on to which Ryle would not necessarily have been willing to follow them. Whose 'intentions' are we talking about? The teacher's, the student's, the parents'? If it is the teacher's, as appears to be the case, is it fair to tie a *student's* mastery to a *teacher's* intentions?

Ascertainment of mastery seems not to be thought particularly problematical; perhaps as Ryle would likely have done, McIntyre and Brown argue that knowledge and abilities can be observed directly, in the spirit of knowing *how* rather than knowing *what*. But judging whether a student knows the difference between a concept and a principle is not at all the same as judging whether a man knows how to shoot (to use one of Ryle's examples). This is true even if one uses the most direct means of ascertaining knowledge, which is presumably oral interrogation coupled with requests to demonstrate; it is patently true if one resorts to using paper-and-pencil tests to ascertain mastery. Evidently the test form interposes itself between knowledge or ability and judgement, and to the extent that it is an imperfect transducer of what the student knows or is able to do, so will the judgement be distorted. The multiple-choice item is particularly questionable in this respect. Robert Gagné (1970) has shown how shaky is the inference from response to mastery. Then there are the arguments concerning recall versus recognition (Brown, 1976) which can only be discussed in psychological terms but which affect judgements as to what is truly *known*: sometimes, too, you find an appeal to psychological reasoning to defend the use of a particular testing technique, for example, Keith Davidson's (1974) defence of the use of multiple choice for testing comprehension in 'O' level English language exams.

It may appear that what has been presented constitutes a more powerful argument against paper-and-pencil tests than against McIntyre and Brown and, indeed, they might retort that they are not interested in what are essentially artifacts of certain forms of testing. However, that would be to evade the point. What was said is true of oral questioning or of any mode of interrogative enquiry, that is to say, of any attempt to understand what is in the other person's head. You have only to read Margaret Donaldson's (1978) descriptions of the difficulties children experience in dealing with the language of questions and engaging in 'disembedded' thought to take the point. It may be possible to purge *content* of psychological contamination but it is hard to see how you can chase it out of educational measurement altogether when it persists in cropping up whenever a judgement about mastery has to be made.

I said that McIntyre and Brown were heard to call for the abandonment of educational measurement. How did this come about? It started with the question, 'Here are data from some tests (or items); what did they measure?' This, of course, is the classic psychometric method of proceeding. Finding no satisfactory answer to their question (and one cannot argue with them for their criticism of dimensionality is faultless), they conclude that there is no such thing as coherent measurement and therefore that quantification in education should be abandoned. I would like to suggest that by posing the question as they did, they were bound to arrive at that bleak conclusion. Ask the 'what' question before testing, as Gagné (1970) has shown,[6] and you have entirely different, and more hopeful, possibilities. What you must have, though, is the willingness to expend enough care on the *single item* to ensure, as far as possible, that unequivocal inferences from response to judgement of mastery can be made. How do you do this? You build in controls which permit the ruling out of alternative inferences; distinctive and distortion-free measurement, he called it. Gagné's ideas for item writing deserve closer study.

If the 'what' question can be tackled, there remains the matter of aggregation, or 'how much'. Finding no answer to the 'what' question, McIntyre and Brown saw no point in asking the 'how much' question. It is a pity Gagné did not deal with the matter of aggregation. For a recent opinion, there is Green (1981) who writes: 'Test work by the weight of numbers ... of course, each item should be carefully designed and as good as possible, but no single item can ever do very much good or very much harm.'

I would not want to dispute this statement but I do wonder if test constructors are not too ready to fasten on to Green's first assertion and use it to justify their lack of attention to single items. Casual treatment of one item is casual treatment of all items. Gagné said you had to start with the single item and work up – there are no short cuts – but I fear such a severe injunction has often proved too much to take.

NOTES

1. I have in mind Meredith's (1974) charge that 'generations of educational psychologists have been reared on a diet of psychometrics whose function is to demonstrate degrees of *ineducability,* to assign educational failure unequivocally to defects in the child, in his home, in his parents, and in his heredity, and *never* to failures of teaching, failures in

school organisation, failures in urban conditions, failures in commercial ethics, or failures in educational legislation.'
2. Bereiter (1970). In a later paper (Bereiter, 1980), he contended that it is the uncertainty introduced by genetic variation – making determinism manifestly unworkable – which is the most important contribution of genetic ideas to education.
3. Was Hamilton (1929) the first to do so?
4. Nunnally (1975) refers darkly to a 'philosophy of education spawned by the Skinnerian movement in operant learning'. Glaser was working on teaching machines and programmed learning at the time he wrote the paper.
5. And the major distinction impossible to sustain. 'The problem of the standard is usually finessed in mastery learning studies through some sort of normative comparison' (Messick, 1981, p. 585).
6. 'This is what I want to measure; how do I construct tests to do it?'

REFERENCES

Bereiter, C. (1970) 'Genetics and educability', in Hellmuth, J. (ed.) *The Disadvantaged Child*, 3, New York: Brunner-Mazel.

Bereiter, C. (1980) 'The relevance of genetic ideas to education', in Van Der Kamp *et al.* (eds) *Psychometrics for Educational Debates*. London: John Wiley.

Brown, J. (ed.) (1976) *Recall and Recognition*. London: John Wiley.

Carver, R. C. (1974) 'Two dimensions of tests: Psychometric and edumetric', *American Psychologist*, 29, 512–18.

Davidson, K. (1974) 'Objective text', *The Use of English*, 26, 12–18.

Donaldson, M. (1978) *Children's Minds*. London: Fontana/Collins.

Gagné, R. (1970) 'Instructional variables and learning outcomes', in Wittrock, M. C. and Wiley, D. E. (eds) *The Evaluation of Instruction*. New York: Holt, Rinehart and Winston.

Glaser, R. (1963) 'Instructional technology and the measurement of learning outcomes: Some questions', *American Psychologist*, 18, 519–21.

Goldstein, H. (1979) 'Consequences of using the Rasch model for educational assessment', *British Educational Research Journal*, 5, 211–20.

Green, B. (1981) 'A primer of testing', *American Psychologist*, 36, 1001–11.

Guy, W. and Chambers, P. (1973) 'Public examinations and pupils' rights', *Cambridge Journal of Education*, 3, 83–9.

Guy, W. and Chambers, P. (1974) 'Public examinations and pupils' rights revisited', *Cambridge Journal of Education*, 4, 47–50.

Jensen, A. R. (1969) 'How much can we boost IQ and scholastic achievement?', *Harvard Educational Review*, 39, 1–123.

McIntyre, D. and Brown, S. (1978) 'The conceptualization of attainment', *British Educational Research Journal*, 4, 2, 41–50.

Meredith, P. (1974) 'A century of regression', *Forum*, 16, 36–9.

Messick, S. (1981), 'Constructs and their vicissitudes in educational and psychological measurement', *Psychological Bulletin*, 89, 575–88.

Monroe, W. S. (1923) *An Introduction to the Theory of Educational Measurements*. Boston: Houghton Mifflin.

Nunnally, J. C. (1975) 'Psychometric theory – 25 years ago and now', *Educational Researcher*, 4, 7–21.

Ryle, G. (1949) *The Concept of Mind*. London: Hutchinson's University Library.

Shayer, M., Küchemann, D. E. and Wylam, H. (1975) *Concepts in Secondary Mathematics and Science*, SSRC Project Report. London: Chelsea College.

Wood, R. (1976) 'A critical note on Harvey's "Some thoughts on norm-referenced and criteria-referenced measures"', *Research in Education*, 14, 69–72.

1.7 | SCHOOL EXAMINATIONS – SOME SOCIOLOGICAL ISSUES

JOHN EGGLESTON

INTRODUCTION

Contemporary sociology of education with its interest in social selection, reproduction and accreditation sees school examinations in modern societies as highly important mechanisms for these processes. But so far there has been little sociological examination of examinations. This chapter will attempt to alleviate this deficiency and in so doing throw some light not only on macro issues such as selection, credentialism and the definition of school knowledge but also on the sociology of the school and the classroom.

HISTORICAL CONSIDERATIONS

[...] It was only in the nineteenth century that the practice of competitive examination with rewarding consequences for those who succeeded became widespread in the schools, thereby reinforcing, as Durkheim (1956) points out, the individualisation that has become characteristic of industrial society which is in stark contrast to most traditional societies. Commenting upon this, Cherkaoui (1977) asserts that 'the examination system is organically connected more with a specific mode of socialisation than with the expressive order in general'.

In their modern form, as a component of mass education, examinations are essentially a product of the nineteenth century and certainly one of the growth industries of the twentieth century. Without them the education systems of our day would almost certainly be fundamentally different: smaller, less structured, less integrated, less influential. Perhaps because of their ubiquity, there has, since Durkheim's seminal work, been little sociological examination of examinations: like curricula they have been taken as given; to be reckoned with but not clearly to be seen as socially determined phenomena. Only recently Broadfoot (1979) in her pathfinding *Assessment, Schools and Society* has begun to focus attention once again on the sociology of assessment. She argues that the institution of formal evaluation procedures in education was contemporaneous with the institution of mass education systems *per se* in industrial societies, and was directly instrumental in rationalising educational provision into a system. In particular, it was linked with four themes which became dominant in the provision of schooling, namely competence, competition, the rationalisation of content and control.

THE SOCIOLOGICAL STUDY OF EXAMINATIONS

After Durkheim's early initiatives, the first sociological study of examinations arose during the revival of specific interest in the sociology of education in the mid-1950s. In the predominantly functionalist orientations of sociology at this time the examination was seen as a crucial instrument for the development of the socially mobile society; by demonstrating that examination qualifications increasingly determined the level of entry to the labour market it was believed that the distribution of class, status and power could be influenced by educational strategies designed to increase the opportunities of examination success. Numerous studies showing correlations between home and community background and examination achievement were not at first seen as casting doubt upon the 'true' selective role of examinations in a meritocracy, indeed they gave rise to ever more educational policies designed to increase examination success, particularly among the 'socially disadvantaged'. The work of the Crowther Committee (1958, see Crowther Report, 1959) was particularly interesting in this approach.

The prevailing views were neatly summed up in the concept of *contest* mobility, a term coined by Turner (1961) to describe the model of open competition for educational and occupational achievement predominantly exercised through the examination system. But Turner contrasted this with an alternative concept – that of *sponsorship*, describing a model in which certain young people were 'chosen', largely by and through their social backgrounds, to compete for educational and occupational achievements. As the early 1960s gave way to the late 1960s and the 1970s, it became clear that the examination systems of most, if not all, educational systems approximated far more closely to a sponsorship system rather than a contest system (see, for example, Hopper, 1968); the point being made most sharply by Bourdieu and Boltansky's (1978) analyses. Even though, partly as a result of the empirical evidence of educational sociologists, educational administrators developed compensatory programmes, introduced comprehensive schools and liberalised entry to higher education, the distribution of examination success remained persistently linked to class, sex and race.

The British experience since the implementation of the Northcote-Trevelyan report, confirmed by research by Little and Westergaard (1964) and Lee (1968), indicates that there has been little overall evidence of social mobility through educational achievement. This is not to say that the examination does not play an important, even inescapable role in reproduction, but rather that this role is essentially a legitimating and not a determining role, an important way in which the ruling classes legitimate the power and prestige they already have. Of course, the ruling classes have privileged access to such legitimation in their virtual monopoly of attendance at the independent (public) schools which typically have higher success rates in examinations – a characteristic explicable not only by their usually superior resources and teacher pupil ratios but by the existing cultural capital and aspirations of their pupils. For most, however, cultural and social reproduction is reinforced rather than determined through examinations – though increasingly it is a reinforcement that cannot readily be dispensed with in the allocation to most sectors of modern industrial societies.

EXAMINATIONS AS INSTRUMENTS OF SOCIAL CONTROL

To view examinations as instruments of legitimation is not, however, to confine their significance to the extent to which they legitimate the status and position of individuals. They are also a crucial component in the selection, distribution and evaluation of knowledge in the curriculum: as Bernstein (1971, p. 47) has written in a well-known sentence: 'How a society selects, classifies, distributes, transmits and evaluates the educational knowledge it considers to be public, reflects both the distribution of power and the principles of social control.' Bernstein's verdict reminds us that the examination system is a crucial instrument in the way in which all modern societies handle their educational knowledge; it is, therefore, a key instrument of social control in a far wider sense than its socially selective role. The examination syllabus, and the student's capacity to respond to it, becomes a major identification of what counts as knowledge; those who determine the knowledge requirements of the examination hold major power positions in society.

The view of examinations as an instrument of social control has been most fully developed by neo-Marxist sociologists of education. Typical are Bowles and Gintis (1976) who see the process of accreditation as a device whereby societies recreate their labour force and in so doing perpetuate the economic and social structure – the so-called 'correspondence' theory. Thus, it is argued, the examination system, like the schools in which it operates, becomes identifiable as a tool of the state. Yet to accept this view is to risk accepting an oversimplification. It is one task of this paper to probe these issues more fully.

Unquestionably there has been a dramatic reconceptualisation between the earlier functional studies of social class and educational opportunity and the more recent studies of education and social control often based on conflict theories. Yet it should be noted that virtually all the contemporary analyses, including those from a neo-Marxist perspective, have links to the functionalist perspective with which we began – that examinations perform basic functions in society, that there are fundamental constants that are susceptible to identification: that there is a 'society' requiring these performances. Human capital theory shares these concepts.

The reality is, of course, quite different. Examinations are, like all other aspects of educational systems, made not given. In large and small detail they are subject to change – change often arbitrary and even unplanned by those who make and use them. If we wish to achieve an adequate sociological perspective on examinations then we must explore the perspectives and interpretations of the actors involved and particularly the conflict between them. This chapter examines three central areas of conflict over examinations:

1 Who should be examined?
2 What should be examined?
3 What value should be placed on examinations?

WHO SHOULD BE EXAMINED?

There is no doubt that decisions, overt or covert, made about access to examinations are still an important issue and one that shows up clearly even in geographical distributions. Taylor and Ayres (1969) have analysed examination results in the various regions of England and Wales. They note that in the northern region barely 10 per cent of all boys and only just over 5 per cent of girls obtained the traditional passport to higher education – two or more A-levels – and that only 16 per cent of all school leavers went on to some form of full-time continuing education. Conversely, in the south-east region (excluding London) 15 per cent of boys and 10 per cent of girls obtained two or more A-level passes and over 22 per cent of all school leavers continued some form of full-time education.

For many years there has been widespread debate over the discrepancies highlighted in such figures and also in those reflecting equally significant class, race and sex differences. Indeed, as we have already seen, concern over access and distribution has dominated the sociological analysis of examinations to date. Essentially the conflict has been seen to be about the search for ways in which the disadvantaged pupils usually associated with lower social class may be helped to achieve greater access and success. This is one of the themes of works such as Lowndes' *Silent Social Revolution* (1969), where the history of education is presented in terms of the slowly increasing entry of elementary school pupils (predominantly working class) to the liberal classical curriculum of the grammar school. An alternative way of presenting the evidence would have been to have demonstrated the way in which almost every major English report on education this century (Spens, Norwood, Newsom) has argued that such pupils remain distanced from this kind of curriculum. As Silver (1973) has shown, it is the conflict over distribution that has also characterised much sociological research springing from the 'political arithmetic' studies of the 1930s through to the major work on social mobility in the 1950s. Yet these studies, like most others, make a fundamental assumption in their analysis of the conflict. They assume that the elite forms of education are appropriate and even desirable for all children. The idea that alternative forms of education could be appropriate and desirable did not feature in sociological discussions. In this way sociologists lent unintentional reinforcement to the prevailing belief that success in elite forms of education offers the best criterion for social and occupational allocation. The research and the debate that sprang from these considerations, for the most part, regarded only the distribution rather than the evaluation or the definition of knowlege as problematic.

Most of the major conflicts over examinations have followed this form. The 'Cockerton Judgement' of 1900 followed the attempts by the London School Board to extend the elementary curriculum and examinations in the higher grade classes ('higher tops') of the elementary school to incorporate aspects of the classical liberal curriculum of the grammar schools – an attempt that was ruled to be illegal. The conflict over secondary education since 1944 has been, for the most part, a conflict of a somewhat similar nature. The implementation of the 1944 Education Act explicitly excluded the pupils of the newly instituted secondary modern schools from the General Certificate Examinations on the grounds that their curricula, designed for more practically oriented pupils and thus being different and shorter, made such examinations inappropriate. The efforts made by a number of secondary modern schools to challenge this restriction and to provide extended and examination courses have been documented by Taylor (1963). It was the same conflict that dominated many of the arguments about the introduction of comprehensive education in the 1960s.

WHAT SHOULD BE EXAMINED?

Unlike the distribution debate, the debate over what should be examined has been to a great extent an 'inside' professional debate. It has been conducted within ministries, government committees, universities admissions boards, examination boards and to a lesser extent within the professional associations such as the Assistant Masters' Association and the National Union of Teachers and most notably within the specialist organisations such as the National Association for the Teaching of English and the National Society of Art Education.

Indeed, the history of some of the professional subject associations is predominantly the history of the struggle to redefine the subject in question as being one that is examinable at school, college or university (commonly in that order) – for example, the development of the Institute of Handicraft Teachers, later the Institute of Craft Education (the change in name is not without significance). Hanson has described the similar history of the Society of Art Masters, later the National Society of Art Education (1971). His account of the affairs of the Society of Art Masters at the turn of the century illustrates the complex paths trodden by many of the 'lower-status' professional groups in their pursuit of the re-evaluation of their area of the curriculum with the aid of examinations:

> The Society was aided in its bid to attract members when it obtained the right to award academic dress. Originally, certification was in the hands of the Department of Science and Art and later the Board of Education, but the Council of the Society of Art Masters was anxious that extra symbols of status and professional respectability should be obtained – namely academic dress and initials to place after one's name. It was decided that the Fellowship of the Society (FSAM) should be awarded to members who produced evidence of their artistic competence and ability to pay a fee. Later the ability to prepare a dissertation upon an acceptable theme was made compulsory. In 1907, when the project was introduced, nine Fellowships were granted, but several Council members had few illusions about the worth of the award. A Mr Fisher stated 'We know the initials are a sham, but they carry weight with non-intellectual bodies' (he was referring to Local Education Authorities and government bodies).

The more recent developments of art as a subject in university degrees, the struggle to establish the Art and Design Board in the Council for National Academic Awards, and the place of art in the polytechnics carry events forward.

Perhaps the major development in the content debate was the gradual incorporation of science into the grammar school curriculum and examinations at the close of the nineteenth century. In the latter half of the century new pressure groups with alternative definitions of knowledge emerged to challenge the classics dominated school curriculum.

Apart from science, only modest success has been achieved by the advocates of redefinition until the past decade (Hammersley and Hargreaves, 1983). New subjects have been successfully introduced into school curricula but almost always these have been subdivisions or modifications of existing high-status subjects, notably in the fields of literature, languages and history; almost always such subjects have had to preserve the form and manner of the original high-status subjects from which they sprang. The social sciences are a particularly interesting case. Though belatedly succeeding in the universities where they were able to adopt a pure science model (Kuhn, 1970), they have made only slight progress as high-status subjects in the schools, with the possible exception of economics which was able to gain an entrée in the slightly more flexible area of the grammar school sixth-form curriculum. Significantly the substantial gains have been in the lower-status areas where subjects such as *social studies* have become widely available for lower-level or non-examination classes.

The conflict over definition may perhaps be seen most clearly in the attempts to bring about the redefinition and re-evaluation of low-status components of the curriculum. Efforts to give higher status to areas such as social, vocational and technical studies, to applied subjects like book-keeping or typewriting and to 'non-academic' studies like art and craft, have been closely bound up with the struggle to have them recognised as O- and A-level subjects, especially by the more prestigious examination boards. This has been the basis of a continuing conflict during the past century. But success has been limited. A typical case is the emergent subject of 'technology', with some fairly consistent advocacy by members of elite groups and some support (but as a minority time subject) in some leading independent schools. Having links with both sciences and craft subjects, technology has found itself in a characteristic dilemma whereby the need to achieve status and recognition has led its advocates increasingly to emphasise its science connections. Yet the enthusiasm to embrace it in the schools has sprung predominantly from the lower-status craft teachers, who, for obvious reasons, have been anxious to achieve the enhanced status that work in this field may bring them. This support has immediately warned off science teachers in many schools. The example illustrates the general problem: the relative failure to bring about significant changes in what should be examined. This has largely been a consequence of the difficulty of achieving substantial redefinition of what counts as high-status knowledge.

The development of working-class education provided an equally consistent challenge to high-status definitions of knowledge embodied in the examination system. Hobsbawn, in his *Labour Aristocracy* (1956), describes a nineteenth-century labouring elite that early began to develop an alternative definition of knowledge that was at variance with the classical model. Williams, in *The Long Revolution* (1961), draws attention to the challenge to the nineteenth-century definition of knowledge offered not so much by the curricula of working-class institutions such as the Mechanics' Institutes with their predominantly technical curricula, but rather through the indirect enhancement of class consciousness and identity that they helped to foster. This consciousness was slowly embodied in a political form, often with the aid of the Workers' Educational Association and the university extension classes and many local organisations, such as the Sunday morning classes of many industrial areas.

ASSESSMENT OF PERFORMANCE

In the mid-1970s a quite different move to test for competence rather than allocation has arisen from the development of interest in accountability, notably in the United States and in England and Wales. The American National Assessment of Educational Progess Project (NAEP) and the Department of Education and Science Assessment of Performance Unit in England (APU) are pioneering assessment strategies that aim to assess national standards of performance across the whole curriculum – not just those areas that formal examinations assess.

The task of the Assessment of Performance Unit is illuminating; it is to 'provide information about general levels of performance in children'. Testing is in process in mathematics, science, English and a first foreign language. However, the attempts to test performance in the wider areas of personal development (areas that have been strongly emphasised in the 'new' curricula of the 1960s and 1970s) have met with formidable technical and professional difficulties. They include personal and social, aesthetic and physical behaviour. The problems of assessing moral responses, musical appreciation and sensitivity are formidable and there is still no commitment to monitor them. Not surprisingly, there is widespread suspicion of a governmental body seeking to explore matters such as children's moral behaviour; this and all other aspects of the APU's work have fundamental possibilities for enhanced central control. However benign the intentions of the DES may be and however light may be the sample (approximately 1 per cent of all children), the very existence of the testing is likely to lead teachers to 'teach' some of the test items; publishers are already independently printing 'APU oriented' school texts. And the possibility of local authorities using similar tests on large sections of their child population is already under discussion. But perhaps the major 'threat' of the APU is its potential contribution to the renaissance of the psychologists who hold a dominant role in the National Foundation for Educational Research, the body so far entrusted with all APU testing except for science. Notwithstanding these difficulties, the approach to testing being developed by the APU may prove highly significant in opening up the possibility of a redefinition of what counts as science – or maths or language – that may transcend not only the traditional subject barriers that exist in many schools but also the newer definitions of knowledge embodied in the new curricula and examinations.

The broadening of the response to 'what should be examined' to embrace, potentially, every aspect of a pupil's behaviour in school has fundamental implications. In particular, the efforts to undertake assessment of the full range of 'personal and social development' activities, if successful, go beyond the realm of Bourdieu's social reproduction and into the area of his cultural reproduction currently dominated by the family. If an examination system were built upon so fundamental a change in the definition of knowledge, it could indeed offer a detailed exploration of competence rather than allocation. It may go further than most radical reformers would wish, however; it would certainly open up the prospect of social control through examinations as a reality.

WHAT VALUE SHOULD BE PLACED ON EXAMINATIONS?

The changes in the distribution and content of examinations that have been reviewed in the two previous sections have, for the most part, rested on an advocacy that has assumed that any 'new' categories of candidates and of knowledge to be examined may not only be valued but valued at least as highly as those already being examined. This is implicit in all recent proposals for examination reform (see, for instance, the Waddell report, 1980, advocating a common examination system at 16 +).

Yet the evidence of Dore (1976) and Berg (1973) suggests that this is not so, rather that the users of examinations – employers, colleges and universities and the students themselves – are remarkably conservative and are unwilling to devote time or effort to 'unproven' qualifications.

We have shown that examinations are relatively unresponsive to educational change, that they play a crucial role in legitimating the allocation of power and status, that they strongly influence the definition of what counts as knowledge, that access to successful performance is unevenly distributed. Yet there is no identifiable locus of elite power that manages all this. The universities are commonly seen by teachers as such a locus but those who work therein find it immensely difficult to identify it. It is equally difficult to identify direct government intervention. Rather it is the consensus of the employers, parents, teachers and above all students who in their search for status and security regularly and predictably reinforce the examination system and enable it with minimal state or capitalist direction to perform its powerful controlling role on schools and their personnel.

CONCLUSION

In our consideration of examinations, of who and what should be examined, we have returned repeatedly to the central concepts of power and control. In the last analysis, examinations are a mechanism for regulating social conflict and for legitimating the use of power by those who succeed in them. Of course, there are other routes to power and these may, in some situations, reduce the effect of the examination to the role of a minor dependent variable. But it is certainly the case that success in competitive examinations is, for most people, an essential prelude to the legitimate exercise of power, responsibility and status throughout modern societies; lack of accreditation constitutes a severe limitation and there is abundant evidence that the examination system, despite its technical and ideological critics, enjoys widespread public acceptance. Broadfoot (1979) paraphrases Marx to claim 'assessment has become the opium of the people'.

It seems to follow that adjustment or adaptation rather than abolition of the examination system offers one of the more accessible ways of redistributing power in society. The extreme difficulty of making such moves, a recurring theme in this chapter, appears to confirm this conclusion. Yet here radical critics of society are presented with their most crucial dilemma. To achieve many desired changes, an attractive route would appear to be to take the examination system apart; to dissolve or abolish it. Yet in doing so the very process where, albeit with difficulty, many such radical critics found their own route to power may be cut off. There may instead be a return to covert, non-competitive recruitment to the power structure. And unlike the use of the Trojan Horse, the examination system cannot be overthrown once the radicals have smuggled themselves within. For to overthrow it would be to destroy the very legitimacy that allows them to be there; their capital investment in it would be devalued; a personal sacrifice that, so far, few have made. Perhaps our consideration of the examination system indicates yet one more area of social behaviour wherein the gradual rather than the dramatic model of social change is inescapable. If so, the careful historical analysis of Durkheim is more likely to provide the basis for a more fundamental analysis than those of many contemporary sociologists.

REFERENCES

Beloe Report (1960) *Secondary School Examination other than GCE*. London, HMSO.

Berg, I (1973) *Education and Jobs: The Great Training Robbery*. London: Penguin.

Bernstein, B. B. (1971) 'On the classification and framing of educational knowledge', in Young, M. F. D. (ed.), *Knowledge and Control*. London: Collier-Macmillan.

Bourdieu, P. and Boltansky, L. (1978) 'Changes in social structure and changes in the demand for education', in Giner, S. and Archer, S. (eds), *Contemporary Europe. Social Structures and Cultural Patterns*. London: Routledge and Kegan Paul.

Bourne, D. (1977) 'Education and the Labour Party', unpublished PhD thesis. University of Keele.

Bowles, S. and Gintis, H. (1976) *Schooling in Capitalist America*. London: Routledge and Kegan Paul.

Broadfoot, P. (1979) *Assessment, Schools and Society*. London: Methuen.

Cherkaoui, M. (1977) 'Bernstein and Durkheim: Two theories of change in educational systems', in *Harvard Educational Review*, 47, 4.

Durkheim, E. (1956) trans. Fox, S. D., *Education and Society*. Chicago: Chicago Free Press.

Hammersley, M. and Hargreaves, A. (1983) *Curriculum Practice: Some Sociological Case Studies*. Lewes: Falmer Press.

Hobsbawn, E. J. (1956) *The Labour Aristocracy*. London: Lawrence and Wishart.

Hopper, E. I. (1968) 'A typology for the classification of educational systems', in *Sociology*, 2, 1, pp. 29–46.

Kuhn, T. S. (1970) *The Structure of Scientific Revolutions*. Chicago: University of Chicago Press.

Lee, D. J. (1968) 'Class differentials in educational opportunity and promotions from the ranks', in *Sociology*, 2, 3.

Little, A. and Westergaard, J. (1964) 'The trend of class differentials in educational opportunity in England and Wales', in *British Journal of Sociology*, 15, 4.

Tawney, R. H. (1922) *Secondary Education for All*. London: Allen and Unwin.

Taylor, W. (1963) *The Secondary Modern School*. London: Faber.

Thurrow, L. C. (1977) 'Education and economic equality', in Karabel, J. and Halsey, A. H. (eds), *Power and Ideology in Education*. New York: Oxford University Press.

Turner, R. H. (1961) 'Modes of social ascent through education: Sponsored and contest mobility', in Halsey, A. H. *et al.* (eds), *Education, Economy and Society*. New York: The Free Press of Glencoe.

Waddell Report (1978) Department of Education and Science, *Report on School Examinations*, Cmnd 7281–1 and 11. London: HMSO.

part two

RECORDS AND PROFILES

INTRODUCTION

The 1980s began for schools and authorities in England and Wales with a series of departmental circulars urging curricular review. In this period many authorities published lengthy discussion papers showing a strong desire to encompass new approaches to assessment. Accountability, in this period before the 1988 Education Reform Act, involved the forceful questioning of long-established custom and practice. The research conducted into the use made of routine monitoring of basic skills was one interesting study of the time. As Caroline Gipps and colleagues show in Chapter 2.1, authorities were often to make vaunted claims for the use of these results. Closer examination showed reality varied from intention. Monitoring was of two kinds: for comparison with national norms and for screening. Even the second rationale was often 'undermined' by a preference to have an 'eyes and ears' approach to schools or students with special needs requirements. Teachers, even head-teachers, felt left out of the monitoring process, but were only occasionally critical. Resource allocations were only tenuously connected to these assessments, and in any case someone must need the records!

The attraction of 'records of achievement' as a form of profiling that entails recording of a rather different kind is the 'promise' it makes to make assessment closer to teachers and students – to an extent they might feel they 'own' it. Secondly, the claim would be that a profile might best provide coherence between different individual assessment needs. For example, a pupil record may have a formative and summative value. In Chapter 2.2 the PRAISE evaluation team, based at Bristol University and the Open University, considers four aspects of achievement under RoAs (records of achievement) – the recording of out of school interests, subject specific achievement, cross-curricular achievement and personal achievement. The success of RoAs would depend on the reliability and simple efficiency of pupil self-assessments. In the second part of the chapter, the team examines this critical issue.

It may seem in the 1990s that records of achievement have not attained the authority that was sought in the previous decade. Yet the democratic character of many of the practices that were encouraged (and which Mary James, in Chapter 2.3, compares to practice in open-ended evaluations) has been sustained and has found favour alongside traditional forms of assessment (in

GCSE, for example). The influence upon assessment in vocational courses is yet more profound.

2.1 THE USES AND PURPOSES OF TESTING

CAROLINE GIPPS

INTRODUCTION

In this chapter we shall discuss in more detail the purposes local education authorities (LEAs) ascribe to their testing programmes and put forward our interpretation of these findings. In the first part of the chapter we shall look at what LEAs say and in the second part at what schools say about the purposes of LEA testing and the uses they make of the results.

THE LEA VIEW

We have grouped local education authorities' reasons for introducing testing into three categories: political, organisational and professional. According to our classification, *political* reasons include the atmosphere in the mid- to late-1970s at the time of the Great Debate, the *Black Papers* and the William Tyndale affair, resulting in pressure from members of Education Committees and a desire by some Chief Education Officers (CEOs) to be forearmed in the event of questions over standards. *Organisational* factors include the ending of the 11 +, school reorganisation and LEA reorganisation, all leading to a demand for information particularly relating to primary/secondary transfer. Lastly, *professional* reasons include concern over the numbers of children being referred for remedial help – both too large and too small – and concern over, for example, reading standards following publication of the Bullock Report. These categories result in testing programmes of three major types:

monitoring programmes for accountability purposes, testing for transfer and screening programmes.

Monitoring involves examining group scores, where groups may be classes, age-groups or schools across an authority, with a view to making comparisons. Screening refers to the process whereby test scores are used either exclusively, or in combination with teacher judgements, to identify children in need of further attention. Testing to give information for transfer is self-explanatory and usually takes place at 11+, but can also take place at 12+ or 13+ in areas where there are middle schools. These are, however, not the only reasons for having testing programmes: they are also used for record keeping and allocation of resources. It is not always clear what the latter term means although, with concern over cuts in educational spending, it is currently in wide usage; we shall come back to this later.

The introduction of testing for organisational purposes can be illustrated by the story of a Northern metropolitan borough whose Chief Education Officer offered the heads of primary schools the possibility of a testing programme after the 11+ was stopped. Almost unanimously they asked for batteries of tests (i.e. not just tests of reading) at 7+, 8+, 9+ and 10+. The LEA has since tried to reduce the amount of testing, which is one of the heaviest programmes we have come across, because it is concerned about the amount of testing, about heads' testing expertise (they told us of one who consistently refused to observe the time limits), and about the actual tests chosen. This move was met by strong opposition from the heads. This highlights two points: first the perceived need for testing following the ending of the 11+ and second that testing programmes, once established, tend to persist.

Testing can be used as a management tool, a concept to which we shall return. A management tool at its most general can be having ready clear, brief figures relating to the performance of schools and children in the LEA, to be used whenever such performance is discussed or questioned. But management in this sense can also mean management of Education Committees and governors as well as schools.

From the questionnaire returns we gained an overall view of what purposes LEAs attribute to their testing schemes.

Table 1 shows that screening and monitoring are the most popular major purposes given by LEAs. Screening and monitoring separately, together or in combination with others are the purposes given for their testing programmes by 73 LEAs out of the 79 for which we have information. They also account for the sole or part purpose of 165 testing schemes out of the 203 described to us. Testing for transfer (which may include selection), record keeping and allocation of resources are secondary purposes, i.e. they were rarely given alone. These accounted for the sole purpose of only 11, ten and four schemes respectively, but in combination with other purposes they were widely mentioned. Of the 120 schemes to which were attributed more than one purpose, record keeping was mentioned for 82 schemes, allocation of resources for 66 and transfer for 11.

Purpose	LEAs	Testing schemes
Screening only	7	23
Monitoring only	5	22
Transfer only	2	11
Record keeping only	1	10
Allocation of resources only	0	4
Screening + Monitoring + / − other	43	81
Screening + other	16	23
Monitoring + other	2	16
Other	3	13
Total	79	203
No information	3	5

Table 1   *The purpose of LEA testing*

Perhaps the most interesting aspect of these figures is the nujmber of schemes for which more than one purpose was given. The data reveals that local authorities seem to believe that testing, and nearly always a single test, can satisfy several purposes. Monitoring plus screening plus record keeping plus allocation of resources is the cover-all answer and this was given as the purpose of 19 schemes; a further five schemes had testing for transfer added to this formidable list. We would not attach significance to this and other not-so-extreme claims of multiple purpose were it not for odd comments received such as 'The tests are administered to monitor performance across the authority, to indicate resource requirements and to enable decisions to be made on appropriate curriculum.' Indeed, the LEA in which the case studies of classroom reading assessment took place made a similar claim for their reading test scheme. There are technical limitations to the efficiency with which the same test can be used simultaneously to monitor and to screen and we were made aware in some LEAs of disquiet about using tests for so many different and sometimes incompatible purposes. There were authorities which were able to differentiate purposes quite clearly: this test is for monitoring, that is for screening, etc., but these were in the minority. Of course, not all combinations are unsatisfactory: combining, for example, testing for transfer and monitoring may be a way of maximising information provided any limitations are understood.

Becher, Eraut and Knight (1981) investigating accountability policies in a small number of LEAs discuss the place of standardised testing in LEA accountability. They distinguish between testing schemes for maintenance of standards and testing schemes for problem solving. The former is to make sure that the system as a whole is in healthy working order; the latter is to identify, possibly to anticipate, particular things that are going wrong. In testing to give reassurance about the maintenance of standards, results at an *aggregated* level need to be made public. In testing to identify weaknesses, steps must be taken to repair such weaknesses but, at the same time, privacy must be observed. Relative performance of *schools* should be kept confidential and in professional hands. In other words, findings from one type of testing should be broadcast, and from the other should be confidential. Becher and colleagues admit that there is a blurring of distinctions in LEAs between these two types of testing for accountability.

We would go further than this and suggest that Becher *et al.*'s formulation is light years ahead of LEAs' thinking about testing. The high proportion of combinations of purposes given to us by a large number of LEAs suggests a serious lack of sharp thinking about purpose in testing. To our concerns about technical limitations on testing programmes being used for monitoring and screening purposes, Becher and colleagues would add what we might term administrative concerns, about the lack of clear distinction between testing for different purposes within monitoring. Different levels of analysis and different policies on the publication of results are needed according to the purpose.

One reason why there is a lack of clear thinking about purpose in testing may be that testing, particularly of reading, has for so long been part and parcel of primary education, that going back to first principles in thinking about it does not come easily to LEAs. What seems to have happened in some authorities is that programmes which set out originally with screening as their main purpose have, as often as not, had monitoring added, perhaps as a political response and then most recently, with cuts to the fore, have had allocation of resources added as well. With regard to special educational provision, the advent of the 1981 Education Act may mean that the next few years will see another expansion of testing for screening purposes.

It is difficult to talk about use of results of testing programmes at the LEA level, since this varies from one LEA to another and because the lack of clear thinking about purpose makes classification difficult. We shall instead describe in more detail monitoring and screening programmes and thereby illustrate some of their uses.

MONITORING PROGRAMMES

Monitoring is of two kinds. There is monitoring of authority results (Becher *et al.*'s testing to maintain standards) which involves comparison with ostensibly national norms and there is monitoring of school results (Becher *et al.*'s testing to identify problems) which involves comparing schools. An authority may do both from the outset or end up doing both, having started with the first kind. Monitoring does not necessarily imply any particular testing plan and it is not necessary to test all children; comparisons can be made using samples. In practice, however, most LEAs which claim to be monitoring engage in blanket testing, partly or perhaps mostly because they wish to screen at the same time, and also because light sampling of the order of 10 per cent is not thought to provide enough information on which to base inter-school comparisons. (We found in our school survey that this view is often very strong in schools.)

As to cause, there is no doubt that the agonising about 'standards' which was a feature of the middle 1970s persuaded some authorities, but by no means all, that they ought to be monitoring. The response took various forms:

1 setting up testing programmes with the object of monitoring alone;
2 setting up testing programmes with the stated object of screening but with the intention of monitoring also;
3 using existing screening programmes for monitoring purposes;
4 augmenting existing schemes on the grounds that, having proved to be workable and acceptable, the machinery is there to extend testing, a 'knock-on' effect.

The point, which will surprise few people, is that no single causal explanation will fit all authorities which claim to be monitoring. The corollary is that there is almost certainly great variation in how results of monitoring programmes are used. It could be anything from a casual inspection of results one afternoon to a full-scale intervention exercise based on the results.

While there is some mystery surrounding the use to which monitoring results are put because of the variation, it looks as if they are not used to make schools or teachers accountable in anything like the classic manner. To our knowledge there is no authority which publishes 'league tables', that is, named school results. A classic 'accountability through testing' model should, we hypothesise, have the following features:

1 monitoring initiated by officers or at the instigation of the Education Committee;
2 results collated centrally and analysed on a school by school basis;
3 school results made available to the Education Committee in 'league table' form, perhaps also to the media;
4 schools said to be performing below par asked to explain themselves.

(We stop short of adding supposed American-style actions such as dismissing teachers or keeping students at school.)

The chief reason why this scenario does not occur is that teachers, individually, on panels convened by LEAs, and through their associations, have made it abundantly clear to officers that 'league tables' are not admissible. Officers in their turn have done everything in their power to dissuade Education Committee members from requesting league tables and, as far as we can tell, have always succeeded. The most members might get, in a large authority, are summarised results at a divisional level. In the words of a (then) senior officer of the National Association of Inspectors and Advisers in

Education: 'much more progress is to be made by slowly establishing mutual confidence and providing steady professional support than by any kind of disciplinary or inspectorial action' (Pearce, 1982).

Maurice Peston (1981) argues that the accountability debate is to a considerable extent to do with a jockeying for position between teachers, officials and politicians and the relationship of all of them to parents, pupils and society in general. In this analysis, monitoring procedures can be seen as a *contract* between officials and teachers aimed at excluding politicians from access to school data, and so prevent unwelcome enquiries. There are trade-offs, of course. Teachers have to accept the tests while officials deny themselves the opportunity, if they ever wanted it, of getting public leverage from test results. Any leverage they do exert has to be private and that, in fact, is the form the contract takes. Typically schools are assured that results will be used confidentially and *professionally* which means, for example, an adviser talking over below par results with the head of the school. It is the significance of such meetings – they may be symbolic – and the consequences, which remain to be explicated. What we can add to Becher *et al.*'s findings is that by and large LEAs *do* treat individual schools' results privately by keeping them in professional hands.

Anyone reading some of the contributions to Becher and Maclure's book *Accountability in Education* (1978) might come away with a strong impression of 'administrators eagerly embracing testing and test data as satisfying their need for administrative neatness and the appearance of objectivity'.

We would not deny that LEAs contain people with this cast of mind, although the consequences might be fairly harmless; or dispute the fact that test results, providing they turn out right, offer a highly convenient way of keeping critics at bay. All the same, as a general description of administrators the quotation will not do. If it did, there would not be LEAs about which it could be said that they could do far more with test results than they do. Several have data on all children but choose to look only at small samples. There are LEAs which do not collect data centrally. We know of one LEA which never got round to making use of test scores gathered several years ago and has had to admit that the data are now worthless. And there is an LEA which each year tests 60,000 children with not inexpensive tests and gives as its sole reason 'to give teachers some idea of the general ability of the children they teach'.

There are officers who use testing for opportunistic reasons; there are officers who subscribe to testing for sincere reasons, believing that schools should be more accountable and that test data, limited though they may be, are part of the evidence. And there are officers who have intellectual reservations about testing, or just plain distaste for it, in both cases perhaps harking back to the 11 +. Some have resisted testing in debate, others have resorted to delaying tactics such as waiting for the APU (Assessment of Performance Unit) and LEASIB. Others have bowed to realpolitik but are working away at converting Education Committees and colleagues to what they regard as a more enlightened outlook, for example, using guidelines.

Finally, there are those officers who have no strong feelings one way or the other about testing as a source of information but who realise that testing can be messy, can cause problems (computers), can store up trouble for the future (with heads and unions), can get out of control (if results fall into the wrong hands) and so on. Testing can spoil administrative neatness as well as enhance it.

SCREENING PROGRAMMES

Screening is the process of testing groups of children to identify individuals in need of special help, and a screening programme requires that all children in the relevant group are tested. The existence of such a programme also implies that there is some follow-up: there is little point in identifying children in need of special help if this help is not then provided. The Bullock Report was, in fact, clear that follow-up should be planned carefully *before* screening policies are adopted. The importance of this seems to be recognised in LEAs: we know of at least one LEA which now plans to drop one of its testing schemes on the grounds that it no longer has the resources to do any follow-up. Follow-up and use of test scores does however vary tremendously in style and quality from one LEA to another.

We found from our interviews that in areas which are geographically large, lines of communication long, and/or the advisory system understaffed, a formalised system of follow-up is most likely to be operated. A 'formal' system is characterised essentially by the presence of rules and in several LEAs the 'rule' is that all children scoring below a certain cut-off point on the screening test must be followed up. For example, in one formal system each child who scores below 80 on the 7+ reading test has a form filled out by the class teacher; the Schools Psychological Service (SPS) see all the forms, and base follow-up decisions on this information. It is, however, also the case that sometimes a cut-off point is used for follow-up in 'informal' systems, but only as a guide. The key to the difference between the two systems is flexibility; in the informal system, in which there is more room for discretion, the cut-off point acts as a guide with the experienced judgement of the head or class teacher coming into play in judging whether follow-up is necessary.

For an informal system to work, it requires that the local authority, or division within an authority, be small and that there be an adequate number of advisers and educational psychologists. For example, it is possible to say, in the small boroughs, 'we know our schools'. This is, of course, much more possible where schools are physically close and advisers and educational psychologists can 'pop in' when they are passing by. If advisers and psychologists are in and out of schools regularly (and therefore informally) because there are enough of them to go round and their schools are within reasonable distance, they can keep in touch with what is going on.

This system works on the 'eyes and ears' approach, that is, school support staff are able to see for themselves what is happening in the schools before it is reported formally. Now in this situation, of course, a corollary is that if the eyes and ears are good enough, maybe testing is unnecessary. This is not a view subscribed to by the eyes and ears themselves: tests, they would agree, clearly take on a less central role than in an LEA with a hopelessly stretched or inadequate intelligence system, but they are still a necessary part of the functioning of the system. It may be that advisers and psychologists do not wish to rely solely on what heads tell them so they need the 'objectivity' of the test score. Perhaps the tests serve a different purpose by legitimating access to schools: a point that some psychologists make is that they find it difficult to go into a school to carry out their work with children unless they have a systematic survey under their arm. In this situation, test scores are useful in that they provide an entry to schools. In an informal system, such an entry ticket would not be necessary, if only because entry to schools is reinforced by habit – if advisers and psychologists are always popping in, they need no excuse to do so.

There is no straight-forward answer to the question 'to what extent is follow-up based on test scores?' Where an authority has a testing programme which is expressly for the purpose of screening then, obviously, they are more likely to select children for further attention on the basis of test scores alone, particularly where LEA officials consider objective test data to be especially valuable. Where officers are less convinced of this, referral is likely to be of the test-score-plus-skilled-teacher's-judgement variety. As might be expected, we came across no LEA in which testing was solely for screening purposes and the resulting test scores were *not* used in referral.

The overall picture seems to be this. About three-quarters of education authorities have some centralised system for testing their children in reading. Most of this testing involves all of the children in a particular age group, usually at the junior school level. Most authorities have some system for providing remedial help in reading and usually (always, when screening is the avowed aim) referral is determined in part, or in whole, by the LEA reading test scores. The reliance placed upon the score varies with other factors. For example geographical size of the LEA and number of support staff (both of which determine how well schools are known); the personal views of the advisers and psychologists concerned about the value of test scores; the relationship between the head and the adviser; and the experience of the class teacher (for it is clear that an experienced teacher's judgement counts for a lot in decisions about placement).

Links between the SPS and the advisory service – which in some authorities form a joint system and in others are quite separate – are important in determining the style of the remedial service, for there are several models: teachers within the school with special responsibility for reading, peripatetic remedial teachers, remedial advisers, reading advisers, and reading advisory teachers (as well as educational psychologists) are all used in various authorities to provide reading support.

Remedial help outside the classroom may, of course, be something that we are going to see less and less with the programme of cuts begun in the early 1980s, though it should be said that concern over the lack of success of current methods of remediation may have played a part here, as well as notions of economy. Testing programmes are already being introduced, or justified, on the grounds that LEAs need to reallocate resources (e.g. remedial teachers) to make the best use of those they still have. As part of this trend there is a move away from remedial teachers to remedial advisory teachers because this is considered a more efficient way of using resources. The rationale here is that if there are several poor readers in a class it makes sense to work with the teacher in that class rather than with the individual children. Another development is that teachers are being encouraged to take more remedial work on themselves and to question whether referral of a child is really necessary. As a result, according to one adviser concerned, the number of referrals is falling because 'straight-forward' problems are being dealt with by the teacher in the classroom. The question which springs to mind here is 'how successful is the class teacher at dealing with these problems?'. It could be that the teacher, although put off referring children by the adviser, does not really have the time or expertise to deal with the child in the class and so perhaps the 'straightforward' problems are just not dealt with. At least one LEA was quite open about the fact that it was encouraging teachers to do more remedial work themselves because of cutbacks: children will still be seen by remedial teachers and educational psychologists but only as a last resort. In fact cutbacks, if they have the effect of removing remedial teachers as was due to happen in at least one county, bring the whole concept of screening programmes into question. In such a situation it will become much more important that the teachers themselves are equipped to do basic remedial work, particularly in reading. If they are not, then testing programmes for the purposes of screening will have little justification, since the resources needed for follow-up will be absent [. . .]

THE SCHOOL VIEW OF TESTING

This information was gained from the interview survey carried out in schools in 20 LEAs.

PURPOSE OF TESTING

We asked primary heads first whether they had been consulted by the LEA about the testing programme. Two-thirds (66 per cent) of the 80 heads interviewed said that they had never been consulted. Of those that had (almost a quarter of the sample), most had been consulted via meetings (54 per cent), some via meetings *and* in writing (14 per cent) and some just in writing (18 per cent). In fact, 'consultation' via writing is more likely to be in the nature of informing than consulting so the high overall proportion (2/3) who had meetings (with or without written consultation) suggests that where consultation takes place at all it is more likely to be face to face and with the possibility of dialogue. Where consultation did take place it was on more than one occasion for over half (59 per cent) the heads. So although a high proportion of the heads reported no consultation, where it did take place it seemed to involve more than just the barest minimum.

Though two-thirds of the heads had not been consulted, only half this number (38 per cent) had not been given a reason of some sort for the testing programme. The reasons most often given by LEAs for introducing testing programmes according to heads were screening, transfer and monitoring/ accountability purposes (36 per cent, 37 per cent and 34 per cent respectively). Breaking down the monitoring/accountability category, responses were fairly evenly distributed among gauging the performance of the authority against national norms, comparing the performance of different schools, and meeting political pressure over standards.

Comparing this with the reasons given to us by LEAs for their testing programmes discussed earlier in this chapter, we can see that there is broad agreement over the importance of screening and monitoring. However, schools mentioned transfer more often and resource allocation less often than did the LEAs. This is perhaps not surprising since one would expect primary heads to be more interested in testing for transfer – an immediate professional concern – than in testing to aid resource allocation which is more properly the concern of the LEA.

When these heads were asked whether they thought there were any other reasons which the LEA had *not* given them, accountability featured most prominently. Almost half the reasons (43 per cent) given related to standards, political pressure, the Great Debate and so on, that is, pressures generated by public debate over education. The heads who had not been given any reasons by the LEA for the testing programme when asked why they thought the testing was introduced gave answers in line with the heads who had been given reasons. Screening, transfer and monitoring/accountability were the reasons most often given, while allocation of resources was not given at all.

Thus, acknowledged reasons for testing were a mixture of professional, organisational and political, while unspoken reasons were assumed to be largely political.

We asked the heads whether they thought the LEA testing programme was serving its purpose and the majority (60 per cent) felt that it was. However, favourable comments made by the heads were mostly in connection with testing for transfer or screening, for example:

'An excellent programme.'
'Unable to think of a better one.'
'As a result there is modification as far as reading and maths programmes

are concerned ... we can have extra [help] ... definite proof for educational psychologists to be brought in ... hence children can go to [the] Reading Centre in town part-time or Special Education.'

'Serves as a part basis for grades on record sheets which help [the] next school.'

'Infant programme very successful at picking up kids at risk – gives some information to classify kids coming to school – can relate to national level. Junior – more difficult as [it's] not used by [the] head – can tell how efficient [your] own school is – with caveats.'

'It serves them [the LEA] because we have figures to give them. We can compare achievement between different years. It also pinpoints various deficiencies and strengths. We can tell if it is a weakness in reading or a weakness in remembering and comprehending.'

Dissatisfaction with programmes included narrowness of the assessment and light or voluntary sampling:

'Partly, but [it] gives a very narrow range of ability of each pupil. If they were used solely it would be most inadequate. We use other tests as well.'

'Programme is too English oriented ... not wide enough. Good in what it does but maths, etc. overlooked.'

On sampling – 'No, because [it's] not covering all schools. Should either all do it or not do it at all.'

As for whether there were any adverse side effects of the LEA programme, most heads did not think this was a problem – 68 per cent gave a definite or qualified no when asked this question:

'Some headteachers do feel so, but I do not. I did have this concern but results are confidential.'

'None whatsoever. That's why I was disappointed with [the] union's attitude to [the] reading test. I don't know why we're frightened of these things. I think we should have more. It's good to have [an] objective view of standards.'

'Not really – very limited anyway. Fairly restrained testing. Feel they don't really want to interfere – they do a minimum. Bend over backwards not to interfere really, but feel they have to monitor standards.'

The adverse effects that were perceived were, however, more likely to be potential than actual:

'If talking of publishing results, then an adverse effect. Good starting lever for politicians. There could be – not at the moment.'

'If results were being used on a table basis where schools were being compared, then that would be a problem.'

'Can be misrepresented by certain sections of community ... too much stress, importance, can be placed on these without complete understanding of what [they're] produced for.'

As a final question about whether heads were happy with the LEA testing programme, we asked whether they would prefer not to have to do the LEA tests. Their answers suggested widespread support for the testing programmes: only 12 per cent of the heads we interviewed wanted to drop their LEA testing and a third of these only wanted to drop parts of the programme:

'They buy the tests I would use anyway. Saves me money!'
'No, I think it's a shame that the ending of the grammar school system lowered standards. There was always this control before ... and, I think that if you took away this final little hurdle that remains, then some schools would fall completely flat. The knowledge that results from their schools go on to secondary schools keeps junior heads on their toes.'
'If it helps them [the LEA] I have no objection to doing it. It's just that I don't like the Gapadol tests.'
'Well, obviously they take up time. In a small school it doesn't come to much. But I think the advantages very much outweigh the disadvantages. As a head I'd say, No, there aren't any disadvantages. But as a classroom teacher faced with 35 Edinburgh tests to mark I'd think differently.'
'I like the tests as long as they don't dominate school life. I think the children enjoy doing them.'

To sum up then, most of the primary heads had not been consulted about the LEA programme and a third had not been given a reason for the testing. Testing for transfer, monitoring and screening were the reasons most often given while unspoken reasons more often related to accountability. The majority of heads felt that the programme was serving its purpose, in particular in relation to screening and transfer. The lack of consultation notwithstanding, most heads could see no adverse side-effects to the testing programme and only a small number would prefer to drop it.

USE OF TEST RESULTS

Both primary heads and teachers were asked how LEA test results were used in the school. Overall, the major use of reading, maths and IQ tests for heads and teachers was record keeping. Another major use of reading and maths tests was to identify children for remedial help, also to provide information to secondary schools on transfer which was the second major use of IQ tests. These are all uses which are essentially for someone else. A further major use of LEA reading test scores for the class teachers was supplementing or confirming their own assessments. Over half the heads found the LEA IQ tests of little or no use, while a quarter felt this way about the reading and maths tests. The teachers were not asked about the IQ tests, but a quarter of them found the maths tests, and a fifth the reading tests, of little or no use.

These findings may seem at odds with the fact that heads were apparently content to have the LEA testing programmes. However, as some of their comments indicate, the heads can see the need for the LEA to test, though the test results are not necessarily useful to the schools themselves. Reasons given for lack of usefulness of the LEA tests were overwhelmingly to do with timing and/or that testing was, in any case, for others. The timing of testing when it is for transfer purposes is nearly always a contentious issue. If testing is carried out at the end of the last term in the feeder school it will have little to offer these schools, although they will have to bear the brunt of giving and marking the tests. If, however, the tests are given earlier, in order to give them some feedback on their performance, then the receiving schools may well consider that the information is out of date by the time the children transfer to them. To test neither early nor late is often to fall between two stools.

Record keeping is in a sense the most passive use of test results. Looking at findings from other research into teachers' use of test scores our finding that this was the most common use is not surprising. Becher and colleagues (op. cit.) found that, though many tests were introduced for diagnostic purposes, their results were rarely used in this way. Teachers welcome the occasional individual check on their judgement but seldom find that standardised test scores provide new information about pupils or useful ideas for classroom strategies. Moreover, they found teachers were reluctant to make detailed analyses of test results as these do not form an integral part of their teaching programme. Work in the USA (e.g. Salmon-Cox, 1981; Yeh, 1978) and Ireland (Kellaghan *et al.*, 1982) found that teachers rely primarily on their own judgement and observations to make assessments about children (and to assign them to groups) rather than test scores, and our findings do not alter this picture. However, we do not know in what subtle ways the knowledge of a 'normed' score may influence a teacher's expectation and hence action.

Up to now we have referred to primary heads and teachers; this is because only seven of the 20 LEAs in which we interviewed had testing programmes at the secondary level. This reflects the national picture which is that testing of whole age-groups or classes is more common at the primary level than at the secondary level. As there were only 14 secondary schools in which we asked about LEA testing, we shall deal fairly briefly with what the staff said. Again there was little consultation between the LEA and heads; as a result there seemed to be rather less idea of what the testing programmes were for. On the whole secondary schools seemed less touched by the testing programmes and did not feel called to account by them, presumably because public examination results are so much more important at this level. On the other hand there was, as in the primary schools, little desire to do away with the testing programmes, as they were felt to be useful to the LEA, that is for monitoring purposes, and were used within the schools for record keeping.

Our interpretation of these findings is that testing programmes, contentious though they may be before introduction, become routine and uncontroversial once established. Though there may be confusion over their purpose and variation in their use, schools are apparently happy to carry on with these externally imposed testing programmes because, while they may do no good, they are seen to do little harm. In effect they are seen as a safety net, whether that consists of the teacher's records of individual pupils or the LEA's data about schools.

The picture we present of test scores being so little used, the use of results from monitoring programmes being difficult to tease out, testing once established becoming routinised and uncontroversial, and programmes for monitoring standards becoming of less interest to politicians once established, indicates to us that testing in some areas has a symbolic rather than a practical role. It seems that it may be the setting up of a testing programme that satisfies, rather than the rigorous use of results, particularly when its purpose is political rather than professional. Given this state of affairs some will view LEA testing programmes as so much wasted time and money. But in our view it is the hidden functions of testing which are important rather than the overt functions. These hidden functions that we have noticed – and because they are hidden what follows is tentative – are: acting as a safety net in the event of questions about standards; providing 'objectivity' for professional assessments (but this 'objectivity' can be relegated in the event of a disagreement between the 'objective' and professional assessments); and legitimating psychologists' and advisers' access to schools.

REFERENCES

Becher, T. (1981) *Policies for Educational Accountability*, London: Hutchinson.

Becher, T. and Maclure, S. (1978) *Accountability in Education*, Slough: NFER.

Kellaghan, T., Madaus, G. and Airasian, P. (1982) *The effects of standardised testing*. Boston (Ma) Klumer – Nijhoff Publishing.

Salmon – Cox, L. (1981) *Teachers and standardised achievement tests: what's really happening?* Phi Delta Kappan, May pp. 631–634.

Yeh, J. (1978) *Test use in schools*. Los Angeles, University of California Centre for the study of Education, (unpublished paper).

Records of Achievement: Report of the National Evaluation of Pilot Schemes

2.2

Patricia Broadfoot, Mary James, Sue McMeeking, Desmond Nuttall and Barry Stierer

Aspects of achievement

Having given a general indication of the range of achievement which RoA (record of assessment) systems attempted to cover, we now turn to the aspects of achievement comprising that range. For the purposes of our analysis we have found it convenient to think of this range in terms of four aspects. We should stress however that we have chosen these categories because they are in common usage; as we shall argue later they are not necessarily theoretically or empirically distinct either within an individual or within a school's recording system. [...]

Extra-curricular and
out-of-school interests and activities

All case study schools have aimed to cover extra-curricular and out-of-school interests and activities in their recording systems. At first view there seems much value in this since choice of leisure time activities and work experience often says much about an individual which is of potential interest to employers and can provide interesting material for discussion at interview (e.g. the Hawthorn RC School girl who runs a pig and rabbit breeding business and wants to make a career in agriculture). It also appears to have value as a way of strengthening pupil–tutor relationships by providing an opportunity for tutors to discover a different side of their pupils and by giving in-school achievement a new perspective.

We have evidence that authentication has been sought within some RoA systems – for example, confirming signatures on the personal record or signatures on verification slips.

Often, however, what pupils say they have done has been taken on trust. Teachers appear reluctant to insist on written testimony from other adults precisely because such an act would imply suspicion and therefore undermine the developing relationship. Teachers also maintained that most pupils are basically honest.

In relation to this aspect of achievement we would wish to make four points. First, placing extra-curricular and out-of-school achievement on the recording agenda may imply an increased responsibility on the part of the school to provide extra-curricular activities. Secondly, teachers need to be acutely aware of the possibilities for social divisiveness and personal intrusion inherent in such an aspect of recording. Thirdly, pupils need to be made aware of the possible uses to which their records might be put to enable them to be both wide-ranging and judicious in their choice of evidence to record. Fourthly, pupil autonomy is an important principle to protect in the context of this aspect of recording.

SUBJECT-SPECIFIC ACHIEVEMENT

With the exception of two schools whose RoA was confined to personal achievement, all of the schools we have studied have, at some point during the pilot period, attempted to include pupils' achievement in their academic subjects within the RoA system. Hence we are able to report an emerging consensus in this area, as we were in the area of extra-curricular and out-of-school activities in the previous sub-section.

However, the scale and nature of such recording varied enormously according to the vantage points from which the recording of subject-specific achievement was carried out, and according to the notions of subject-specific achievement which underpinned it.

This diversity can be represented by describing *three broad types of recording of subject-specific achievement*. These are not 'ideal' types in any pure sense, and aspects of more than one type may be found within a single school. Nevertheless, we have found them to be a helpful way to understand the range of practices and definitions which abound in this area.

Within the *first type*, pupils' achievement in their subjects was recorded from a 'tutorial' vantage point. This type was generally built upon the responsibilities of form tutors for keeping an overall 'watching brief' on pupils' academic progress. Hence, whilst this vantage point held the potential for a comprehensive view of a child's experience of the academic curriculum, in the cases we studied it tended to be generalised and partial, lacking the specificity of assessment concepts relevant to each subject or course area. Often such records had the familiar character of the form tutor's overview found in conventional reports to parents or school leavers' testimonials. Certainly this type did not in itself require changes in the way that individual subject departments conceptualised achievement in their areas or in the way they organised teaching, learning, assessment and recording.

Within the *second type*, pupils' achievement in their subjects was recorded by subject teachers, but the emphasis of the RoA system was on *summarising* achievement and *reporting* that portrayal to particular outside audiences at certain times in a pupil's school career (we are not referrring here exclusively to summative RoAs). Reporting frameworks were generally devised to reflect and incorporate existing methods of teaching, learning and assessment, and internal recording. For example, course work would be taught and marked by teachers in a traditional way, often using marks or grades, but achievement over a given period would be expressed in the form of positive prose comments, and discussed with pupils, at the point when summary reports were required.

Within the *third type*, recording grew out of a reappraisal by subject staff of notions of subject-specific achievement and a restructuring of teaching, assessment and record-keeping. The emphasis here was on such formative processes as the explication of learning objectives, the development of modules or units of work, continuous criterion-referenced assessment, the grounding of records in evidence of pupils' work, teacher–pupil dialogue and a systematic approach to the diagnosis of strengths and weaknesses.

It would not be appropriate for us to advocate the universal adoption of one of these types, because to do so would not only be to judge one kind of RoA system as superior to another but to say that one form of curricular organisation is to be preferred. We hesitate to do this because we recognise that this would have far-reaching implications which schools may not be in a position to take on board and which may be more than is required for the development of a satisfactory RoA system. On the whole we have chosen to concern ourselves with what is possible and sufficient, although we do not wish to deny the possibility of an ideal for which schools might aim.

None of these types, for example, necessarily precludes the adoption of a wide definition of achievement which goes beyond the knowledge of subject content to include conceptual, practical, process, personal, social and attitudinal achievement. Neither does any type necessarily preclude a central role for formative processes of self-assessment, review and target-setting, although these are more clearly formalised in the last. Realistically, any decision about which of these types a school can be expected to adopt will need to recognise current organisation and starting points including the relative emphasis given to the role of form tutors, the need to communicate a synopsis of pupil achievement to outside audiences, and the development of formative processes within subject areas. Schools' ability to adopt one or another of these types will also be constrained by the availability of resources to enable fundamental change in their forms of organisation.

We now turn our attention to the different *conceptions of subject-specific achievement* which have underpinned recording systems in our case study schools. In this respect, our evidence suggests that systems developed to record subject achievement, within any of the types outlined above, pay attention to one or more of the familiar trilogy of knowledge, skills and attitudes.

By *knowledge* we mean propositional knowledge specific to the subject which is assessed by requiring pupils to demonstrate recall and understanding. Traditionally this has had a prominent role in education and, according to our evidence, is still an important focus for assessment, recording and reporting.

Attitudes constitute another aspect which has always been a prominent focus for recording in relation to subject achievement, in particular the interest in, and disposition towards, work within the subject as demonstrated by effort, commitment and motivation. Assessment of a pupil's 'effort' has had a long history in education in England and Wales although the assessment of attitudes *deliberately fostered within the curriculum* (such as those promoted within, for example, health education) is a different matter.

Skills constitute the third aspect and it is this area which has received particular attention in some schools and schemes, in keeping with the current prominence of skills-based approaches to curriculum and course design and development. Indeed 'skills' has become something of an educational buzzword, the meaning of which has been obscured by possible overuse. This observation applies equally to the term 'processes' to which it is closely allied, sometimes to the extent of being used synonymously. For the purpose of clarification, variations in the meanings attached to the term 'skills' can be conceptualised according to definitions on three dimensions. On the first dimension, narrow definitions of achievement in terms of skills often focus on performance of some generalised operation (or process) devoid of reference to specific content and context (e.g. problem-solving) although more comprehensive definitions acknowledge that skill also involves knowledge of ends and the means to achieve them (propositional knowledge) and a disposition to use means to achieve ends (attitudes). On the second dimension, the concept of a skill developed in subject contexts can be restricted to what might be termed practical or craft skills (e.g. ball control in physical education; manipulation in craft, design and technology) or it can be broadened to take in intellectual skills (e.g. critical analysis, investigation) and personal and social skills (e.g. empathy, collaboration). On the third dimension, skills can be singular and discrete (e.g. asking questions, hypothesising, collecting data, categorising) or they can be composite (e.g. investigating, researching) indicating different orders of skills in which higher order skills subsume lower order skills.

We do not wish to get into an extended discussion about the nature of skills, although we think it is worth noting that the place of skills in the curriculum is an area of considerable debate. Neither do we wish to advance one interpretation to the exclusion of others, although, as we shall argue, our evidence suggests that, at least for summary purposes, a broad definition on all of these dimensions is to be preferred, i.e. that the skills of most interest are higher order, inclusive skills defined as practical knowledge in personal, social and intellectual areas as well as craft skills.

Although most of the schools which we studied implemented RoA systems which incorporated subject-specific knowledge, attitudes and skills, to a greater or lesser degree, a few chose to make skills (or processes) a principal focus for recording. In these contexts what was identified, assessed and recorded as skill or process achievement varied widely both between and within institutions, along the lines described above. A number of issues of special interest emerged but the greatest problems were experienced when skills were recorded as atomistic, general competencies devoid of reference to the content and context of demonstration.

On the basis of this evidence, our judgement is that subject achievement which is recorded in terms of skills will need to include reference to the content and context of performance if it is to have validity and meaning. While skills may have similarities in different contexts they are also distinguished by their content. It cannot be assumed therefore that they are entirely transferable.

Similarly, although it may be helpful to record the performance of numerous discrete skills (e.g. in comment banks) at the formative stage, the indications are that these need to be summarised in more holistic ways when there is a summative intention to report to other audiences. Thus ways need to be found to order achievements in some kind of hierarchy such that atomistic skills, if it is felt that there is value in recording them, are subsumed within more holistic categories at the stage of reporting. This is important because the constraints on space in any summary document create a need for selection, but limited selections of atomistic skills tend to trivialise and misrepresent achievement.

Our evidence also points to a growing recognition that a wide range of skills is brought into play in learning within subject contexts. This range is likely to include intellectual, social and personal skills as well as manipulative skills. Indeed, the experience of teachers in some schools suggests that curricular opportunities for demonstrating social and personal skills are best provided within the formal academic curriculum where they arise naturally and are often an essential element (e.g. skills of collaboration).

On the basis of our evidence, our judgement is that a broad definition of skills appropriate for development and recording in subject areas should be encouraged, and that this should include skills of a personal and social kind which have an important bearing on subject-specific achievement. Indeed we feel that this is an important and valid way of approaching the recording of cross-curricular achievement and personal qualities, which is more specifically discussed in the next two sections.

CROSS-CURRICULAR ACHIEVEMENT

Although many of our case study schools have expressed an interest in incorporating recording of cross-curricular achievement as a distinct element in their RoA system, and some have established working groups with this in mind, there has been comparatively little progress towards implementation in this area. This appears surprising but can be accounted for by the theoretical difficulties in defining cross-curricular achievement and by patterns of departmental organisation which tend to inhibit cross-curricular deliberation in secondary schools.

In our case study work we encountered two basic approaches to understanding the term 'cross-curricular' and we feel that these need to be taken into account in the continuing debate on recording pupil achievement. First, there was the approach to cross-curricular which centred on the *pupil*. This approach was grounded on the assumption that general processes, concepts and skills can be identified which do not appear exclusively related to the substantive content of subjects. They are recognised to have a level of generality although they do not require some common agreed attempt across subject areas to foster the same skills in different contexts. Thus cognitive skills of investigation, social, personal and psycho-motor skills, and attitudes to learning, have all been referred to at one time or another as cross-curricular achievements. Such achievements may be developed, demonstrated and recorded in subject-specific contexts without reference to other subject areas. In some cases, as mentioned in the previous section, they may be considered *essential* to achievement in those contexts, in which case aspects of subject and cross-curricular achievement become indistinguishable and the term 'cross-curricular' becomes simply a way of indicating a level of generality beyond the particular. The substitution of terms such as 'general competencies' for 'cross-curricular skills' is significant in this respect.

The second approach appeared to centre on a notion of cross-curricular which related to *school organisation*, and suggested skills which could be fostered, assessed and recorded in two or more departments and which were therefore identified as a shared objective.

In practice, there was sometimes movement from one approach to the other and the skills framing both kinds of approaches were often roughly similar. The strength of the first approach was that it allowed for the possibility that no two departments could foster precisely the same skill because skills have a knowledge content which is to some degree context specific, even though they may have much in common at a general level of analysis, for example drawing conclusions from evidence. On the other hand, the second approach had the advantage of encouraging fruitful discussion and collaboration between departments. Ideally, some combination of these two approaches should be possible – they are not mutually exclusive. However, in the light of the evidence from our case studies that cross-department agreement is difficult to achieve and that transferability is a questionable assumption, our judgement is that the first approach has the greater potential in this area. There is a strong implication in this that the term 'cross-curricular achievement' is a misnomer for which an alternative should perhaps be sought; it is perhaps significant that the DES policy statement refers to general learning skills.

PERSONAL ACHIEVEMENT

From what has been said already readers will be aware that, in addition to extra-curricular and out-of-school interests, RoA systems in case study schools often included reference to personal and social achievements within subject-specific and cross-curricular recording. Indeed, as our analysis progressed, what had at first seemed to be clear conceptual categories became increasingly blurred. However, in keeping with their interest in portraying the whole person, all schools consciously developed a 'personal' element as part of their recording procedures, either as a separate record or within the curricular elements of the RoA. Although one can argue that all recording is personal because it focuses on individuals, schools in pilot schemes appeared to use the term in a more restricted sense to refer to achievements, experiences and qualities which were assumed to be pupil-specific rather than curriculum-related. Sometimes the reference was to personal qualities or attributes and sometimes it was to personal skills. The distinction is an important theoretical one but need not concern us here because in no case was there any interest in recording immutable individual characteristics which could not be fostered, developed or influenced by educational experiences. It is interesting that what in one place was labelled a personal quality (initiative, reliability, punctuality) was elsewhere described as a skill. On the whole any lists of such qualities or skills developed by schools or schemes to guide recording exhibited a remarkable degree of similarity. The proscription of comments on a pupil's honesty was widely advised; and the need to include some comment on attendance was also usual, although this was neither a quality or a skill.

Our evidence suggests that schools regard personal qualities and/or skills as an important aspect of achievement which deserves recognition within the RoA because personal and social development is held to be an important purpose of education. However it does not seem to us that universal agreement over what counts as personal achievement should be considered a pre-condition for objectivity, any more than it is in any other area (language, mathematics, or science, etc.). Criteria are, of course, implicit in the public form of discourse that teachers participate in for assessing such development. In other words the kinds of categories and criteria which have emerged through trial and review in the DES pilot phase are likely to have value in a record of achievement. As long as they are publicly accessible they are also likely to be used as starting points for discussion in other schools wishing to develop recording systems appropriate for their own special contexts. If criteria emerge and evolve in this way it is unlikely to be necessary to prescribe a list of qualities or skills to be recorded.

However, experience in pilot schools strongly suggests that, in order to be fair, personal qualities or skills should be recorded with sufficient detail of the content and context of demonstration to indicate that what is recorded is bounded achievement rather than fixed and immutable personality traits. There was also a considerable degree of agreement within pilot schools that comments should only be made on those personal qualities and skills which can be demonstrated in relation to the school's education programme. This of course has implications for curriculum planning and demands that opportunities for fostering personal qualities and skills should be part of curricular and/or extra-curricular provision. Some of the pilot schools we studied made deliberate efforts to enhance curricular provision in this respect.

Overview

In our discussion of aspects of achievement we adopted a categorisation which often framed professional discourse in case study schools. However, the terms 'extra-curricular', 'subject-specific', 'cross-curricular' and 'personal' have strong associations with the way the curriculum is *organised* in secondary schools and this may be misleading. At various points we have said that these categories are not distinct or mutually exclusive in terms of what constitutes achievement. For example, personal qualities are not distinct from social skills since they may only be demonstrable in social contexts; what are called cross-curricular skills, such as co-operation and taking responsibility, are often indistinguishable from formulations of personal achievement; and both so-called cross-curricular and personal achievements are integral, even essential, to subject-specific achievement.

We are impressed therefore by the way in which the Hargreaves Report, which influenced the development of the London Record of Achievement, avoided tying the discussion of aspects of achievement to the organisational structures of schools. Instead it created categories of analysis labelled simply aspects of achievement I, II, III and IV. Aspect I related to propositional knowledge as assessed by examinations with an emphasis on an individual's ability to memorise and organise content; aspect II related to practical processes and skills involved in applying knowledge, e.g. problem-solving, investigative skills or manual skills; aspect III related to personal and social skills such as communication, co-operation, initiative, self-reliance and leadership; and aspect IV related to positive attitudes associated with motivation and commitment.

According to this analysis it is possible to see that what we have referred to as subject-specific, cross-curricular and personal achievement can incorporate more than one of aspects I to IV. Indeed the authors of the Hargreaves Report argued that subject-specific achievement properly encompasses all four. The fostering of all these aspects of achievement therefore transcends organisational boundaries; recording in relation to most aspects can, and perhaps should, take place in relation to all elements of the educational programme of schools. Although the practice may fall short of the theory, as indeed our evidence suggests, this was the thinking underlying the development of units and unit credits in ILEA. In so far as units and unit credits can in principle be developed to cover all aspects of achievement in relation to any curriculum unit – academic or pastoral – we feel the approach has much to recommend it. Of course, if Hargreaves' four aspects were to be used as straitjackets for the development of skills in every curriculum unit, classified under four reporting headings, rather than simply as categories for analysis, then their effects could be deleterious. The advantage of the Hargreaves approach, as we see it, is that it provides a reminder of the comprehensiveness and multi-dimensionality of subject achievement, and has some potential to erode the hard-and-fast academic and pastoral divide which has been erected and sustained by essentially organisational boundaries. The implications for curriculum planning, for teaching and learning, for assessment and recording and for in-service and other forms of support are of course substantial. However, our evidence leads us to the conclusion that this broadening of the scope of recording across the whole curriculum is the only valid way to portray the educational experience of the whole child within the existing organisational structures of schools. [. . .]

PUPIL SELF-ASSESSMENT

We use the term 'self-assessment' to refer to specific judgements or ratings made by pupils about their achievement, often in relation to teacher-designed categories. These tended to be more abbreviated than continuous records or statements, and were often expressed in grids rather than in free prose. We have observed self-assessment taking place in relation to personal qualities, cross-curricular skills and (perhaps most often) subject-specific achievement. These self-assessments, together with teachers' assessments, often provide a basis for teacher-pupil discussion.

For many of our case study schools, pupil self-assessment has constituted one of the most significant elements of the RoA system, holding as it does the potential for realising a number of central RoA principles. Moreover, unlike some of the other processes which have been developed as part of RoA systems, it promises eventually to reduce the time demands of RoAs on teachers while serving valid educational purposes, although in the short term the reverse sometimes appears to be the case.

We have, in our case study work, encountered a number of imaginative uses to which pupil self-assessment has been put. Virtually without exception, all of these uses fit into one of three categories: feedback, specific judgements and self-evaluation.

First, *feedback* is, strictly speaking, more of a consumer's review of particular aspects of a course than a self-assessment as such, except in so far as pupils are invited to reflect critically upon their personal response to the course and to think analytically about what aspects of the course engendered the response. Feedback also includes pupils' responses to their teachers' comments on profiles.

Secondly, *specific judgements* are what is probably most commonly understood by the term 'pupil self-assessment' – that is, pupils' rating or estimation of their attainment or competence with respect to a specified aspect or level of achievement.

Thirdly, *self-evaluation* refers to those instances when pupils are invited to appraise their performance in a mainly diagnostic way – that is, to reflect upon their strengths and weaknesses in relation to specific work and to give thought to ways in which they could in future improve their performance or derive more out of the work, but not to assess themselves in terms of specific aspects of achievement or levels of learning which were given priority by teachers.

Evidence we have collected highlights problems experienced by pupils in making their assessments.

SUPERFICIALITY

We have evidence that pupils are strongly influenced when making assessments of themselves by their perceptions of the kinds of assessments teachers will find acceptable.

MODESTY

The difficulties described above may be compounded by the fact that pupils report that they underestimate their achievements in order not to lose face if they are subsequently downgraded. Teachers seem to attribute this latter phenomenon to the unwillingness of some pupils to appear boastful.

PERSISTENCE OF NORM-REFERENCING

A further problem arises from the fact that pupils appear to have no clear frame of reference when making their assessments. Although presented with specific categories or criteria for assessment, many judge their achievement in relation to their perception of the range of achievement in their teaching groups.

Pupils have a natural inclination, through years of experience within the educational system, to base their views of their own achievement on perceived teacher expectation, on perceptions of what is socially acceptable, and on conceptions of 'average' relative to a familiar group. What seems clear is that, if pupils are to become more autonomous and discerning in their assessments of themselves, teachers must provide abundant and supportive opportunities for them to gain practice and experience. In this respect the introduction of self-assessment processes probably requires an investment of a great deal *more* time by teachers, rather than representing a time-saving innovation, at least in the short term.

PUPIL DIFFERENCES

Many of the questions which concerned us in our case study work related to the ways in which differences between pupils might affect their experience of RoA processes. Like many others working in this area who are committed to improving the educational opportunities of girls and of pupils from social and ethnic groups who have generally been less successful within the education system, we have been interested to examine the extent to which participation in RoA systems might serve to improve such opportunities. We have also had an interest in the ways in which pupils of different ages and different levels of attainment might vary in their ability to participate in RoA processes, and the extent to which those processes have been adapted to meet different needs.

Like a number of other issues in the area of records of achievement, most of these questions relating to pupil differences were long-term, research-type questions which were difficult to resolve within the terms of reference framing our evaluation. It has, for example, been difficult to isolate one dimension of pupil difference (such as gender) from others (such as writing ability), and to isolate RoA processes as a causal factor. A great deal more research needs to be done before we have satisfactory answers to these kinds of questions, but we hope that our work may at least begin to cast some light upon them.

AGE

Because of the diversity of starting points for RoA projects in schools, we have been able to observe the experience of pupils spanning the whole secondary age range. One difficulty we face in analysing our evidence, however, is that the period of our investigation has not spanned the full five years of secondary education for any one group of pupils. We have certainly found, not surprisingly, that many pupils who have been introduced to the principles and practices of recording in their fifth year have found it difficult to understand the programme and to support it enthusiastically. However, this is a management issue concerning the phasing in of RoA systems.

It remains to be seen whether, as so many teachers we have interviewed believe, pupils introduced to these principles and practices early in their school careers are able by the time they leave school to participate in the processes with confidence, understanding and skill. We have found that, despite the difficulties which younger pupils have experienced in recognising and reflecting upon their achievement, younger pupils have taken to the processes of recording with more enthusiasm and less self-consciousness than older pupils. However it does not necessarily follow from this that these younger pupils will be less inhibited, as fourth and fifth year pupils, than pupils who are not introduced to RoA processes until the fourth and fifth years. The culture of self-deprecation which seems so prevalent among teenagers may well be more powerful than the impact of participation in RoA processes at an earlier age. More knowledge in this area will be available as more and more cohorts of pupils experience a full five years of RoA-related work.

GENDER

Our evidence relating to girls' and boys' experience of RoA processes – and in particular teacher–pupil discussions, statement-writing and diary-keeping – is unexpectedly consistent. Bearing in mind that differences are rarely very sizeable, and that generalisations are difficult to draw, we have found that these RoA processes tend to appeal to girls more than to boys. In teacher–pupil discussions they are generally more forthcoming, better able to appreciate the purpose of this exercise, and more skilled at sharing responsibility for the conduct of the discussion. In this sense teacher–pupil discussions may capitalise upon the particular strengths of girls in the secondary age range such as social awareness, maturity and competence in one-to-one conversations.

In terms of statement-writing and diary-keeping, girls tended generally to demonstrate a clearer understanding of the purpose of the exercise, to write more and in greater detail than boys, and to place more value on both the process and the product. Here again, it may be that these kinds of activities build on the more positive orientation of girls towards writing, their enthusiasm for comparatively private and solitary activities, and their apparently boundless capacity to plan for nostalgia.

In this sense we can speculate tentatively that RoA processes, and in particular teacher–pupil discussions, statement-writing and diary-keeping, may go some way towards rectifying the imbalances between boys and girls which have been associated with such traditional school processes as large-group and whole-class question-and-answer sessions and concentration upon propositional knowlege as opposed to personal experience.

On the other hand, the growing tendency to use formative records to serve public reporting purposes might erode this possible advantage, since boys tend to have a keener sense of external audience in their writing and to concentrate on concrete achievements rather than feelings and relationships.

The issue here may be particularly acute in situations where male tutors are expected to conduct one-to-one discussions with Asian girls. Alternative arrangements may, however, be difficult to make within the existing tutorial arrangements of most schools.

The second point relates to the common assumption that girls tend to underestimate achievement in self-assessment, while boys overestimate achievement. We have some evidence to support this.

However, most of our evidence led us to conclude that the undoubted tendency to underestimate achievement was shared roughly equally by both boys and girls and indicated, not a gender-specific phenomenon, but a cultural norm associated perhaps with acquired national characteristics such as 'British reserve'.

CULTURE

ETHNICITY

We have to report that our data in this area were insufficient to permit even speculative remarks of a general nature on the experience of pupils from ethnic minority backgrounds. This is due in large measure to the way in which the sample of schools and schemes taking part in the pilot programme was skewed significantly away from inner-city areas with large proportions of ethnic minority pupils. Added to this have been the constraints, of both resources and methodology, on our ability to pursue research questions in this area. For the record, however, we present the little evidence we have in the following extracts from our case study reports.

WELSH LANGUAGE DIMENSION

Welsh was the main language of the catchment area of one of our case study schools. [The insights gained with respect to the language issue in this school were summarised in the extract from the case study that appears in the main research report. Ed.]

SOCIAL CIRCUMSTANCES

The main issue emerging from our evidence which relates specifically to RoAs and social circumstances, and not to the general problem of education and social disadvantage, is the apparently wide variation among pupils from different social groups in the kinds of out-of-school activities, experiences and interests which they may bring to the recording process.

Although the rhetoric of RoAs emphasises that positive recognition should be given to the way in which *all* pupils spend their time outside school, regardless of their social background, this ignores the powerful forces operating within schools which communicate to pupils the kinds of activities which are, and are not, acceptable. Notions of 'cultural deficit' are deeply ingrained, and teachers are quick to impose (unintentionally) those notions on pupils and to accept the reports by pupils from 'disadvantaged' or rural backgrounds that they do nothing out of school worthy of recording. On the other hand, teachers may be justifiably torn between their wish to draw out and give real recognition to their pupils' out-of-school achievements, and their concern that outside users of an RoA document may react negatively to descriptions of activities which attract social disapproval.

The task of drawing out and placing genuine value upon the out-of-school activities of *all* pupils therefore involves far more than training in interview techniques, however important these are. An attitude of mind is needed which can accommodate the widest possible range of interests and experience, and an ability to communicate that attitude without condescension. Finding strategies to cope with the issue of user prejudice is even more difficult, and our evidence offers us no easy or immediate solutions. For this reason we can do little more than indicate this as an area for further research and deliberation.

ATTAINMENT

LOW-ATTAINING PUPILS
PROBLEMS IN ASSESSMENT

The most notable way in which low-attaining pupils might be disadvantaged by assessment frameworks devised as part of RoA projects has been in the tendency of the more structured assessment frameworks (e.g. comment banks and staged assessment systems) to be hierarchical in their treatment of attainment and therefore to prohibit some pupils from gaining many statements or stages, or indeed any at all. For example, some pupils are unable to reach the lowest stage of some staged assessment frameworks, and the small number of statements out of some comment bank systems which can be applied to low-attaining pupils contrasts dramatically with the large number which can be applied to other pupils.

While it is inevitable that assessments will differentiate between pupils, or at any rate enable differentiation between pupils, the implicit normative principles of these frameworks emphasises the differences between high- and low-attaining pupils and makes it difficult to realise the RoA purpose of giving positive recognition to all pupils when their records are compared.

WRITING DIFFICULTIES

One prominent feature of many of the RoA systems we have studied was the considerable writing demands they make on pupils. Diary-keeping, statement-writing, self-assessment and other methods of self-accounting, add to the already substantial requirements for pupils to produce written work at school. Moreover, the increasing use of portfolios which contain 'best' pieces of work extend even further this emphasis upon writing. We have already mentioned the possible ways in which this emphasis may give girls some advantages. Nevertheless, it is important to recognise that a large proportion of pupils experience writing difficulties of one kind or another – either through their relatively low level of language development, or problems with handwriting, or simply a dislike of writing – and that this will affect their attitudes towards RoA processes.

Several attempts have been made in case study schools to minimise the alienation of pupils with writing difficulties from RoAs. First, giving pupils the option of preparing their work on a word processor has in many cases broken through their antipathy.

Secondly, schools have discovered ways of using pieces of writing prepared in the context of RoA processes for some other additional purpose such as GCSE coursework, which may in time rationalise the writing demands overall and provide greater integration of RoA processes with other school work.

Finally, teachers have enabled pupils with writing difficulties to dictate, for example their statements, either directly to a teacher or into a tape recorder for later transcription. This has been transcribed to provide a first draft, thus overcoming the initial hurdle.

HIGH-ATTAINING PUPILS

This section concentrates on the reaction of high-attaining pupils to the process of recording. We have evidence that this group of pupils seemed more likely than others to question the relevance of aspects of the process, in particular the personal element. Since high-attaining pupils tend generally to be prepared to conform to school expectations, they have on the whole participated conscientiously in RoA processes as they would in any school task which was expected of them. However, a number have questioned whether they would benefit directly from the process when they were single-minded in their intention of going on to higher education, and have in some cases resented the loss of revision time caused by participation.

Any reservations on the part of high-attaining pupils may well become less strongly felt when RoA processes are extended into sixth forms and FE institutions, and when all pupils become better informed about possible users of RoAs other than post-school destinations.

It must also be said that some high-attaining pupils reported that they enjoyed the opportunity to talk to their teachers on a one-to-one basis about themselves. In this sense they placed particular value on the process as opposed to the product. This was especially true in the selective school in our sample, where opportunities for formal one-to-one discussion with teachers had previously been rare.

VALIDATION AND ACCREDITATION

We are now in a better position than we were in July 1987, when we published our interim evaluation report, to say something about the impact of developments in validation and accreditation on case study schools. However, our account remains mainly descriptive because the evidence is not yet available that would enable an analysis in terms of distinct models emerging *at school level*. Neither are we yet able to draw general conclusions about the relative effectiveness of different approaches. [...]

We would wish to preface our remarks in this area by emphasising that there was no unambiguous definition of, or clear distinction between, validation and accreditation as concepts underpinning practice in case study schools. However, the term 'validation' appeared less frequently and we have no evidence of procedures designed *to validate the records of individual pupils*. The terms validation and accreditation were thus generally applied to the *processes* which schools have adopted to develop records of achievement. Nevertheless, when these processes involved examination of samples of documents, which were the product of the process, as it did in some cases, the procedure came close to *validation of records* in the stricter sense.

With regard to the range of experience of validation and accreditation at school level we encountered considerable diversity. In some schools the terms were rarely if ever used, reflecting the low priority of development in this area. In others, though no specific procedures had been developed, there seemed to be an assumption that 'quality control' would be ensured by a combination of fairly strict county guidelines regarding principles, processes and products, by in-service education and training, and by routine inspection by the county inspectorate. Elsewhere explicit and detailed procedures were initiated. Within this last group of schools, a common pattern, as far as one can be detected, was for schools to apply to the scheme for accreditation by preparing a submission based on a review of their current and projected practice and provision in the light of scheme criteria or principles. These submissions were then scrutinised by a specially appointed accreditation group composed of representatives from the scheme project team, the LEA's officers and advisers, and sometimes an examining board and colleagues from other schools. Often the procedure involved some members of this group visiting the school. If the school satisfied the group that it had met the criteria, or that it had established a development programme to achieve these ends, then the school was given accredited status which usually entitled it to use the crest or logo of the local authority or scheme.

Negotiation and Dialogue in Student Assessment and Teacher Appraisal

2.3

Mary James

Introduction

The literature of naturalistic inquiry in general, and democratic evaluation in particular, explores many of the methodological and ethical issues surrounding the case study researcher's interest in gaining access to data of a personal, and therefore sensitive, nature. Similarly, it addresses many of the problems associated with the need to make reports, especially evaluations, publicly available without exposing the most vulnerable to invidious social control (e.g. Simons, 1979; Kemmis and Robottom, 1981). In both contexts, 'negotiation' has emerged as an important concept and has assumed considerable prominence in social contracts which provide a basis for working relationships among researchers, sponsors and research subjects.[1]

The fact that the term 'negotiation' also features prominently in some new student assessment and teacher appraisal schemes may be entirely fortuitous, but there are distinct parallels with forms of naturalistic inquiry. In most cases, a teacher or senior colleague is interested in eliciting information of a personal nature from those who are likely to have less power. The purpose of this is partly diagnostic or developmental but there is usually also an intention to make an agreed statement about the individual, available to others. How access to, and release of, information is negotiated is therefore as crucial in assessment and appraisal of individuals as it is in naturalistic inquiry and evaluation at institutional or programme level. It would be reasonable to suppose that theory and practice in the latter might have something to contribute to the former. Such a possibility provides the focus for this chapter.

NEGOTIATION AND DIALOGUE IN NEW FORMS OF STUDENT ASSESSMENT

Student profile assessment and records of achievement schemes have developed with such rapidity that they seem to bear the stamp of an evangelical movement. As with many such movements, emphasis on development and action often outweighs critical reflections (see Broadfoot, 1986, for a critique of some of the issues arising). Even a cursory examination of profiling practice reveals a confusion of purposes, processes, concepts and principles. On the one hand, processes aspire to be formative, developmental and confidential; on the other hand, they have a summative element and claim public currency. One can argue that this dichotomy represents a fundamental division of purposes that is not easily reconciled.[2]

Similar tension is manifest in the almost arbitrary use of the terms negotiation and dialogue as labels for what goes on in the process of reviewing the experience and achievement of individual students. The following definition of negotiation, for instance, makes passing reference to aspects of social control but, by treating them as unproblematic, implicitly denies the need for negotiation in the sense in which the term is commonly understood, i.e. with an assumption that the parties involved have different interests and values:

Negotiation
A process of discussion between pupil and teacher, either to draw out and nourish a view of significant experience and achievement in the past or to plan some future action, course or curriculum. A progress [*sic*] whereby aims, objectives, goal and content of a training programme are agreed jointly by tutor/trainee/student.

Negotiation presupposes open relationships between students and staff where discussion of issues can come to mutually agreed acceptable conclusions without undue pressure or prejudice by one party or the other and where due allowance is made for inexperience, lack of maturity or inarticulateness (National Profiling Network, 1985).[3]

Elsewhere, as in the illustration given below, even this minimal recognition that negotiation has something to do with power relations is absent. 'Negotiation' and 'dialogue' are therefore often used interchangeably.

I will begin by examining a recorded and publicly available example of negotiation/dialogue between a teacher and two of her students, then I will comment on some of the issues raised. In subsequent sections I will develop the idea that negotiation and dialogue are logically distinct processes which assume different contexts, have different purposes and need to be governed by different sets of principles and procedures. This is where I perceive the methodology of naturalistic inquiry to be potentially very helpful.

The critical question that emerges is whether negotiation, as more appropriately applied to summative assessment, and dialogue, as appropriate to formative assessment, should be considered as two entirely separate and polarised activities or whether they can both be accommodated in a unified profiling assessment or appraisal scheme. My feeling is that the latter is possible provided that the worth of formative and summative aspects or stages is judged according to different, though not conflicting, criteria. In other words, formative dialogue could be expected to contribute to understanding and development, while summatively oriented negotiation should aim to promote credibility, acccountability and justice. My argument is mainly for greater clarity and an end to some of the muddle that threatens the baby as well as the bath water.

AN INSTANCE

The following is a transcription of an excerpt from an Open University television programme.[4] A teacher of French is conducting one-to-one review sessions with students. She talks first with Michelle, then Kelly, about their achievements. Before each interview the teacher prepared an assessment sheet and the student wrote a self-assessment. Teacher and student sit side by side and the teacher refers to the two assessment sheets during the interview.

Voice: One of the main objectives of this kind of assessment is to make students and teachers more equal partners in the learning process. So, instead of the teacher merely completing her side of the form by herself, she discusses her judgements with each student. There's a process of negotiation.

Teacher: Let's have a look. [Reads] 'Have you enjoyed your work in this subject?' 'Yes, I have enjoyed this subject very much, especially the oral work.' Why especially the oral work?

Michelle: I just like speaking it. Y'know, it's good.

Teacher: You like the language? You like the sound of it?

Michelle: Yeah.

Teacher: Yeah. Well, you've got a *wonderful* accent, as I've always told you, and you really sound very good indeed. What do you think you would deserve for your grading and for your attitude?

Michelle: Um ... One?

Teacher: Well, I agree with you. Yes, very good. [Reads] 'Presentation of your work.' What would you say about that?

Michelle: It's O.K. Say about Two.

Teacher: Mm, absolutely agreed. Yes, Two. Different pieces of work are different, aren't they? ... in the neatness, and so on. But generally it's fine; it's lovely. [Reads] 'Your general ability in the subject: strengths and weaknesses'. You can 'speak it O.K.'; yes, I agree. But you are 'not very good at writing it down'. But you are not that bad, Michelle; you are really very good, aren't you?

Michelle: I suppose I am. I don't know.

Teacher: Well, I've given you a One.

Michelle: A One!

Teacher: Mm.

Michelle: Oh.

Teacher: Do you agree with that, or do you want me to put it down?

Michelle: O.K.

Teacher: I'd like to keep it as One because I believe that. And how good do you think you are at writing? [Reads] 'Not that good. I have trouble with my verbs.' Um ... I would say Two, because I think you're good. You're not excellent, and you're not sort of just fair. You're just in the middle. So a Grade Two for that, and you agree?

Michelle: Yeah, I agree, yeah.

Teacher: Good, lovely. That's it then, Michelle. I'll hang on to this.

Michelle: O.K.

Teacher: Thanks very much. (Michelle leaves.)

Voice: As with Michelle, so with Kelly.

Teacher: I think we'll try and do this fairly quickly because if I look at my own gradings I'm fairly certain of the good gradings that I have given you, all right? So I don't think really we need to discuss it that much. I feel that you enjoy this subject generally very much, yeah?

Kelly: Yeah.

Teacher: You do? Good. And you're fairly good at speaking it so I am going to leave out the first few questions and then just ... We can come back to it another time. How good are you at speaking? [Reads] 'There are some words that I find difficult to understand, but most of them are O.K.' Well, I think you are very good at speaking and I've given you a Grade One for that. Would you agree?

Kelly: I don't think I'm that good.

Teacher: You don't think you're that good! Do you want me to change it to a Two, or a One/Two?

Kelly: I don't mind.

Teacher: You'd prefer I kept it at a One, I'm sure. Well, I'll just pencil in a One/Two, all right? Then I'll have another think about it later on. How good are you at understanding? [Reads] 'If the teacher talks to me using all French words there would be quite a few I wouldn't understand.' Well, of course, yes, but do you generally get the gist of what I'm saying?

Kelly: Yeah, I do really.

Teacher: Yeah, you won't understand every single word but, I mean, if you understand the basic ...

Kelly: Yeah, some words I know what it means, but then the little words I don't.

Teacher: Yeah, O.K. What would you give yourself for that then?

Kelly: ... Three.

Teacher: A Three! I wouldn't. I've given you One/Two again. Well, I'm sticking to that because I believe in it anyway. And your homework? How have you got on with the homework? [Reads] 'Sometimes I think we get a bit too much.' Ha, ha! I don't! ... Um, regularity: do you always do it?

Kelly: I do do homework. Sometimes it's hard.

Teacher: Yes, even if it's hard, but you always do it, and it's always given in when you should do?

Kelly: Yes.

Teacher: Yes. And the quality of it? ... What do you think? And do you always try to do your very best, even though you find it difficult?

Kelly: Yeah. Some of them are hard and I don't understand 'em, so I try as much as I can and if I can't do the rest I just sort of leave it.

Teacher: Mm.

Kelly: I would always do most of it.

Teacher: Yes, O.K. Well, I agree. I have been fairly pleased with that and I have, in fact, given you a One for each of these. Right. And you would like to take it next year? [Reads] '... think I would because I enjoy most of the work.' I would like you to take it next year as well ... [Fade out]

Voice: Surely a useful conversation.

COMMENTARY

This example of a reviewing process invites a number of comments, and poses several questions regarding the nature of the process itself and the validity of the assessments made.

ISSUES OF POWER AND AUTHORITY

The teacher sets the pace and tone of these interviews, especially the second: 'I think we'll try to do this fairly quickly because if I look at my own gradings I'm fairly certain of the good gradings that I have given you, all right?' This has the effect of giving priority to the teacher's assessments but it also means that she has no time to explore the learning difficulties that the student is signalling to her. Thus she passes up the opportunity for diagnosis and planning of future action on both her part and the student's.

Eight grades are assigned in the course of these two interviews. On three occasions the teacher invites the student to state her self-assessed ranking before offering her own judgement, and on three occasions the teacher offers her grading first but asks whether the student agrees. Yet on two occasions the teacher assigns a grade without discussion. If a teacher gives her assessment first, will it inevitably be established as 'authoritative' and invite acquiescence on the part of the student?

On three occasions the assessments of students and teacher are clearly at variance (regarding Michelle's 'general ability in the subject' and Kelly's 'speaking' and 'understanding'). In each case the teacher disagrees, sometimes quite forcefully, with the student's judgement and substitutes her own assessment, twice without change and once with only minor modification (from Grade One to One/Two, with the option of changing it back later, possibly without the student's explicit agreement). On all three occasions the student's 'agreement' looks like capitulation. Is this an inevitable consequence of the value traditionally ascribed to the professional judgement of teachers, and claimed by them? Would this be undermined if they 'compromised' their judgement in areas of special expertise, for example subject areas? Can they 'afford' to concede to the judgements of students?

In each case of disagreement, the students assessed their achievement less favourably than did the teacher. Are these students deliberately underselling themselves to avoid risking any loss of self-esteem, which might be occasioned by downgrading by the teacher? Is this one way of ensuring that they retain some power in a situation that is weighted against them? Or do they deliberately undervalue their own worth in order to encourage a favourable assessment by the teacher, who will probably approve of their modesty? (Such an interpretation may appear to ascribe a high level of conceptualisation to students' analyses of the situation but it is quite possible that they act on intuitive understandings.) Alternatively, in interviews such as these, is there a tendency for teachers to 'upgrade' students, either because they do not wish to do anything to destroy motivation, or because they find it too difficult to be totally honest when face-to-face with the person they are assessing? Whatever the reason, is downgrading of self by students, or corresponding upgrading of students by teachers, a common phenomenon, and is it particularly characteristic of the profile assessment process experienced by girls?[5]

The teacher enthusiastically reinforces occasions when the student's self-assessment agrees with her own. There is no further discussion. Are we to assume that agreement or consensus is equivalent to a valid assessment, or should the evidence for both agreed and disputed assessments be examined more fully in the light of tangible evidence? Is the main purpose of the review session to agree assessments that can be made public, or should it aim to deepen mutual understanding? Can these two goals be pursued simultaneously, or will one inevitably pre-empt the other?

Is anything of value, therefore, being learnt in these exchanges, apart from the interpersonal skill of predicting the kind of things the other wants to hear? Are they merely ritual exercises in how to keep everyone happy?

DISCUSSION

The terms 'negotiation', 'conversation' and 'dialogue' are all used in the Open University programme to refer to the face-to-face interaction that is part of this assessment process. Although profiling or records of achievement schemes vary in many respects, most regard a formative process of one-to-one review as essential. Indeed, although sponsors, for example, DES, MSC, examination boards, and some 'consumers' (e.g. parents and employers), may still conceptualise profiles and records primarily as summative documents, there is some evidence that they are taking on board the fact that many developers attach much importance to the formative process. Thus, for instance, the DES Policy Statement (1984, p. 4) made the point that: 'Regular dialogue between teacher and pupil will be important.' Moreover: 'Such discussions should be of direct benefit to pupils. They should also help schools to improve their organisation, curriculum and teaching and the range of opportunities open to pupils' (DES, 1984, p. 5).[6]

Interestingly, the DES favours 'dialogue' and 'discussion' over 'negotiation'. I have no doubt that this was a deliberately neutral choice, for 'negotiation' has political overtones which make its use controversial. Whereas, according to the *Oxford English Dictionary*, 'conversation' simply means talk, and 'dialogue' means conversation between two parties, 'negotiation' has the sense of 'conferring with another with a view to compromise or agreement'. Therefore, although agreement does not necessarily assume compromise, the term 'negotiation' implies differences of perception, interests and values. Certainly, in any encounter between teachers and students there are likely to be differences in these respects. Moreover, the distribution of power is manifestly unequal.[7] Given this reality the major issue seems to be whether to recognise these differences and try to develop structures for making mutually acceptable agreements/compromises, or whether to relinquish any claim to do more than raise students' self-esteem and motivation by spending some time talking with them individually. To choose the first option risks disturbing the status quo by countenancing radical change in relationships between teachers and students and therefore in the nature and control of schooling. The second option is easily dismissed as merely cosmetic, although it may have considerable intrinsic value, as evidence from the national evaluation of pilot schemes indicates (see PRAISE, 1987, p. 30).

The majority of profiling and records of achievement schemes have a liberal/progressive aspiration to improve pupil self-esteem and motivation without appearing to have anything very much more radical in mind. Some, for instance, refer to 'counselling', 'guidance' and 'tutoring' rather than 'negotiation' or even 'dialogue'. However, one suspects that those profile developers who emphasise negotiation feel this does not go far enough. They would indeed like to change the nature of the relationship between teachers and students in a radical direction. The trouble is that few are prepared to take the radical argument to its logical conclusion, so it tends to fall between two stools. Even the eminently reasonable definition quoted above is too bland. It conveys no sense of the difficulties associated with the resolution of differences that we are familiar with in industrial relations. If 'negotiation' is to be more than a pleasant social encounter, but with the less powerful ultimately acquiescing to the views of the more powerful, it must be more hard-nosed. It must acknowledge that there will be stated or unstated disagreements, and if students are to be given real power their judgements should not be explicitly or implicitly overridden by teachers.[8] Without the exercise of judgement in real situations it is unlikely that students will learn to have the autonomy that is so frequently stated as an educational goal. Moreover, if they begin to perceive the process as a hollow exercise, it may turn out to be not only a waste of time but educationally counterproductive. So what are the possibilities for developing situations conducive to genuine negotiation?

If the problem is unequal distribution of power, with students being relatively powerless, then it can be argued that the need is for structures or procedures that will create a better balance. Three possibilities present themselves. First, the student's hand could be strengthened by a third party who takes the role of an advocate committed to supporting the student's position. Such a person might be a school counsellor, another teacher or tutor, a parent or another, perhaps older, student. Secondly, students could operate systems of rewards and sanctions that would give them more power. The most obvious device, given current trends in the UK, would be to link student assessment with teacher appraisal. In this way it would become a reciprocal, and symmetrical, activity. Thirdly, various kinds of 'assertiveness training', which find a place in life skills courses, could be developed for application in teacher student negotiations. In the last analysis, however, all these 'solutions' appear negative and profoundly depressing. With the exception, perhaps, of the second, they rest on a conflict model of interaction, invoking notions of 'trade-off', having little to do with education. Is it possible to find a more positive and educational conception of what negotiation might be?

A WAY FORWARD

This is where the literature of naturalistic inquiry is pertinent, especially the methodology of 'responsive' and 'democratic' evaluation which pays particular attention to political and ethical dimensions. Since the mid-1970s, when MacDonald (1977) developed his political classification of evaluation studies,[9] evaluators working within a 'democratic' mode have acknowledged multiple perspectives and value-pluralism in the framing and exchange of information. Thus they have sought principles and procedures to safeguard those who are least able to protect themselves from the effects of exposure. According to MacDonald: 'The key concepts of democratic evaluation are "confidentiality", "negotiation" and "accessibility".' These concepts or principles are not entirely discrete since they all relate to a superordinate concept of ownership.[10] The assumption is that participants in an evaluation study have a right to control the dissemination of *personal* information about themselves and, therefore, privacy must be respected and access and use of such data should be negotiated. To meet these requirements evaluators have derived practical procedures from these principles and advocate 'negotiation of access' to data sources and 'negotiation of clearance and release' of reports (see Simons, 1979; Kemmis and Robottom, 1981). With this I have no problem. However, they also suggest that evaluators should 'negotiate the boundaries' of studies in terms of what should be included or excluded, and likewise 'negotiate accounts' in terms of accuracy and relevance. In both cases validity is the issue, which raises a question about whether it is appropriate to 'negotiate' truth and relevance.

If one adheres strictly to MacDonald's position that valuators should act as 'brokers' in exchanges of information and judgements, then the task is to ensure that they have accurate accounts of the truth *as participants perceive it*. If, on the other hand, evaluators give any interpretations of their own, and I personally think this is unavoidable since some interpretation is implicit even in the organisation of accounts, then validity is crucially important. However, to talk of negotiating the validity or truth of accounts with participants implies a consensus theory of truth that is naive and relativistic. As I suggested in relation to the transcribed teacher–student review session, the fact that two people agree a judgement does not guarantee its truth.[11] The grounds for an interpretation or judgement need to be scrutinised and this is not a matter for negotiation. It is an epistemological activity, concerned with meaning, understanding and the ascription of value. In this context the term 'dialogue', with all its Socratic associations, seems more appropriate.

It takes little imagination to see how closely the relationship of evaluator to participant corresponds to the relationship between teacher and student in the process of recording achievement. In both contexts, the individuals concerned are characteristically involved in both a formative and summative activity, that is deepening mutual understanding during face-to-face interaction and preparing accounts for possible public consumption. Since the second of these activities may place the student in a vulnerable position, it is appropriate to establish procedures for negotiation of access to information, including such things as personal diaries, and release of summary accounts, records or reports. However, when defining the bounds of relevant discussion (e.g. how far teachers should enquire into personal qualities or out-of-school achievements in making an *educational* record), and certainly when examining the evidential bases for assessments, then dialogue seems the better description of a process that is educational in intent. This distinction is presented in Table 2.

Purpose	Concepts	Process	Procedures
Formative (developing understanding of experience on the basis of evidence)	Validity, understanding	*Dialogue*	Discussion of relevances (i.e. boundaries); discussion of facts, interpretations and judgements
Summative (preparing mutually acceptable accounts possibly for public consumption)	Ownership, currency	*Negotiation*	Negotiation of access; negotiation for release

Table 2 *Negotiation and dialogue: purposes and processes*

One major question remains. Is it possible for negotiation and dialogue to be associated with different sets of concepts, principles and procedures and yet continue to co-exist within one activity, for example profiling or recording activity?

There are those, like Don Stansbury (1985), who have for a long time been saying that the formative and summative elements of profiling are uneasy bedfellows. The pressure to produce an 'agreed' summative document, of use to employers and the like, could so easily come to dominate and therefore diminish the potential for genuine educational dialogue between teachers and students concerning, not only students' achievements, but curriculum content and processes in institutional and social contexts. Certainly, the rather inadequate and superficial attempt by the French teacher to 'negotiate' assessments with her students could be explained by reference to the conflicting pressures inherent in the situation. Somehow she had to juggle her roles as subject expert, assessor, diagnostician, facilitator of learning, authority figure, manager of time and resources – and television star! Even in the absence of a television crew, could any teacher be expected to do very much better? One feasible suggestion might be to develop further the distinctions made above, and put them into practice as entirely separate but complementary activities. Together they could still be described as recording achievement but the process would be plural rather than singular.

NOTES

1. PRAISE conducted 23 case studies of schools as one strand of its evaluation strategy. Access to all schools was negotiated on the basis of a 'site brief' and a set of ethical guidelines concerning access, storage and reporting of data (see Murphy and Torrance, 1987, pp. 291–3).
2. This parallels the tension in school self-evaluation schemes between demands for accountability and aims of educational improvement. The question of whether a single activity can serve both purposes is also similar.
3. National Profiling Network (1985). A glossary of terms used in profiling: First draft. *Newsletter*, 2. Available from David Garforth or George Pearson, Advisory Service, Education Department, County Hall, Dorchester, Dorset DT1 1XJ, England. By January 1986, the NPN held a register of 79 profiling schemes generated at national, regional, county or school level.
4. Open University (1978). *Course E206, Personality, Development and Learning*, TV 10 '*Measures of Success*', Milton Keynes, OU/BBC Productions. The school and teachers involved in making this programme have pointed out that they have now moved on in their thinking and practice. This should be taken into account, as should the obvious constraints placed on students and teachers by the presence of a television crew.
5. This observation is confirmed by evidence from the national evaluation of DES-funded pilot records of achievement schemes (PRAISE), although underestimation of achievement by students appears to be characteristic of both boys and girls.
6. See DES (1984). The point about the importance of planned discussion between teachers and pupils was reinforced in DES (1987).
7. Andy Hargreaves (1986) examines the ideological implications of records of achievement schemes.
8. Some profiling schemes place the teacher's and student's assessment side by side, instead of presenting an agreed statement. It is likely that many adults, though not all, would automatically give greater credence to the teacher's assessments.
9. Earlier versions of this paper were published in MacDonald and Walker (1974, see MacDonald, 1974) and Tawney (see MacDonald, 1976).
10. Ian Stronach criticises the commodity and exchange metaphor that dominates much thinking in this context. The concept of ownership must be considered part of that same metaphor and, therefore, subject to the same criticism.
11. It can be argued that people can reach agreement without reaching consensus. However, this is a fine distinction that the users of profiles or records of achievement are not likely to make.

REFERENCES

Broadfoot, P. (ed.) (1986) *Profiles and Records of Achievement: A Review of Issues and Practice.* London: Holt Educational.

DES (Department of Education and Science) (1984) *Records of Achievement: A Statement of Policy.* London: HMSO.

DES (Department of Education and Science) (1987) *Records of Achievement: An Interim Report.* London: HMSO.

Hargreaves, A. (1986) *Two Cultures of Schooling*, Basingstoke: Falmer Press.

Kemmis, S. and Robottom, I. (1981) 'Principles of procedure in curriculum evaluation', *Journal of Curriculum Studies*, 13, 2, 151–5.

MacDonald, B. (1974) 'Evaluation and the control of education', in B. MacDonald and R. Walker (eds), *SAFARI I: Innovation, Evaluation, Research and the Problem of Control*, pp. 9–22.

MacDonald, B. (1976). In D. Tawney (ed.), *Curriculum Evaluation Today: Trends and Implications*, pp. 125–36. Schools Council Research Studies. London: Macmillan Educational.

MacDonald, B. (1977) 'A political classification of evaluation studies', in D. Hamilton, D. Jenkins, C. King, B. MacDonald and M. Parlett (eds), *Beyond the Numbers Game*, pp. 224–7. London: Macmillan.

Murphy, R. and Torrance, H. (1987) *Evaluating Educational Issues and Methods.* London: Harper and Row.

National Profiling Network (1985) Newsletter No 5, Dorset County Council, Dorchester.

PRAISE (1987). *Interim Evaluation Report, 1987.* Milton Keynes and Bristol: Open University School of Education and Bristol University School of Education.

Simons, H. (1979). 'Suggestions for a school self-evaluation based on democratic principles', *CARN Bulletin 3.* Cambridge: Cambridge Institute of Education.

Stansbury, D. (1985). *Programme to Develop Records of Experience as an Element in the Documentation of School Leavers: Report on the Preliminary Phase, March 1984 – July 1985.* Totnes: Springline Trust.

Turner, G. and Clift, P. (1985). *A First Review and Register of School and College Based Teacher Appraisal Schemes.* Milton Keynes: Open University School of Education, mimeo.

part three
THE CASE OF READING

INTRODUCTION

As Caroline Gipps and colleagues made clear in Chapter 2.1, reading is the skill that is regularly and almost universally monitored on teachers' own initiatives or as a result of the intervention of public bodies. According the topic of reading a section of the reader is appropriate in terms of the importance of the issue – but reading assessment has not always shown the vitality of assessment in other topics.

Elizabeth Goodacre considers the relationship between models of learning and teaching on the one hand and methods and procedures for assessment on the other. She considers that as a model of reading is an abstraction from reality, this may imply that those involved with the testing of reading – teacher, researcher or test constructor – *impose* a view of learning. There is as a consequence no commonly held view of an appropriate reading model.

In the first of three chapters, Barry Stierer gives an increasing focus on work in classrooms. He discerns that the purposes of testing established by 'outsiders' (including here the local educational authority) alter within and between schools. Thus test results may have consequences for resource allocation in one locality but not another. In Chapter 3.3, Barry Stierer considers three criticisms of tests – that they are out of date, that they fail to diagnose individual difficulties, and that they do not measure 'real reading'. Among several interesting findings is the high level of selectivity teachers adopt in 'taking seriously' test results. The common accusation that teachers who so react are not facing the facts is examined by a questioning of the notion of validity in testing and the invitation of many teaching tests.

In Chapter 3.5 the authors, who had responsibility for introducing the ILEA Primary Language Record in 1988, sought to bring unity to various 'interests' in the reading process. The Record invites contributions from parents and the children themselves – extending in scope to writing, speaking and listening too.

3.1 | WHAT IS READING: WHICH MODEL?

ELIZABETH GOODACRE

This is a most difficult and complex question to answer, and to some extent it depends on who is asking the question. In this chapter I intend to examine first the researcher or theorist's view of the reading process and the fact that the emphasis, until recently, has been more on the way that children are taught to read rather than how they learn. Secondly, I shall look at the test designer's construct or model of the reading process and show how the test designer makes certain assumptions about motivation in the testing situation, which may be very different from those of the teacher. Thirdly, I shall describe some of the ways in which the teacher's model differs from those of the researcher and the test constructor, particularly in regard to the way in which the teacher perceives his role and function in children's school learning. Finally, I shall try to relate changes in the three types of models of reading to sociological changes, so that the reader may realise that it is not only important *who* asks the question 'What is reading?' but also *when* this question is asked in a society's cultural and economic development.

THE RESEARCHER'S MODEL OF THE READING PROCESS

The reading researcher tends to operate with a reading model because her experiments and studies are set up to provide answers to questions that she is asking about the phenomena she is studying. Models in research thus tend to serve a guiding and exploratory function. 'If it was like this ... I should expect so and so to happen, or to find evidence of such and such.' Such models can be *descriptive*, dealing for instance with the identification of the characteristics of reading behaviour, or *explanatory,* examining and offering explanations of the relationships between characteristic behaviour patterns. Using a model of reading, in either way, leads the researcher to expect certain types of outcome, to perceive some things and ignore others. Models, therefore, typically become overviews of a science's subject matter.

Essentially though, a model of reading is an abstraction from reality. It is intended to order and to simplify our view of that reality, while still keeping to the fore the essential characteristics of the process. Therefore, the researcher's model of reading isolates and brings together her ideas, beliefs and knowledge about reading, which have been formulated on the basis of her own experience with reading in the 'real' world. The ordering involved in such model making will be selective, and models inevitably become *perceptual filters* (Forcese and Richer, 1973) shaping the individual's experience, influencing the kinds of questions asked, leading to particular expectations. The model or construct of reading held by the researcher, test constructor or teacher all have this characteristic in common – they impose a pattern on experience which is the result of experience for, in George Kelly's words (Britton, 1973):

> Man looks at his world through transparent patterns or templates which he creates and then attempts to fit over the realities of which the world is composed. The fit is not always very good. Yet without such patterns the world appears to be such an undifferentiated homogeneity that man is unable to make any sense out of it. Even a poor fit is more helpful to him than nothing at all.

In reading research, a number of models have been formulated (Singer and Ruddell, 1976). All isolate particular aspects of the reading process and seek to describe their interrelationship as explanations of how the reader responds and processes printed/written matter, but they differ in structure and in emphasis, usually on the basis of the discipline of study and experience of the researcher, for example whether they studied experimental, cognitive or perceptual psychology, computer studies or linguistics. Such models of reading can provide insights into the possible working of the process and therefore have implications for teaching, and for the diagnosis of reading difficulties. However, such partial models may be highly selective; also, some are more applicable to the beginner than the mature reader.

Williams (1972) has suggested that until the 1970s there was little interest in the development of a comprehensive theory of reading. She considered that models had been mainly formed on the basis of improving *teaching* of reading, particularly for beginners, rather than in relation to the study of how this skill is acquired by the learner. As the result of a targeted research programme (Gephart, 1970) emanating from the United States 'Right to Read' campaign (which assumed that *all* citizens could learn to read, unless physically impaired), the focus changed. Williams reported a greater tendency for researchers to work towards the development of a reading model geared more nearly to the generation of research hypotheses, that is questions that could be asked about the working of the reading process rather than studies of the effects of changing teaching techniques. Since then most of the model building in reading research has focused on the cognitive aspects of the process, with little attempt (until very recently) being made to incorporate affective factors into such models. Athey and Holmes (1969) made a substantial review of the latter area in the late 1960s and Lawrence's work (1974) in this country, on the effects of counselling on reading disability, seems to have led to a revival of interest in personality factors and reading progress. Whitehead's School Council project (1975, 1977) on children's reading interests has also helped to highlight the importance of motivation factors.

THE TEST MAKER'S MODEL

Test constructors are, of course, aware of research trends although, in reading assessment, there seems to be more delay in new ideas about the reading process reaching test makers than ideas regarding test measurement and construction. Pumfrey (1977) has outlined how certain assumptions about the nature and distribution of mental abilities underpinned the testing movement in this country during the last century, influencing the type of reading tests produced. Certainly reading tests need to be viewed in relation to the reading models current at the time of their construction. It is not just a question of the ever changing nature of language and the way in which words in tests can 'date' (e.g. refrigerator over several decades becomes more familiar in its contracted form fridge), but also that the content of the test (what the testee is asked to do in terms of reading behaviour) provides evidence of the test maker's model of reading. The graded word reading tests have been increasingly criticised during the last decade because they sample a very limited form of reading behaviour, that is the pronunciation of words without the help of contextual information. When the graded word reading tests were originally designed, nearly forty years ago, models of reading were in the main based on 'decoding', and instruction methods emphasised the performance aspects of reading. Such tests, at that time, were probably adequate measures of reading achievement in the light of instructional objectives. However, test users must be aware of the changing nature of teaching aims and goals and therefore the need to assess the content of tests in relation to *current* objectives.

To some extent, there is always likely to be a certain degree of mismatch between the model of the test maker and that of the test user, since the former tries to sample, under well-defined conditions, a *sample* of pupils' reading behaviour. *Standardised* reading attainment tests measure a pupil's reading performance, such tests often being paper and pencil instruments given collectively to a group or class of children. Every aspect of these tests has been standardised so that, if all the directions are followed correctly, it should be possible to interpret the results in the same manner regardless of where the test is given; that is, the results should mean the same thing to different people. 'Standardised' therefore means that the methods of administering, recording, scoring and interpreting have been made uniform. *Norm-referenced tests* are those which are used to compare the relative position of individuals in different groups, whereas *criterion-referenced tests* are used to determine whether an individual or a group has achieved a certain level of mastery. The standardised test should have validity and reliability. A valid test should measure what it sets out to measure and, to be valid, reading tests must be reliable in that they must be able to produce consistent results. The test maker is therefore very concerned to achieve conditions which ensure standardisation, and such control is likely to limit the type of reading behaviour which is amenable to such forms of assessment. For instance, teachers who claim that reading is a holistic act may consider the aspect of reading measured by a particular type of test as a minor or relatively unimportant part of the total reading process. Certainly, the limitations involved in producing commercial reading tests, which are cheap and easily administered, may lead the test maker to settle for a test design whose content suggests a one-sided or partial model of the reading process.

THE TEACHER'S MODEL

Helen Arnold (1977), as a result of working on the Schools Council project 'Extending Beginning Reading', has suggested that there are three main factors which shape teachers' perceptions of reading behaviour. These are, first, the teacher's own concept of what the reading process constitutes (his model of reading); his expectations of pupils will depend on how far they measure up to this concept. Secondly, through experience the teacher builds up general expectations of pupils' reading at certain stages of development. He has constructs of different types of reader, and his perception of each pupil in the role of reader is likely to be influenced by his assessment of that pupil in general terms of attitude and ability; for example 'a sensible boy', 'a clever child', 'a good worker'. The teacher may, for instance, expect a child from a 'good home' to be a 'good reader' (Goodacre, 1967). Thirdly, achievement in reading is assessed in various ways and such results will in turn help to shape a teacher's ideas about 'reading' and the characteristic signs of progress. Arnold thought that such assessment often involved those aspects or elements of reading which are most easily measured (the types of reading behaviour sampled by standardised tests and the practice of 'hearing') and that therefore teachers' constructs of the reading process are more likely to be influenced by these more formal or 'ritualistic' reading assessments than their attitudes to children's choice and use of reading.

For instance, she reported that primary teachers seemed to see reading mainly as the mastery of initial decoding skills:

They look for certain specific signposts to gauge achievement, for example the mastery of key-words (sight words), the ability to 'sound out' words (phonic attack), and the successful completion of a reading scheme. The word most often used by teachers to signify mastery of reading is 'fluency'. This is seldom defined, but appears to mean the ability to read a given passage orally with expression.

This finding is supported by earlier work with infant teachers (Goodacre, 1970) which showed that their model of reading was closely related to one based on the behaviour of the mature, competent reader reading aloud, that is reading fluently with expression, making few if any corrections or repetitions. However, individual teachers differed considerably in the criteria they adopted when assessing children as 'ready' for the next stage in a reading scheme. For example, some demanded accurate reading of *all* words, in order, from the lists at the back of the book, while others only asked children to identify a random selection of such words. Pupils in the 'hearing' situation, as opposed to formal testing situations, seem to be assessed in relation to criteria based on the teacher's model of reading which stresses fluency and expressive oral reading, characteristics of the mature reader's *performance* level. In other words, the learner is judged on the extent to which he can produce oral reading which is similar to the teacher's model of reading based on adult performance.

Maxwell (1974) discussed different definitions of 'reading', identifying three elements which he suggested emphasised: (a) what is read (the content), (b) for what purpose it is read (the reader's motivation) and (c) how it is read (the process of reading). He outlined the way in which children acquire the reading skill, suggesting that the activity at each stage involves the three elements in different combinations. He cited evidence from the SSRC (Social Science Research Council) study of teaching reading in Scottish primary schools in which the teachers' reading aims were analysed in relation to these different emphases. He reported that, for instance, the teachers of the younger children tended to define reading more frequently in process terms. Arnold, in the Schools Council study referred to above, also found that those teachers teaching 7 to 9 year olds were preoccupied with initial skills, stressing instruction and practice in phonics. She reported that these teachers generally tended to see reading as a hierarchy of subskills which can and should be instructed sequentially. However, the project's results showed clearly that, at that age, pupils were using all levels of language simultaneously when reading aloud to make sense of the text – they made use of phono-graphemic, syntactic and semantic cues. She suggested that children usually work through their strengths and that a sequential model of reading does not allow for that. She claimed that, when teaching, the teacher generally followed 'an accepted pattern which chops up the process of reading into discrete compartments' such as phonic rules, spelling patterns, vocabulary, comprehension, etc. As explained earlier in regard to formal testing, the teachers' perceptions of pupils as readers tended to be formulated on their impressions of pupils' achievement in separate subskills. So that teachers could, for instance, refer to pupils being 'good at reading' but 'poor at comprehension', suggesting that 'reading' was being defined in terms of performance rather than as a thought-getting process. She suggested that 'teachers' perceptions of their pupils' reading are often based on intuitive, generalised judgements at one extreme, and assessment, which concentrates on a narrow spectrum of the whole skill, at the other'.

THE TEACHER'S CONCEPT OF THE TEACHING ROLE

The teachers' reading model may also involve the way in which they see themselves as teachers. They can perceive their role mainly in terms of *facilitator* of a child's learning of literacy skills or as *guardian* and dispenser of a skill highly valued by society. From a sociological viewpoint, it is more likely that the former role operates in an open society, the latter in an elitist system where reading is the key to knowledge and the means to secure power and status. Reading is a means to an end, not an end in itself. Pupils are instructed and if they fail to acquire the skill, the fault lies more with them than with their instructor. In the more open society the teacher is unable to depend to the same extent on the pupil's motivation to acquire the skill for reasons of prestige, and therefore needs to rely rather more on the learner experiencing satisfaction from the actual use of the skill. Changes in the economic and political structure of society are reflected in changes in the literacy standards of that society. Such changes must inevitably affect the reading models of researcher, test maker and teacher.

CHANGES IN READING RESEARCH MODELS

During the last decade it is possible, in the theoretical explanations of reading, to trace a move away from emphasis on reading as performance and from explanations stressing the transformation of printed/written matter into speech sounds (as illustrated in Gibson's, 1965, definition which refers to the reader as speaker, *then* hearer) to models implying direct access by the reader to the meaning of text. If reading is viewed as mainly a process of decoding text to speech, it is logical that knowledge of phonic 'rules' and word attack skills are considered important components of reading, often as ends in themselves, and stressed by the teacher in the role of instructor. Venezsky (1963), for instance, suggested that learning to read was learning to correlate grapheme and phoneme (written symbols and speech sounds). This type of model described reading mainly in terms of what linguists refer to as 'surface-structure phenomena' as opposed to 'deep-structure phenomena' which are concerned with underlying meanings, 'the writing between the lines'.

A second model was suggested on the basis of interpretation of reading as a search for information (Hochberg, 1970), a view that was paralleled by Goodman's (1970) description of reading as the reduction of uncertainty. Hochberg distinguished between reading as decoding symbols to sounds and reading as a search for information. He saw the reader as mainly extracting the information necessary for understanding from a display of information which was largely irrelevant and redundant. If the reader had to extract the necessary information from a display containing irrelevant and redundant information, an efficient processing strategy would entail sampling of the text. As long ago as the end of last century (Pillsbury, 1897), it had been noted that the proficient reader read materials without detecting errors such as letter substitutions, transpositions, omissions or additions. Empirical evidence that the mature reader does not process all the information available to him was reported by Kolers (1970). He found that, if the reader had to adopt a letter-by-letter strategy, his reading rate dropped to about a tenth of his normal reading speed. Smith (1968, 1973) has also stressed that a reader *allocates* his attention to the text and that increases of reading rate facilitate extraction of meaning from the text. Venezky and Calfee's (1970) information processing model drew attention to the more proficient reader's ability to 'tag' information (to identify and deal with potentially informative areas of the material to be read). The use of parts of words as cues was suggested by the work of Marchbanks and Levin (1965) and Weber (1970). Levin and Cohn (1968) showed that the reader uses processing units of different sizes as his reading task changes.

Such findings suggest that there may be no one model of the reading process; different factors assuming varying importance at different ages. This led to a modification of the search-for-information model to the view that reading is a search for units, and also that this may be related to the developmental nature of reading acquisition involving, as it does, the learner's cognitive and linguistic faculties.

Schlesinger's (1969) finding that readers pick up and process phrase units, seems to be a characteristic of mature rather than beginning readers. This led to a more general interest in segmenting and 'chunking', and the development of the idea of the 'mapping' of oral language on to written language (Clay, 1972). Word matching, in this type of model, may also involve letter string/speech sound matching which leads to workable phonemic/graphemic generalisations on the part of the learner.

Levin and Kaplan (1970) described a reading model which incorporated the idea of hypothesis formation (informed guesses on the part of the learner), confirmation or disconfirmation of the hypotheses being major elements in the model. This type of model suggests that efficiency in reading is charac-terised by the operation of reader expectation and the confirmation that such expectations are correct. To some extent such reading models parallel models of speech production emphasising the gradual nature of the acquisition of communicative competence and the 'naturalness' of the process. The emphasis on readers' expectations and attitudes also, of course, leads to revived interest in the affective aspects of the reading process.

Description of the stages in cognitive and linguistic development have helped in the understanding of how children learn to talk and to think. A similar advance in understanding could come from the identification and study of stages in the acquisition of literacy (Goodacre, 1977; Vernon, 1977).

ARE READING TESTS CHANGING?

Research suggests that reading models have changed taking cognisance of the changing roles of teachers and pupils; the more recent models allocating a more active, participating role to the learner. How far is this change paralleled by changes in the reading models of test makers? Are there changes apparent in the content of more recent tests?

In fact a number of published tests in current use have been with us a considerable time. It may well be that such tests retain their popularity because they fit in with teachers' ideas about the reading process, which research suggests are slow to change. The Schonell Graded Word Reading Test and the Burt (rearranged) Word Reading Tests were reported in the 1975 Bullock Report as being used in 72 per cent and 34 per cent respectively of primary and middle schools. Both tests are measures of a pupil's ability to pronounce isolated words without help from contextual cues. They involve a model of reading which places more emphasis on performance than meaning, stresses the correspondence between speech sounds and printed/written symbols and concentrates on a part of the process rather than the operation as a whole. They are used to categorise pupils by level of achievement; they cannot provide diagnostic information – they were not designed to do so. Of the more recent tests coming onto the market however, the Edinburgh Reading Tests seek to measure more than one aspect of the reading process and two experimental versions of tests (the London Reading Test and the NFERS Reading Level Tests) are based on the 'cloze' procedure, which involves deleting or omitting words in a text on a systematic basis. The reader is required to insert appropriate words with contextual help thus indicating his understanding of what he has read.

Pumfrey (1974) suggested that teachers have limited knowledge of the range of reading tests available to them and that more could be done by LEAs to promote more sophisticated uses of reading tests, particularly through the medium of in-service education. Awareness of their own ideas about reading, and the way in which such models influence their assessment of pupils' abilities and potential, should enable teachers to evaluate more completely the assessment measures they use, and to reach conclusions about the aspects of reading which, to them, seem worth testing; that is, which will provide them with information that is useful in facilitating pupils' learning. Test manuals should provide the answers to the questions teachers ask as the result of such evaluation of their teaching objectives, and the content of manuals should be expected to improve in line with the criteria suggested by the British Psychological Society (1960).

REFERENCES

Arnold, H. (1977) 'Teachers' perceptions of their pupils' reading ability', in J. Gilliland (ed.) *Reading: Research and Classroom Practice*. London: Ward Lock Educational, pp. 165–9.

Athey, I. and Holmes, J. (1969) 'Reading success and personality characteristics in junior high school students', *University of California Publications in Education*, 18, 1–80.

British Psychological Society (1960) 'Technical recommendations for Psychological and Educational Tests prepared by the Committee on Test Standards of the British Psychological Society', *Brit. Psycho. Soc. Bull.* 41.

Britton, J. (1973) *Language and Learning*. Harmondsworth: Penguin.

Clay, M. (1972) *Reading: The Patterning of Complex Behaviour*. London: Heinemann Educational.

DES (Department of Education and Science) (1975) Bullock Report *A Language for Life*. London: HMSO.

Forcese, D. and Richer, S. (1973) *Social Research Methods*. London: Prentice-Hall.

Gephart, W. (1970) 'The targeted research and development program in reading: a report on the application of the convergence technique', *Reading Research Quarterly*, 5, 505–23.

Gibson, E. (1965) 'Learning to read', *Science*, 148, 1066–72.

Goodacre, E. (1967) *Teachers and their Pupils' Home Background*. Slough: NFER.

Goodacre, E. (1970) 'The concept of reading readiness' in Chazan, M. (ed.) *Reading Readiness*. University College of Swansea Faculty of Education Occasional Publication.

Goodacre, E. (1977) *Stages in Literacy*. Centre for the Teaching of Reading publication, School of Education, University of Reading.

Goodman, K. S. (1970) *Reading: Process and Program*. Illinois: National Council of Teachers of English.

Hochberg, J. (1970) 'Components of literacy: speculations and exploratory research', in Levin and Williams (eds) *Basic Studies in Reading*. New York: Basic Books, pp. 74–89.

Kolers, P. (1970) 'Three stages of reading', in Levin and Williams (eds) *Basic Studies in Reading*. New York: Basic Books, pp. 90–118.

Lawrence, D. (1974) *Improved Reading Through Counselling*. London: Ward Lock Educational.

Levin, H. and Cohn, J. (1968) 'Effects of instructions on the eye-voice span', in Levin *et al.* (eds) *The Analysis of Reading Skill*. Ithaca: Cornell University.

Levin, H. and Kaplan, E. (1970) 'Grammatical structure and reading', in Levin and Williams (eds) *Basic Studies in Reading*. New York: Basic Books, pp. 119–33.

Marchbanks, G. and Levin, H. (1965) 'Cues by which children recognize words' *J. of Educ. Psychol.*, 56, 57–61.

Maxwell, J. (1974) 'Towards a definition of reading', *Reading*, 8, 2, 5–12.

Pillsbury, W. (1897) 'A study in apperception', *Amer. J. of Psychol.*, 8, 2, 315–93.

Pumfrey, P. (1974) 'Promoting more sophisticated use of reading tests: a national survey', *Reading*, 8, 1, 5–13.

Pumfrey, P. (1977) 'Reading measurement and evaluation: some current concerns and promising developments', in Gilliland (ed.) *Reading: Research and Classroom Practice*. London: Ward Lock Educational, pp. 205–27.

Schlesinger, I. (1969) *Sentence Structure and the Reading Process*. The Hague: Mouton.

Singer, H. and Ruddell, R. (1976) *Theoretical Models and Processes of Reading*, 2nd edn, Newark, Delaware: International Reading Association.

Smith, F. (1968) 'The use of redundancy and of distinctive features in the identification of visually-presented words', unpublished doctoral dissertation, Harvard University.

Smith, F. (1973) *Psycholinguistics and Reading*. New York: Holt, Rinehart and Winston.

Venezsky, R. (1963) 'A computer program for observing spelling-to-sound correlations', in Levin (ed.) *A Basic Research Program on Reading*. Ithaca: Cornell University.

Venezsky, R. and Calfee, R. (1970) 'The reading competency model', in Singer and Ruddell (eds) *Theoretical Models and Processes of Reading*. Newark, Delaware: International Reading Association, pp. 272–91.

Vernon, M. (1977) 'Varieties of deficiency in the reading process', *Harvard Educ. Review*, 47, 3, 396–410.

Weber, R. (1970) 'First-graders' use of grammatical content in reading', in Levin and Williams (eds) *Basic Studies in Reading*. New York: Basic Books, pp. 147–63.

Whitehead, F. *et al.* (1975) *Children's Reading Interests* Schools Council Working Paper No. 52. London: Evans/Methuen Educational.

Whitehead, F. *et al.* (1977) *Children and their Books*. London: Schools Council Research Studies, Macmillan Education.

Williams, J. (1972) 'Learning to read: a review of theories and models', in Davis (ed.) *The Literature of Research in Reading with Emphasis on Models* Targeted Research and Development Program in Reading Project No. 2, The Literature Search, Contract No. OEC-70-470 (508) Project No. 0-90-36.

3.2 THREE STUDIES OF READING TESTS IN THE CLASSROOM

BARRY STIERER

THE STUDY

This chapter draws on a range of ethnographic data arising from long-term participant-observation case studies in three junior classrooms. These were carried out between September 1981 and March 1982, and consisted of about one full day spent in each classroom each week for the six-month period. Their purpose was to describe teachers' everyday assessment practices for reading based on regular classroom observation, tape-recording and discussion with teachers.

All three schools were located within the same LEA, a large non-metropolitan county in southern England. The target classes were selected from the same LEA to permit observation of three teachers' responses to the same LEA testing programme, which consisted of an annual reading survey of 7 + and 10 + year olds. Although the three schools showed great variations in intake, size, organisation and atmosphere, all rising 8 year olds in the three schools were tested for reading during the period of fieldwork. This provided a testing 'base-line' common to the three classes in the study. Some information included in this chapter relates to the purposes behind the authority's testing programme and is derived from interviews with senior officers in the LEA advisory and psychological services, and from documents produced by the authority and provided to the project.

The three schools and classes (pseudonyms are used for the names of schools and persons throughout) which comprised the study were:

Ms Braithwaite, Oak Lane County Primary School

The school:
- Primary school for 5–11s in a small provincial town near the south coast.
- The school roll had fallen steadily for several years, from about 450 to under 300.
- A strong sense existed among the staff that the school was working under exceptional pressure brought about by the 'deficient' language and social skills of children coming into the school. This chronic problem was felt to be the cause of the school's allegedly poor reputation in the town and disproportionate falling roll compared to other schools in the area.
- The headteacher had encouraged regular testing of reading in the school in an effort to show the town that 'we have nothing to hide or be ashamed of here'.
- All classes in the junior department were vertically grouped, with three first/second year classes and three third/fourth year classes. This was partly an adaptation to uneven patterns in the fall in pupil numbers and partly a positive preference among the staff to teach mixed-aged classes.

The class:
- 31 children, in a vertically-grouped first/second year junior class; 17 second years (rising nine year olds) and 14 first years (rising eight year olds).
- The majority of classroom time was organised according to a fluid independent work pattern, in which children worked through a set of 'jobs' during the day, largely at their own pace.

Ms Harvey, Beaufort County Junior School

The school:
- The only junior school in a large village near the south coast which was dominated by owner-occupier housing and professional London commuter families.
- About 270 children aged seven to eleven, drawn from the only infant school in the village.
- The school was described initially by the headmaster as 'very traditional' due to constant pressure on the school, from a vocal body of parents, to achieve parity with the many local independent schools. The school's testing policies and practices were described as a product of this pressure, in that tests were used moderately heavily to satisfy parents that standards in the school were being maintained and monitored.

The class:
- 34 first year junior pupils (rising 8 year olds).

– Dominant pattern of classroom organisation was that brief instructions were issued at the beginning of each long session, and children then worked at their tables individually or in small groups. Children wishing to make contact with Ms Harvey during these times joined a queue at her desk.

Ms Tate, Greenacre County Primary School

The school:
– A very large primary school for 5–11s in a small provincial town near the south coast, with over 700 pupils and over 25 members of staff.
– The school drew from a varied catchment area which included council estates, private estates, older terraced and semi-detached houses and caravan sites for travellers' families.

The class:
– 34 first year junior pupils (rising 8 year olds).
– A varied classroom style was used, featuring both teacher-centred lecture/questioning and independent work.

TESTING 'ATMOSPHERE' AND INTENSITY OF TEST USE

One of the factors informing the selection of these three classrooms for observation was that they appeared to be situated in an LEA and school context which was not only uncritical of tests but was in fact strongly in favour of regular and routine testing. First, there was a strong expectation emanating from County Hall that children's reading should be tested frequently. The official LEA guidelines for primary curriculum, drawn up by working parties of teachers and distributed to all schools, stated that:

> It is customary for teachers to check children's level of progress at regular intervals, by the use of recognised reading tests. By relating the child's score to his chronological age it is possible to establish his rate of progress.

The Senior Primary Adviser reinforced this expectation when asked in interview for the LEA's view on classroom uses of reading tests:

> If I, or any of my colleagues in the Advisory Service, visited a school and discovered that an up-to-date reading age was not entered on children's record cards, we would certainly want to know why not.

Whereas many of the LEA officers we interviewed elsewhere expressed the hope that their county-wide testing programme would obviate the need for schools to conduct their own testing, and therefore reduce what was sometimes seen as an excess of testing, the local authority within which the three case study schools were located clearly favoured regular testing of reading over and above the annual county reading survey at 7 + and 10 +. Although there are inevitable disjunctions between official formulations and actual practice, it was felt that the *absence* of any misgivings on the part of the central LEA administration over the regular use of reading tests was likely to promote an atmosphere in which the authenticity and respectability of testing was taken for granted.

Secondly, testing was characterised by all three headteachers as central to and instrumental in their schools' most pressing objectives. The headteacher at Oak Lane, for example, portrayed testing in the school as one element in a campaign to restore local confidence in the school. The headteacher at Beaufort Juniors placed testing in the context of a constant need to demonstrate the school's high standards to parents. And the headteacher at Greenacre described testing as an essential part of a sound and systematic curriculum.

Although all these official pronouncements of the value of frequent testing raised the possibility that a great deal of testing would be found in the three case study classrooms, close observations of the three classrooms over a six-month period revealed a very different picture. Certainly nothing like the routine and regular testing of reading expected by the local authority and suggested by the three headteachers was in evidence. In fact, apart from the LEA reading survey, for which all rising eight year olds were tested in November, the use of reading tests was confined to a very few cases where individual children were tested for special reasons.

The fact that none of these three teachers seemed to want reading test data during this study, in addition to that generated by the LEA survey (despite the expectations of the LEA and the school) is not entirely surprising. First, official formulations inevitably simplify the variations and eccentricities of actual practices. Secondly, only teachers who used reading tests very extensively indeed would be likely to test an entire class more than once in a six-month period, and it may have been the case that teachers of other year groups within the case study schools which were not tested by the LEA would have been observed to make more use of tests.

As a result of these circumstances, the descriptions which follow of teachers' specific testing practices are based exclusively on a single test event, the LEA reading survey in November. What is unfortunately missing from the analysis is an examination of teachers' decisions to use, or not to use, reading tests. Teachers did not view their implementation of the LEA reading survey as a personal or professional decision to use a reading test: their reasons for giving the test were considered to be self-evident, since the test was a part of LEA policy. Cooperation with the test was problematic only for Ms Harvey, who described the survey as 'nothing but a public relations exercise for the County Council', and her sense of compromise reflected her objection to LEA edicts as well as to using tests. Similarly, teachers' reasons for not testing children's reading during the study, over and above the county survey, were seen as equally self-evident: there was simply no need, and therefore no decision was involved. Teachers did not perceive pressure for testing, emanating either from the LEA or from headteachers, which was not satisfied during the period of observation by the LEA reading survey.

Although these circumstances precluded an analysis of teachers' reasons for testing or for not testing, they had the advantage of focusing attention on the dynamics of teachers' practices with *respect* to testing, rather than on the more abstract area of teachers' justifications for using or not using tests.

THE LEA READING SURVEY

The LEA guidelines for primary curriculum, already mentioned, stated that the objective of the annual reading survey:

> in addition to identifying individual children with difficulties, was to identify particular areas of need and aid decisions concerning the allocation of scarce resources. Within schools, the same information can help teachers to evaluate the effectiveness of teaching arrangements and methods already employed.

The survey was therefore seen by the authority to fulfil a wide range of educational and managerial purposes. It was, first, a *monitoring* device, generating information which can be used statistically to show trends between groups rather than to measure individual performance. It was, secondly, a device to aid decisions on the *allocation of resources,* that is, it was seen to enable the authority to 'determine if its resources in materials and personnel are being deployed to the best advantage in the context of its obligation to pupils, parents, the community and central government'. Thirdly, it was a *screening* device, enabling 'individual children with low scores to be identified and followed up'. Fourthly, and most pertinent to the concerns of this chapter, the survey was seen to provide *individual schools* with information to 'help teachers to evaluate the effectiveness of teaching arrangements and methods already employed'. [. . .]

The test used in the survey was the Reading Test A produced by the NFER. It is described by the NFER as 'a simple test of reading comprehension of the sentence completion type ... designed for use with children in the first year of the junior school.' Users of the test are reminded by the NFER that 'while ... generally effective as a means of screening with large numbers of pupils of widely varying attainment [the test] tells little about the readers themselves.'

This important caveat raises questions about the authority's fourth objective in the reading survey, that is to provide schools and teachers with information which will aid their teaching and evaluation. Although the LEA curriculum guidelines fall short of positively encouraging teachers to use the LEA test scores to facilitate actual classroom decision-making and teaching for individual children, the document's ambiguity on this point makes it possible to interpret the authority's intentions in this way. Certainly no attempt was made, in the guidelines or anywhere else, to discourage teachers from using the survey results for individual diagnosis and teaching. It is of course unrealistic to expect busy classroom teachers to familiarise themselves either with the technical limitations of a test they are required to administer for the local authority, or with the subtleties of the authority's policy on within-school uses of the test. In the absence of a clear and positive statement to teachers from County Hall on the unsuitability of the test for individual diagnosis and teaching, it is not surprising that the results from the county reading survey were observed in some cases to be used for purposes which the NFER warns against, but which the local authority tacitly supports.

THE TEST EVENT

The manual of instructions for the NFER Reading Test A emphasises that the reliability of standardised scores generated by the test is dependent upon adherence to the uniform and impersonal administration and marking procedures set out in the manual. Wide variations in administration and marking procedures were observed in the classroom however, and teachers' background knowledge about individual children was sometimes observed to inform their procedures for both test administration and test marking.

In terms of administration, at one extreme all first year children at Greenacre Primary were given the test together in the school hall under austere conditions more common to public examinations. Such was the rigour of this school's test administration procedure that the researcher was physically excluded from the hall during testing and was not allowed subsequent access to the test results despite assurances of confidentiality. At the other extreme the 11 first-year children in a mixed-age class at Oak Lane were tested by their own teacher in their own classroom. The researcher was encouraged to observe the test session, and the scores and test papers were subsequently shown to him and discussed. The following extract from observation notes produced during the test event at Oak Lane gives some impression of the atmosphere in the classroom. The fragment begins immediately after the teacher had completed her oral instructions and worked through the examples on the test booklet cover:

11.11 am Ms Braithwaite notices that Zanda has yet to open the test booklet and is strugglng through the examples, even though she has already marked them once. Ms B. gently opens the booklet, whispers something to Zanda, moves away.

11.12 am Mark is already showing signs of strain and distress. He looks up at Ms B. with desperation and panic.

Ms B. circulates round the room, points to something in Luke's booklet, turns the page for Gary.

11.13 am   Mark's face is now contorted with agony. He cries out, 'I can't read any of these sentences!' Ms B. gently shushes him, goes to him, whispers, moves away. Mark continues more calmly.

11.17 am   David, Jessica and Pieter all gliding through, apparently effortlessly.

11.19 am   Ms B. comes over to me to report on her chat with Mark (11.13 am). She says she told him he could stop if he wanted to, and gave him a piece of scrap paper to do a drawing when he decided to stop. This apparently cheered him up and he decided he wanted to carry on.

11.20 am   Gary: big sigh, sits back, gazes out of the window.

11.21 am   Pieter is finished (10 minutes); looks very pleased with himself. Zanda has turned over to p. 2, without apparently attempting any questions on p. 1. Ms B. goes over, whispers, turns back to p. 1.

11.24 am   Ms B. takes Zanda's booklet away; looks over to me and silently indicates 'tears'. Ms B. gives her a reassuring smile and scrap paper for drawing.

11.25 am   Mark now on the verge of tears again. Ms B. takes his booklet away and he begins his drawing, humming to himself cheerfully.

Ms B. stops at my chair again briefly on her rounds. Both Mark and Zanda, she says, hadn't really a clue what they were meant to be doing. She points out what a terrific effort Luke is making – almost comical in his earnest determination.

11.26 am   Jessica is finished (15 minutes). Ms B. allows Wendy, Nicola and Gary to stop. Gary looks especially relieved.

11.31 am   Claire finished.

11.32 am   Nick finished.

11.33 am   Luke has the look of total determination on his face, his whole body involved in the effort, tongue out. He begins measuring with his fingers the blanks in the uncompleted sentences and tried to find which of the four alternative answers best 'fits' (there is in fact no relationship). Ms B. offers to let him stop, but he perseveres. Ms B. looks over to me and winks.

As can be seen, interaction with the teacher was an important and integral part of many children's experience of taking the test. Ms Braithwaite circulated round the room, making herself available to the children and gently intervening when they showed signs of strain. Whether these procedures actually contradicted the terms of the administration instructions printed in the test manual is a matter we discuss more fully elsewhere, but it was certainly the case that they created an entirely different atmosphere from the almost clinical arrangement at Greenacre, and reflected a very different attitude toward the reading survey and testing generally.

The fact that some children in Ms Braithwaite's class were observed to find the demands of the test and the test situation stressful raises important questions about the suitability and validity of standardised testing conditions for mixed ability classes of this age group. Apart from the possible technical implications of children's anxieties, that is the effect on test scores, there are attendant ethical questions related to the advisability of employing testing methods which cause serious discomfort for some children.

Similarly, marking procedures for the test were observed to vary. Several children at Beaufort Juniors, for example, answered test questions ambiguously, for example with more than one response partially indicated, and these children were generally 'given the benefit of the doubt' despite instructions to the contrary in the test manual.

In one sense of course these examples of variation and personal judgement within testing procedures are both inevitable and unimportant. Many teachers will inevitably wish to prevent children from experiencing unnecessary upset during a test and will automatically respond to requests for help and comfort. It is difficult to ensure uniform testing conditions across large numbers of schools and classrooms, particularly for very young children. Many teachers will naturally not mark a particular item incorrect if they feel certain they 'know' what a child intended on the basis of how the child responded to the item and on the basis of their own accumulated understanding of the child. And where teachers have no serious interest in the outcome of the test, or only require individual children's raw scores for individual assessment, these variations and subjective influences will not matter a great deal. Where they do matter is where standardised scores are taken seriously, by teachers, schools and LEAs, since they call into question the way in which scores on a standardised test are achieved and then related to the population on which the reading test was originally standardised. Despite the inevitable diversity of procedures for test administration and marking, standardised scores from the county reading survey were sometimes observed to be given great importance at many levels of the system, with slight differences between children, between classes, between schools, and over time, taken to be educationally significant.

USE OF TEST SCORES

Referring back to the four purposes given by the local authority for its annual reading survey at 7+, that is screening, allocation of resources, monitoring and within-school uses, we can see that some of these purposes were rendered ineffective due either to prior action or to economic constraints.

SCREENING

Senior officers of the local authority described the county reading survey as chiefly a screening device. By identifying children in need of special help with reading – help from a remedial teacher based in the school, or, in exceptional cases, from a member of the psychological service – the test was reportedly used to set into action the chain of procedures for remedial identification and placement. However, procedures for allocating children to remedial groups, as well as for referring children to the psychological service, were observed in the three case study classes to operate entirely independently of the LEA reading survey.

As has been said, the LEA reading survey was administered in November of the children's first year in junior school. In all three case study classes, however, remedial allocations had been made long before the children moved to the junior department or junior school in September, and in one school remedial groups had been withdrawn for special help since Easter of their final year in the infant department. The procedures used for making these allocations varied from school to school, but usually involved a combination of testing and teacher recommendation. Although criteria used for identifying children requiring remedial teaching varied from school to school, the number of places available in the remedial groups was invariably established prior to the selection process, which inevitably governed the criteria used. By the time the results of the LEA survey became available to teachers in late November these remedial groups were well established. No new children were allocated to these groups on the basis of their scores on the county screen, despite the fact that some children not in a remedial group scored within the same range as children receiving remedial teaching.

Similarly, while teachers were observed to refer individual children to the psychological service in the months preceding the LEA reading survey, on the basis of their own observation that these children were experiencing severe difficulties, no new children were either referred by the school or followed up by the psychologists on the basis of test results from the annual survey in November.

It would therefore appear that, at least for the three classes studied here, the 'screening' element of the LEA survey was superfluous to other procedures for identifying children in need of special help with reading. Although in a few cases the survey results were used as a nominal 'check' to confirm the accuracy or validity of these independent procedures, this was never seen to be done systematically since teachers appeared to have a basic confidence in their own methods for selecting children for remedial teaching.

ALLOCATION OF RESOURCES

In addition to its screening functions, the county survey at 7 + was described by senior officials as the basis upon which the part-time teachers constituting the county's remedial service were assigned to schools. The weekly timetables for part-time remedial teachers were established in response to schools' needs as demonstrated by the survey results, and these allocations were reviewed annually. However, as the county's overall level of remedial staffing was reduced during the period of this investigation it was impossible for the LEA to respond to cases of increased need with an improved allocation. At Oak Lane, for example, the school mean dropped in the 1981 survey from 105.0 to 100.4, and yet the school's remedial allocation was actually reduced during the same school year from 0.6 to 0.5 of a full-time remedial teacher. These changes have to be understood in the context of the authority as a whole, where Oak Lane's falling norm may not have seemed especially salient and where a cut of 0.1 in remedial staffing may in fact have represented a rise in the school's *share* of available resources. From the school's point of view, however, the authority's response was seen as a departure from the original intention of the survey, that is to enable schools with severe problems to be recognised and helped. Although there is of course some doubt as to the nature of the relationship between variations in the level of remedial provision and variations in test scores, the LEA had implicitly encouraged schools to view this relationship as a direct one by linking resource allocation to test scores. In a contracting service it was no longer possible to fulfil the expectations which this policy had promoted in the schools.

MONITORING

This is the only area in which the LEA's objective was unambiguously achieved. County norms for 7 + and 10 + are established each year and these are reported to the Education Committee. The fact that county norms at both 7 + and 10 + have increased slightly each year since the survey began is cited as support for the LEA's claim that 'standards in the authority are rising'.

WITHIN-SCHOOL USES

The three case study teachers displayed a wide range of responses to, and uses of, the scores from the reading survey for children in their classes. Ms Harvey at Beaufort Junior was very sceptical of testing in general and felt no need for information about her pupils' reading beyond her own professional judgement; she viewed the test exclusively as a bureaucratic exercise required by the local authority. The test scores from the LEA survey were therefore of no use or interest to her in terms of her own classroom teaching.

Ms Tate at Greenacre Primary placed much more importance on testing in general, and on the scores from the county survey in particular, than did Ms Harvey. In several cases the assignment of certain children to reading groups and the identification of particular children for special help, both of which were done in advance of the beginning of the school year, were characterised as 'provisional', pending confirmation by scores from the November test. Unfortunately, however, scores for children in this class were not made available to the researcher on the grounds of confidentiality, and so it was impossible to document the extent to which the test results confirmed or challenged earlier decisions on grouping and identification. Although no changes were observed in the constitution of reading groups or of groups receiving special teaching, it was not possible to determine whether this maintenance of the status quo was supported by test scores. These constraints notwithstanding, the serious anticipation of test results as validators of class-room decision making, together with the unexpected decision to deny the researcher access to the results, illustrate the degree of significance given to these scores within the school and classroom at Greenacre.

The most complex response to the results of the reading survey was shown by Ms Braithwaite. Although distrustful in principle of the value and sensitivity of standardised testing, Ms Braithwaite nevertheless found her pupils' results on the reading test extremely worrying. Ten of her 14 first-year pupils scored below the national average, and the average standardised score in her class was 90 compared to a national average of 100. Despite the fact that Ms Braithwaite found 'no surprises' among the scores, the results were felt to be 'depressing' in that they 'confirmed the worst' and clarified that she had her 'work cut out' for her. Her misgivings about testing not-withstanding, Ms Braithwaite felt compelled to take action on the basis of the test results. This action consisted of a significant re-formation of reading groups and attendant decisions about suitable teaching strategies for certain children.

At the beginning of the school year the 14 first-year pupils in Ms Braithwaite's class were divided into two groups. One group of eight was composed of all first-year children who were withdrawn from the classroom for two lessons per week of small-group remedial teaching. The other group of six consisted of all other first-year children in the class: these children were considered to have achieved a degree of fluency and independence in their reading, but their membership in the second reading group was technically defined by their 'non-remedial' status. Grouping for the 14 first-year pupils, prior to the LEA survey, was as shown in Table 3. These 14 children then scored as shown in Table 4 on the county reading survey.

At the beginning of the spring term, that is, shortly after the LEA survey, Ms Braithwaite formed a new reading group composed of four children she considered 'borderline' readers, that is, children requiring special attention and teaching but not in need of specific remedial withdrawal. The necessity

Remedial reading group	Other reading group
Daniel	James
Mark	David
Grant	Nick
Gary	Claire
Zanda	Jessica
Wendy	Pieter
Nicola	
Luke	

Table 3 *Reading group assignments for first-year pupils, Ms Braithwaite, from September 1981*

Remedial reading group	Score	Other reading group	Score
Daniel	0	James	89
Mark	78	David	97
Grant	82	Nick	109
Gary	82	Claire	116
Zanda	84	Jessica	122
Wendy	89	Pieter	123
Nicola	92		
Luke	97		

Table 4 *Standardised scores on LEA reading survey for first-year pupils, Ms Braithwaite, November 1981*

for this new group was, according to Ms Braithwaite, demonstrated by the test results. The new alignment of reading groups from January is shown in Table 5 (children's test scores are also shown) [overleaf].

The purpose of the re-shuffle was characterised as two-fold: to enable the remedial teacher to concentrate her attention on the most 'critical' children by removing those whose special needs were 'demonstrably' less acute, and to provide concerted and suitable teaching for 'borderline' children within the classroom by grouping them together. Ms Braithwaite presented this reorganisation to the researcher as a test-based decision, that is, the test results had demonstrated its necessity. And yet the scores from the reading test did not *in and of themselves* appear to 'back up' the decision. Looking at the children in the new 'borderline' group (Table 5) we can see that:

Group	Score
Remedial reading group	
Daniel	0
Mark	78
Grant	82
Zanda	84
Wendy	89
'Borderline' reading group	
Gary	82
James	89
Nicola	92
Luke	97
Other reading group	
David	97
Nick	109
Claire	116
Jessica	122
Pieter	123

Table 5 *New reading group assignments for first-year pupils, Ms Braithwaite, from January 1982*

Gary was 'promoted' from the remedial withdrawal group to the new borderline group, but in fact scored level with Grant and below Wendy and Zanda, all of whom remained in the remedial group.

James was moved down from the 'independent' reading group to the new 'borderline' group but scored the same (89) as Wendy, a member of the remedial group. However, Ms Braithwaite did not 'promote' Wendy to the new group or recommend that James be withdrawn (with Wendy) for remedial teaching.

Luke was moved up from 'remedial' to 'borderline' on the basis of his standardised score of 97. This score was in fact identical to David's, a member of the 'independent' group. David's reading group status was never reconsidered however, and Ms Braithwaite did not consider the possibility of moving Luke directly from the remedial group to (David's) independent reading group.

Of the four children comprising the new 'borderline' group therefore, only one child, Nicola, appeared to have a test score which supported her new group status unambiguously. Test scores for the other three children in the group were not straightforward evidence for the changes made.

Similarly, the kinds of teaching strategies considered by Ms Braithwaite to be suitable for this newly-formed group did not follow directly from the test itself, despite Ms Braithwaite's assertion that it had been the test which had demonstrated these children's teaching requirements. These four 'borderline' children were placed on a programme of work which concentrated on the phonic analysis of words, for example the effect of the final 'e' on short vowels (rat, rate; bit, bite). It will be remembered however that the test used in the county reading survey was, according to the NFER, 'a simple test of reading comprehension' which 'tells little about the readers themselves'. A test intended as 'a means of screening with large numbers of pupils' was therefore cited as the source of diagnostic information about individual children's reading. Moreover, that information was related to children's deficiencies in specific phonic skills, despite the fact that the test was only claimed by the test constructors to measure general comprehension ability.

What sense can be made of these events? Ms Braithwaite's decisions about grouping and teaching for reading have the superficial structure of test based decisions. She claimed that the test results from the county reading survey had pointed to the need for forming a new reading group composed of four children, three of whom were removed from the remedial withdrawal group and one of whom was removed from a group of relatively independent readers. The test was furthermore seen to provide diagnostic information about the teaching requirements of individual children.

At this level, Ms Braithwaite's decisions can be viewed as a source of some disquiet for several reasons. First, the apparent reliance on the test to dictate changes in classroom organisation and in teaching strategies for individual children is incompatible with the purposes for which the test was designed. The test constructors themselves warn of the test's limited applicability, but this warning is not reinforced by the local authority in its curriculum guidelines and apparently not taken into account by the classroom teacher. Secondly, these events, at first sight, would appear to provide an example of a teacher modifying her specific teaching strategies, with respect to reading, in response to 'messages' about what constitutes suitable teaching transmitted by a standardised reading test. This latter possibility indicates the subtle influence which testing may exert on the way in which reading is taught in schools.

Looking more closely at these events however, we saw that the actual linkages between the test used in the county reading survey, and Ms Braithwaite's subsequent decisions about grouping and teaching, were tenuous. Comparing children's test scores with their eventual placement in groups revealed little direct relationship between the two. Clearly, Ms Braithwaite's own professional judgement of the children's reading, based on her everyday interaction with them in the classroom, was the guiding force behind her decision. Prior to the LEA surveys she had expressed to the researcher her concern over James' ability to cope with the demands of the 'independent' group as well as her suspicion that Nicola and Luke would probably be 'better off' out of the remedial group. The test did not 'alert' her to a problem she had not previously recognised, since there were 'no surprises'

among the scores and since she had been dissatisfied with grouping arrangements prior to the test. Nor did it indicate that certain children ought to be
moved to a new group, since the test scores – were they consulted in the way
described – raised questions about four other children whose reading group
status was not reconsidered. The only clear sense in which the test was related
to Ms Braithwaite's decision to regroup was that it provided – or imposed –
a symbolic impetus which galvanised a decision that had been contemplated
indistinctly for some time.

Similarly, the kinds of teaching strategies applied to the children comprising
the new 'borderline' reading group were, according to the class teacher,
suggested by the test, but they could not in fact be easily traced back to the
test content or format. Ms Braithwaite clearly had her own views as to what
constituted suitable teaching for this group of 'borderline' readers. Having
isolated four children for this purpose, these teaching strategies for reading
came naturally into operation. Here again, the test merely catalysed, in the
most general sense, a decision which in fact stemmed from the teacher's
notions about reading and about these particular children, rather than from
anything actually suggested by the test. Instead of the testing *modifying*
teaching, testing in this case was used to *reinforce* the teacher's own notions
about the teaching and learning of reading, which in fact bore no relation to
the notions which could be gleaned from the test.

Therefore, far from the test-based chain of decisions which these events
superficially appeared to be, Ms Braithwaite's decisions and actions can be
seen to have been an example of a teacher exercising her own professional
judgement about the grouping and teaching needs of a small group of children.
The only glaring anomaly in the process is that the test was cited as the
rationale and source of information guiding decisions and actions which in
fact had no clear or direct relationship with the test or the test results. These
decisions and actions could have been taken without recourse to the test, but
the test served to galvanise and legitimise the decisions and actions in a way
which day-to-day judgement might not have done. Test scores were seen as
objective evidence, and yet that objectivity was contingent on the meaning
provided by Ms Braithwaite's background knowledge about the children and
her own notions about the teaching and learning of reading. The episode
confirms the analyses of Leiter (1976) and McKay (1978) who concluded
that teachers' interpretation of test scores is in fact an elaborate process of
contextualising information from tests within the social reality of the classroom. Leiter writes that: 'Numbers have an equivocal sense when they are
simply presented to somebody. It is only when they are provided with a scenic
source that they begin to take on meaning' (p. 64). For Ms Braithwaite, this
'scenic source' or operational context was her pre-existing dissatisfaction with
grouping and teaching arrangements for four readers in the class. The test
scores did not 'mean' that these four children ought to be grouped together
and taught in a particular way; Ms Braithwaite *rendered* the scores meaningful
by virtue of her 'scenic source'.

Viewing teachers' analyses of test scores as a process of interpretation, sense-making and contextualisation goes some way toward explaining the way in which results from the county reading survey were 'used' by Ms Braithwaite to support her decisions and actions. What it does not explain is *why* a test should be used to support a decision which would have had more internal 'logic' had the test not been invoked. Here one can only speculate, but the prestige and scientific respectability enjoyed by standardised testing provide a likely explanation. No matter how inappropriate or inapplicable testing may be to classroom decision-making and teaching, and no matter how sceptical teachers and test constructors are about the suitability and applicability of testing, there is still a feeling among some that tests should be used and their results seen to be taken into account. This example from the classroom demonstrates the almost irresistible power of testing, and the way in which that power can in some instances undermine teachers' confidence in the legitimacy of their own judgements.

SUMMARY AND CONCLUSIONS

Despite some indications that heavy use of reading tests might be found in the three case study classrooms, the test administered in the Autumn Term to all pupils of 7 + in the county for the annual reading survey was the only testing carried out during the six-month observation period.

Distinct variations were observed in procedures for administration and marking of the standardised reading test used in the LEA survey, revealing that teachers' background knowledge about, and interaction with, individual children contributed significantly to the quality of the test event. This raises questions about the way individual standardised scores are 'achieved' and then related by teachers and others to the population on which the test was originally standardised. The stress experienced by some children raises further questions about the suitability of testing conditions for young children.

If we consider the four purposes which the local authority gave for its annual reading survey at 7 +, the following points emerge. The *screening* element was found to be largely superfluous to school-based procedures for identifying children in need of special help with reading in the three classrooms. Cutbacks in the remedial service prevented the authority from responding to the results of the county reading survey by *allocating increasing resources* to school with worsening reading scores. The resource constraints did not, however, modify schools' belief in the direct relationship between quantity of remedial provision and variations in test performance – a belief promoted by the authority.

Individual teachers' attitudes towards the LEA reading survey, and responses to the results, differed widely. One teacher viewed the survey solely as a bureaucratic exercise and made no use of the results for her own classroom decision-making and teaching. The other two teachers in the study were observed to place much more importance on the test results. The reading test used in the county reading survey had been devised as a large-scale screening instrument but, in the absence of a clear lead from the LEA to the contrary, test scores from the reading survey were observed to be put to a wide range of *within school uses*. Where these could be observed in detail however, it appeared that the test merely provided a symbolic licence for changes in grouping and teaching rather than direct support for such changes. It would appear therefore that testing can sometimes exert an almost irresistible power which makes it virtually impossible to avoid taking test scores into account, however inappropriate or symbolic their use may be. The only exception to this pattern within this study was in the case of a teacher whose resistance to the influence of testing was based on a well-developed objection to testing and to outside interference with the autonomy of teachers.

County norms from the reading survey were reported to the county council each year as part of a *monitoring* exercise. Of the four purposes for which the LEA's testing programme was adopted this was the only element which was achieved without complications, or without competing procedures conducted in the schools. It would seem therefore that the county reading survey was in principle a multi-purpose programme but was in practice exclusively a system for producing a single statistic each year for the county council.

REFERENCES

Leiter, K. W. (1976) Teachers' use of background knowledge to interpret test scores, *Sociology of Education*, 49, 59–65.

Mackay, R. (1978) How teachers know: a case of epistemological conflict, *Sociology of Education*, 51, pp. 177–87.

|3.3| READING TESTS

BARRY STIERER

The debate over the use of reading tests is one in which reading tests begin with a substantial advantage. First, they promise an objective and consistent form of assessment which eliminates the variability and subjectivity of teachers' judgement. It's often said that no two teachers make the same judgement about the same child, and that each teacher's judgement is partly determined by preconceptions about the likely abilities of their pupils, and in this sense the tests offer a 'scientific' solution. Secondly, the prominence of reading tests in national and local programmes for monitoring school 'standards' lends the tests a political respectability which reinforces their scientific prestige. Here I refer not only to the Assessment of Performance Unit at the DES which tests the reading of 10 per cent of the country's children every year in an apparent attempt to measure changes in reading standards over time, but also to the practice in at least three-quarters of local education authorities of carrying out an annual LEA reading survey, often involving every primary-age child in the authority every year. Third, reading tests are often used in educational research as 'outcome measures' in studies of teacher effectiveness, thus bestowing an academic status on the tests. Fourth, at the school level, many teachers, parents and pupils use reading test scores as self-evident indices of pupils' achievement and schools' effectiveness. Finally, the tests' considerable technical infrastructure goes a long way towards pre-empting critical debate. There are few other areas of the educational scene where one can observe the same degree of deference to an 'expert' elite by the majority of 'unknowledgeable' laypersons (usually teachers). Debate is often confined to technical issues which leave deeper questions about the tests' underlying assumptions and their functions within the educational system unasked. So, the critics and the sceptics enter the debate with the cards already heavily stacked against them.

Principles underlying the tests

Critics of reading tests generally rally round one or more of the following three battle cries:

1 *Most reading tests are out of date.* The tests which most teachers have access to, or are required to administer, are generally at least 10 years old and often much older. Norms become outdated and misleading, vocabulary and language structures become stilted and off-putting. Models of reading and reading acquisition change over time, rendering the models built into the tests obsolete.
2 *Most reading tests provide little or no diagnostic information.* The tests which most teachers have access to, or are required to administer, provide little more than a single figure for 'reading'. This figure *may* indicate how well a group performs relative to a larger sample, or relative to each other, or how well an individual performs relative to a past performance on the same test. However it does not enable a greater understanding of an individual as a reader: his or her strengths and weaknesses, strategies and responses, attitudes and habits.
3 *Reading tests do not measure 'real reading'.* Critics point out that the reading demands of standardised reading tests are considerably different from the reading demands which children encounter in and out of school, and therefore produce a distorted picture of their reading ability. 'Real' reading, the critics argue, is a complex thinking process which will vary in its effectiveness from context to context according to the reader's need to read, the content and structure of the text, and the reader's background knowledge and interests. A child's successful performance on a reading test does not depend on these vital aspects of the reading skill, any more than a child's poor performance indicates a weakness as a reader in the fullest sense.

The psychometric 'industry' has a number of defences against these kinds of criticisms. In response to the charge that the tests are out of date, it is possible to answer that the 'industry' cannot accept responsibility for the use of outdated tests. Newer tests are available, based on more up-to-date standardisations and reading models, and the industry promotes the use of these tests over older ones.

A similar defence can be offered in response to the complaint that the tests provide little or no diagnostic information. Tests produced in recent years do generate profiles which enable a greater understanding of an individual reader. In fact it has been argued by some that the sophistication of diagnostic information generated by some reading tests now exceeds that of many teachers' own understanding of the reading process. It can also be said that there is *some* diagnostic information available from even the most rudimentary reading test if one is sensitive to it. Again, the testing industry cannot be held responsible if their new, more diagnostic instruments are not widely used, or if test users do not make use of the diagnostic information provided by whatever tests they use.

I think that these two counter-arguments are only valid up to a point, which I shall discuss presently, but they do serve to undermine considerably the first two of the critics' criticisms.

The psychometric response to the third charge, that the tests do not measure 'real' reading, is a much more elaborate one. This response centres on the assumption that what appears on the surface to be a narrow and artificial reading experience may merely 'stand for' the more complex process. A reading test is, after all, no more than a brief sampling of a small fraction of a child's reading. No test constructor would claim that what a child actually does when she or he takes a reading test is the same thing as other kinds of reading, or a complete range of reading tasks likely to be met. That kind of sampling would require months of careful observation, and one of the main attractions of reading tests is that they offer to carry out the longer operation in an abbreviated fashion. In theory, then, a test constructor has demonstrated a test's validity if it can be shown that children with high scores on the test are *rarely* poor readers, and that children with low scores are *often* poor readers. Taken to its ridiculous extreme, a task such as distinguishing between high-pitched and low-pitched whistles would be considered to be a valid reading test if it could be shown that good readers were especially good at it and poor readers were particularly unadroit. It is a tremendously appealing idea: no need to take the time, expense and risk of organisational upheaval to observe children carrying out 'real reading' tasks if their performance on a quick test correlates highly with the more elaborate exercise.

This notion, that the limited and stylised demands of reading tests 'stand for' reading in a broader sense, is the most difficult psychometric defence to refute, since it requires an understanding of the obscure canons of reading test validity theory. Some aspects of psychometric theory are, as yet, almost impossible to refute, since we do not have the empirical evidence necessary to do this. For example, what would happen if test constructors could demonstrate, to our satisfaction rather than to theirs, that word recognition ability correlated extremely highly with an acceptable construct of 'real reading' competence? That is, what would happen if 'good readers', identified by our own criteria, were only very rarely found to be unable to score well on word recognition tests, and if 'poor readers', identified by those same criteria, were very often found to be unable to score well on the tests? Would we then be obliged to accept the tests as reasonably accurate discriminators between good and poor readers? Of course, such a demonstration would still beg a number of crucial questions. For instance our need for rich diagnostic information about individual readers would remain unfulfilled. The fact remains however that certain principles of test validity cannot be discredited, in the absence of relevant evidence.

However, the fundamental weakness of one central aspect of validity theory must be exposed, and this relates to *assessment reference points*. Two courses are open to the test constructor when attempting to establish that children's scores on a new reading test reflect their 'real' reading competence. First, the scores achieved on the test by a large number of children would – according to the rules of psychometrics – have to be shown to correlate very highly with their scores on some *other* test of reading which was widely considered to be a measure of that aspect of reading which the new test aimed to measure. I find the circularity of this procedure absurd, and I am alarmed at the distinct possibility that the validation of reading tests simply serves to perpetuate a descending spiral of mutually-reinforcing assessments. This is still the dominant method for demonstrating tests' validity: often test manuals simply report that the correlation between results obtained on the new test and results on some other popular test was such and such, without providing any reason why we should believe that the earlier test was valid. Kenneth Goodman has called this the 'sky-hook method' which ensures that new tests are anchored to old models of reading: 'If the new test in in fact measuring what the old test did, then why is a new test needed? And if the new test employs new insights, why expect it to correlate with the old?'

Secondly, human judgement is, at least in theory, the ultimate reference point in the validation of reading tests. Even if test constructors do not attempt to validate a new test with reference to assessments by professional teachers of reading, there is in principle some point at the beginning of the spiral where human judgement was consulted. In practice very few test constructors carry out an exercise of cross-referencing with teachers' assessments as part of their validation procedures, because this dimension of validity is so problematic. On the one hand, many psychometricians object to the practice of consulting teachers, since it is the subjectivity and inconsistency of teacher judgement which the tests aim to transcend. After all, test constructors would have a much more difficult time justifying their existence if tests merely reproduced teachers' assessments! On the other hand, even in cases where teacher judgement is treated as a legitimate standard of reference, the test constructor invariably defines the terms which will frame those judgements. Asking teachers to place children in rank order according to the teacher's estimate of their reading ages is a very different kind of question from asking teachers to convey their assessment of individual children as readers. In the first kind of consultation, test constructors are asking teachers to fit a form of evaluation which had already been prescribed, that is the reading age. In the second kind of consultation, test constructors would be asking teachers to nominate a form of assessment which was compatible with their judgements as well as the specific content of assessments for particular children. Reports of validation procedures in test manuals never specify the extent to which teachers found the *form* of assessment employed in the test appropriate or consonant with their own judgement; they only report the extent to which the *content* of the assessments agreed.

So, close scrutiny reveals the inherent weaknesses in the 'assessment reference points' aspect of reading test validity theory, based as it is on the assumption that test scores can be anchored to circular, extraneous and contrived assessments.

TESTING IN CONTEXT

Important though it is to scrutinise the principles underlying the construction of reading tests, it is equally important, I think, to examine the ways in which reading tests are *used*. It is exceedingly difficult to prove empirically that reading tests exert a widespread and nefarious effect on the teaching and learning of reading in schools. There are so many influences impinging on teachers that it would probably be impossible to isolate the tests and to evaluate the damage (if any) for which they alone are responsible.

However, it is possible to indict the tests in one important respect relating to their use in the education system. Apologists for the tests often argue that *reading tests are neutral with respect to their use*. The tests cannot *in themselves* be misleading or damaging. They are only misleading or damaging when they are *used incorrectly*. For competent and well-informed users, fully aware of the tests' limitations, reading tests are an important part of the assessment process. Many advocates of reading tests bemoan the allegedly widespread 'misuse' of the tests, and adopt the posture of the teachers' champion by exhorting the profession to 'improve its ability to use tests effectively' (Pumfrey, 1977) rather than by discouraging the use of tests altogether.

I should like to scrutinise this principle, since I think it is here that some of the contradictions and underlying values inherent in the tests can be found. There are certainly countless documented instances where reading tests have been used in ways which the tests' advocates might regard as 'incorrect'. During our work for the Evaluation of Testing in Schools Project, for example, we found through interviews and case studies of teachers' attitudes and practices that examples of 'incorrect' uses of reading tests abound.

We found teachers exercising considerable selectivity in the test scores they 'took seriously' and those they ignored. We found some teachers using test scores as the basis for critical decisions of organisation, such as the setting of classroom reading groups and the identification of children for special remedial teaching, even when the tests used were explicitly not designed to enable that kind of small-scale decision-making. We found some teachers administering and marking reading tests in unorthodox ways. And we found some teachers 'reading into' some single-figure test scores elaborate diagnoses of individual pupils' teaching needs, such as the need for more training in phonic decoding skills, the need for more group reading work, the need to play more 'reading games', and the need to progress through the reading scheme by means of oral reading to a teacher rather than by means of independent silent reading.

Can we dismiss these examples as failures to appreciate the expressed limitations of reading test technology, or do they begin to cast a shadow over the technology itself? I should like to suggest as a suitable topic for further discussion, investigation and thought, the proposition that it is impossible ultimately to separate the principles underlying the construction and advocacy of the tests from these and other instances of reading test 'misuse'.

SOCIAL CONTEXT OF READING TEST 'MISUSE'

To support this proposition, I would point out first that the social context of each instance of 'misuse' must be taken fully into account. In schools, heads and classroom teachers are continually taking important decisions which require a wide range of information about the reading competence of pupils. Heads in our survey reported their need for some form of 'external calibration' by which to judge their own school's achievements in relation to other schools. They often require an impersonal focus when discussing pupils with teachers and parents. And increasingly they need persuasive evidence when 'making a case' for additional resources for the school. Classroom teachers also work under terrific pressure which appears to intensify every year. A list of their needs for information about pupils' reading competence might include the following:

1 They need to identify children in need of special teaching at a time when need may be found to exceed provision.
2 They need to match individual children to suitable tests and tasks even though time for sensitive observation is at a premium.
3 They need to meet the 'particular needs' of bilingual children and the special educational needs of children with disabilities when all that may be available is traditional 'remedial' teaching.
4 They need general feedback on teaching and learning.
5 They need frequent catalysts for action.
6 They will soon need to satisfy new teacher appraisal criteria.
7 They need evidence to support controversial practices or special requests.
8 They need to meet high professional standards with diminishing resources available for replacing outdated materials or for in-service education and training.

I have tried here to outline some aspects of the social context in which reading tests are used. I suggest two things at this point in relation to this social context. First, I suggest that the promotion of reading tests as suitable measures of reading competence, however cautious, cannot be abstracted from the real world in which that advice might be taken. A technology which is, on the one hand, limited in what it can measure but which, on the other hand, holds out the promise of valid, comprehensive and context-independent information about a reader's competence, *invites* the kinds of 'misuses' I described earlier in the far from idealised settings where tests are used. Similarly, tests which, by definition, soon go out of date and need replacing cannot easily be abstracted from the impoverished educational world in which they are used.

Secondly, and conversely, I suggest that the constructors and advocates of reading tests are partly responsible for (inadvertently) *creating* some of the contradictory and over-simplified needs for information which give rise to 'misuse' of tests. Reading tests are the product of a technology which, for example, claims the power to enable comparisons of reading 'standards' over time and across varied populations, and which appears capable of measuring narrow skills in a brief and artificial context and then generalising, on the basis of that performance, about a wider competence in a wider range of contexts. This has contributed significantly to an atmosphere in which needs for information increasingly outstrip the current limitations of the technology itself, and in which the respectability and scientific prestige of the tests are axiomatic. In this sense reading tests may function to create the need for further testing of reading.

Would our resources and energies not be more productively deployed by developing and promoting assessment techniques for reading which meet the real educational needs of real teachers and children in real classrooms, rather than by promoting a technology which appears to satisfy needs which are in part artifacts of itself?

INTERPRETATION AND 'SCIENCE'

Following on from this observation about the inseparability of reading tests from the social context of their use (or 'misuse'), it is vital to consider as well the nature of *interpretation* as it relates to scores derived from reading tests. Many of the examples of 'misuse' cited above centre on the interpretation (or 'misinterpretation') of test results by teachers. In my own study of classroom reading assessment, for example (Stierer, 1983), I found that the same score on the same test can carry very different meanings, about readers' competence and needs, for the same teacher. And similar scores on the same test suggested different teaching strategies for different teachers, depending on their own views about reading and about teaching and learning generally.

In a fascinating study, Kenneth Leiter examined teachers' use of background knowledge to interpret test scores. He points out that one of the reasons for the use of standardised tests is to eliminate the teachers' use of subjective knowledge when assessing their pupils. And yet Leiter found that, in order to render test scores meaningful, teachers invariably embedded the scores in just the kinds of knowledge the scores are supposed to replace. The professional judgement needed by teachers to 'make sense' of their pupils' test scores consisted of 'using background knowledge to form a context for interpreting the scores' (1976, p. 64). That background knowledge comprised details about, for example, pupils' home backgrounds, pupils' classroom behaviour, and views about curriculum, pedagogy and learning. Teachers' experience of administering and marking the test, and their understanding of the particular test, were also invoked when accounting for the meanings given to test scores.

Teachers' relationships with their pupils also helped to shape the precise meanings they ascribed to their pupils' scores. Teachers' use of that background knowledge was found moreover to be both heterogeneous (i.e. different kinds of knowledge were used in the interpretation of different pupils' scores) and situation specific (i.e. the same kinds of knowledge were sometimes used to derive different kinds of meanings from different pupils' scores).

Leiter's conclusions were far from judgemental in respect of teachers. Rather than upbraid teachers for their subjective approach, and entreat them to be more 'scientific', Leiter suggests that the use of subjective knowledge is the only possible way in which sense can be made of 'objective' test scores. Indeed he asserts that it is this subjectivity that gives the test scores their objective and factual status (1976, pp. 64–5):

> Numbers have an equivocal sense when they are simply presented to somebody. It is only when they are provided with a scenic source that they begin to take on meaning. The use of background knowledge not only provides the numbers with their specific sense, it is in and through the use of background knowledge that their 'objective' character is accomplished ... Because the test scores are potentially equivocal, background knowledge is used to resolve that equivocality and thereby provide the scores with their factual properties. While sociologists and educators imply that the use of background knowledge undermines the objectivity of the test, I have shown that it is through the use of background knowledge that the objectivity of the test is *secured* by rendering an otherwise truncated account of the student's capacities into a rich and immediate context of tacitly and explicitly known matters.

Leiter's analysis should be considered seriously by anyone promoting the use of reading tests as 'objective' measures of pupils' reading competence. Test scores, in and of themselves, are not meaningful. They must be *rendered* meaningful using knowledge and information derived from sources outside the test itself. In agreeing with Leiter's argument I am not suggesting that the use of background knowledge to interpret test scores is simply a weakness of human nature which can be guarded against. I am suggesting that the recourse to an elaborate social, professional and subjective context is intrinsic to *every* act of making sense of numerical information, however 'scientific' the particular circumstances may be. There is therefore a real sense in which the promotion of numbers as indices of readers' competence actually invites and authorises subjectivity in a way which less quantifiable assessment measures may go some way towards preventing. By recommending assessment techniques which require their users to go outside the techniques themselves for the information which makes them intelligible, the advocates of reading tests may inadvertently be encouraging judgements and evaluation which draw upon information which is far from reading-specific, and in so doing perform a disservice to teachers and pupils alike.

This relates back to my earlier point about the pressures under which teachers work. The current atmosphere is one in which many teachers are required to administer reading tests, or feel that reading tests should be used, and one in which teachers feel that scores should be taken into account. As I have said, the psychometric industry must take some responsibility for this atmosphere. In such an atmosphere, test users will inevitably feel that there is meaning to be derived from test scores, and will be encouraged implicitly to engage in the kind of subjectivity which is intrinsic to the interpretation of numbers.

It seems that, on the basis of this analysis, educationalists are faced with an important choice. We can make it absolutely clear, whenever we promote reading tests, that the interpretation of test scores is an inherently subjective process. But is it not possible that the scarce resources currently available to the education service would be better deployed in the development and dissemination of processes for reading assessment which are perhaps more *explicitly interpretive* but less 'equivocal' (to use Leiter's term)? Building upon teachers' existing expertise and knowledge, rather than intensifying pressures to adopt a spurious scientism, may be a more appropriate and effective approach to improving the quality of literacy teaching.

REFERENCES

Gipps, Caroline, Steadman, Stephen, Blackstone, Tessa, and Stierer, Barry (1983) *Testing Children: Standardised Testing in Local Education Authorities and Schools.* London: Heinemann Educational Books.

Goodman, K. S. (1973) 'Testing in reading: a general critique', in R. B. Ruddell (ed.) *Accountability and reading instruction: critical issues.* Illinois: National Council of Teachers of English.

Leiter, K. W. (1976) 'Teachers' use of background knowledge to interpret test scores', *Sociology of Education*, 49, 59–65.

Pumfrey, Peter (1977) 'Reading Measurement and Evaluation: Some Current Concerns and Promising Developments', in J. Gilliland (ed.) *Reading: Research and Classroom Practice.* London: Ward Lock Educational.

Stierer, Barry (1983) 'Reading Tests in the Classroom: a Case Study'. Paper presented to the Symposium on Testing and Assessment at the Annual Conference of the British Educational Research Association, London.

Testing Teachers? A Critical Look at the Schools Council Project 'Extending Beginning Reading'

3.4

Barry Stierer

The *Schonell Graded Word Reading Test* is by far the most widely used test of reading in primary schools today. The Bullock Committee reported in 1975 that the *Schonell* was administered in 73 per cent of primary schools – its nearest rival being the *Burt Rearranged Word Reading Test*, used in 34 per cent of schools. There is no reason to suspect that the popularity of the *Schonell* has faded dramatically since the Bullock survey; certainly nothing which has emerged so far from our national survey of teachers' testing practices suggest a drop in *Schonell's* use.[1]

Ask teachers what they think of the *Schonell GWRT* however, and this clear picture of the test's unrivalled prominence becomes complicated by an array of criticisms and caveats. The *Schonell* arouses ardent denunciation from its opponents and a considerable degree of embarrassment from many of its users, and yet it still remains the most often administered test of reading in schools. Familiar though this contradictory state of affairs may be, it is nevertheless a phenomenon which needs exploring. As a beginning in this direction, I would like first of all to discuss what scores from the *Schonell* mean, and then go on to look closely at the way the test was used in a recently reported national research project.

THE DEBATE

Let us start by reviewing the state of play in the vexed debate over the use of the *Schonell*. On one side of the debate are The Critics, whose arguments usually take the form of three main battle cries:

1 *The test is out of date.* Fred Schonell published his *Graded Word Reading Test* in 1945. The words in the list were therefore selected over 35 years ago and it is inevitable that some of them have now fallen into comparative disuse.

2 *The test does not measure 'real reading'.* Critics point out that the reading demands of the *Schonell* are considerably different from the demands of 'real reading', and therefore produce a distorted picture of children's reading ability. In order to succeed at the task of reading the list a child must be able to pronounce single words in isolation from a meaningful context, and critics say that a child's ability – or inability – to perform successfully at this task may be explainable by any of a number of factors which have little to do with the child's actual competence as a reader.

3 *The test has little diagnostic value.* It is further argued that a 'reading age', calculated on the basis of a child's performance on the *Schonell* list, tells teachers little except how well their children perform relative to children in a national sample, or relative to each other. The score tells the teacher even less about an individual child except perhaps how well the child has performed relative to a past performance on the same test. It certainly does not provide the teacher with a picture of a particular child as a reader: strengths and weaknesses, attitudes and habits, strategies and responses. The test, critics argue, does not supply teachers with answers to the guiding question in assessment, namely 'Where do I go from here?'.

A look at the arguments put forward in defence of the *Schonell* by its advocates, apologists and users provides a clue to its tenacity in the face of prevalent criticism. The Defence generally assembles in two camps – The Pragmatists and the Psychometrists.

Pragmatists justify the continued use of the *Schonell GWRT* on grounds of expedience: the test is cheap, quick, familiar, easy to administer, and provides a rough guide to children's reading. It is important to accept that for a lot of teachers the *Schonell* fits in well with their classroom practice and organisation, and that it would be difficult to stop using the test without some disruption.

Psychometrists are not especially interested in whether a reading test like the *Schonell* requires a child to carry out 'real reading' tasks. What counts for the psychometrists is that the results of the test should correlate highly with some notion of actual reading. So long as they can be shown that children with high scores on the *Schonell* are rarely poor readers, and that children with low scores are often poor readers, psychometrists can recommend the test with confidence.

This second line of argument is the crucial one, since it underpins much of test construction theory and in fact provides the basis for the pragmatists' rationale. After all, it is a tremendously appealing idea: no need to take the time, expense and the risk of organisational upheaval to observe children carrying out 'real reading' tasks if their performance on a quick list of words correlates highly with the more elaborate exercise. But does it?

THE SCHONELL TEST AND 'REAL READING'

Let us have another look at the cornerstone of the psychometrists' creed: *poor readers rarely do well on the Schonell, and good readers rarely fail*. What is the notion of 'actual reading' with which *Schonell* scores supposedly correlate so highly? And how do psychometrists go about establishing this validity?

In order to establish the validity of *Schonell* as a measure of children's competence as 'real readers' one would have to carry out a careful study of many thousands of children to observe how closely their scores on *Schonell* correspond to one or both of the following criteria:

1 Their scores would have to be shown to correlate very highly with their scores on some other test of reading which most teachers would agree measured 'real reading'; or
2 Their scores would have to be shown to correspond to their teachers' own assessments of them as readers.

As far as I am aware, and I should be grateful to anyone who can provide me with evidence to the contrary, no one has ever demonstrated the *Schonell's* validity as an index of 'real reading' for emerging readers; but then Fred Schonell never intended his *Graded Word Reading Test* to be used as a measure of 'real reading'. He cautions (p. 211) that 'studies of the test's use show that this type of test can be a reasonably accurate way of estimating the level reached by a pupil in the *mechanics of reading*' (his italics). He published a further six tests, in fact to provide practitioners with measures of more complex reading.

So, in the absence of any conclusive evidence to the contrary, all of us (psychometrists included) must abide by Schonell's original specification that the test is only valid as an indicator of children's dexterity in the mechanics of reading. In other words, we must endeavour not to confuse *Schonell* scores with 'real reading' competence.

But it is so easy to confuse *Schonell* scores with real reading competence! Can any of us really look at a class list, with *Schonell*-related reading ages tagged to each child's name, and with the best will in the world not begin to make the leap from the mechanics of reading to what we understand to be real reading? If you, like me, find this difficult not to do, take some comfort from the fact that we are not alone. A no less prestigious and informed group than the research team at the University of Manchester, who carried out the

Schools Council Project '*Extending Beginning Reading*', made use of the *Schonell Graded Word Reading Test* in a way which clearly illustrates exactly how easy – and dangerous – it is to confuse *Schonell* scores with 'real reading'.

SCHONELL SCORES v. TEACHERS' ASSESSMENTS

The project team in Manchester first of all asked 291 first and second-year junior teachers to estimate the reading ages of the children in their classes. The teachers were asked to take into account their knowledge of each child's work for the previous six months, but they were furthermore asked to base their estimates on any previous test results where these were available. The teachers were then asked to test their pupils, using the *Schonell GWRT*, and to send both sets of results to the project team for analysis.

What did the researchers do with these two sets of information? Basically, they used the test scores to judge teachers' accuracy as estimators of children's reading ability. In order to do this, the team labelled *Schonell* test scores for selected groups of children 'Children's Reading Ability'. They then took the teachers' assessments for the same groups of children and called these 'Teachers' Estimates'. From there it was only a simple matter of interpreting the pattern of teachers' 'estimates'. And with the cards lined up like this it will come as no surprise that teachers come off looking pretty erratic.

Before looking specifically at some of the conclusions drawn by the project team, let us not overlook the assumptions about teachers, tests and reading which guided the researchers in this exercise. Scores from the *Schonell* are taken by the team to be synonymous, in an absolute sense, with 'reading ability'. Throughout the chapter in the project's final report dealing with this exercise, terms such as 'reading proficiency', 'actual reading age', 'reading performance' and 'reading ability' are used interchangeably with 'test scores' and 'test results', while teachers' assessments are treated as precarious approximations of the true value. By setting the test up as the final arbiter, teachers are put on trial and, in many cases, found deficient. But which set of results really does represent children's reading ability? The teachers' assessments or the test scores? As I mentioned earlier, teachers' own assessments are sometimes used to establish the validity of reading tests by observing the degree of correspondence between test scores and teachers' judgements. In this exercise, however, variations between teachers and tests are explained exclusively in terms of teachers' inaccuracy. Now, I'm certainly not suggesting that we take teachers' assessments as unimpeachable and conclusive evidence of the test's limitations, but it seems to me that the Extending Beginning Reading team had an obligation to call the test into serious question at the same time as they raised questions about teachers' accuracy as estimators of children's reading.

For the sake of argument, and to illustrate the one-sided assumptions informing the researchers' analysis, I have taken a selection of the conclusions the project drew from the data in this exercise, and re-written them below. I have tried to preserve the language of the project's report, but rather than equating *Schonell* scores with 'reading ability' and putting teachers' assessments on trial as the EBR team have done, I have taken teachers' assessments to be the true value of 'reading ability', thereby reversing the emphasis and putting the *test* on trial. The original texts are on the left; my re-written versions are on the right.

Original	Re-written version
Teachers in the first Teachers' Reading Research Group were very willing to co-operate in forecasting their pupils' performances on Schonell's *Graded Word Reading Test*, and to forward these estimates, alongside the actual test results, to the project director. Lists were obtained from 291 classes, referring to 3381 first and second-year junior pupils.	*Teachers in the first Teachers' Reading Research Group were very willing to co-operate in appraising Schonell's Graded Word Reading Test as an estimation of their pupils' reading, and to forward scores derived from this test, alongside their own actual assessments, to the project director. Lists were obtained from 291 classes, referring to 3381 first and second-year junior pupils.*
The general pattern of teachers' estimations was as follows: (a) Almost half of all teachers were classified as 'inconsistent' estimators, as they over-estimated the reading proficiency of about half their pupils, and under-estimated the remaining half. (b) Similar proportions of teachers were categorised as inconsistent in the two age groups (just under 50 per cent in each case). Of the remaining teachers, more of those in the first year tended to be under-estimators than those in the second year.	*The general pattern of the test results was as follows:* *(a) For almost half of the classes tested, the test was classified as 'inconsistent' as it under-estimated the reading proficiency of about half the pupils, and over-estimated the remaining half.* *(b) The test was categorised as inconsistent in similar proportions of classes in the two age groups (just under 50 per cent in each case). Of the remaining classes, more test scores for first-year pupils tended to be over-estimations than those for second-year pupils.*
The teachers who were least successful in estimating their pupils' reading performances showed errors ranging from an over-estimate of three years six months to an under-estimate of three years.	*Instances in which the test was least successful in estimating pupils' reading showed errors ranging from an under-estimate of three years six months to an over-estimate of three years.*
The fact that a minority of teachers were quite seriously in error when estimating their pupils' performances on a well-known reading test, must surely cause all teachers to re-examine their own procedures for monitoring children's reading progress.	*The fact that a minority of scores on a well-known reading test were quite seriously in error when measuring pupils' reading must surely cause all teachers to re-examine their own procedures for monitoring children's reading progress.*

Not surprisingly, there were certain indications that teachers who had based their estimates on previous reading test results were somewhat better at estimating their pupils' reading proficiency than teachers without such results available.

Not surprisingly, there were certain indications that the test was somewhat better at estimating the reading proficiency of those pupils whose teachers had available previous test scores than it was at estimating assessments made by teachers who had relied entirely on their own judgement.

The teachers in this study who had access to previous reading test results had been asked to base their estimates of children's current reading performance on their knowledge of their earliest results – and they proved more accurate estimators than teachers who lacked earlier test results. This finding might well cause those teachers who tend to regard testing as a waste of time to reconsider the prognostic value of prior test results. Alternatively, teachers who had available earlier test results resting unnoticed in drawers or record books might well consider the value of referring more frequently to such records. (Southgate *et al.* 1981)

The teachers in this study who had access to previous test results had been asked to base their assessments of children's current reading on their knowledge of the earlier results – and the test proved less inaccurate at estimating these teachers' assessments than at estimating assessments made by teachers who relied entirely on their own judgement. This finding may well cause those teachers who tend to base their judgements of children's reading on the scores from graded word reading tests to reconsider the prognostic value of such scores. Alternatively, teachers who have available earlier test results resting unnoticed in drawers or record books might well consider the distortion of their judgement which may come about by referring more frequently to such records.

I present these two versions, not because I think mine is necessarily more logical than the original, but because I think that together they highlight many of the serious consequences inherent in equating *Schonell* scores with real reading competence. Consider for a start the many crucial factors which are not considered by EBR in this study. We don't know, for example, whether teachers classified by the team as 'under-estimators' worked in parts of the country where most children achieve fluency in reading relatively early and easily, in which case their conception of 'average reader' – even on the level of mechanical reading – is bound to correspond to another teacher's idea of 'above average reader.' The team does not provide us with persuasive reasons for expecting teachers to base their judgements of individual children on national averages, when their local experiences and expectations are usually more helpful. And after all we are given no evidence that teachers termed 'inconsistent' by the researchers were necessarily less sensitive to the needs of individual readers than any other group of teachers.

CIRCULARITY

But it is the unpardonable circularity of the researchers' conclusions on appropriate uses of tests which should cause us the greatest alarm. We are told that teachers predict children's test performances better when they take previous test scores into account; therefore teachers should test *more*, so that they may be more accurate at estimating future test scores. What comes across as the model of reading assessment advocated by the EBR project is one in which teachers should endeavour to approximate as closely as possible a score on the *Schonell Graded Word Reading Test*. Is this what we are aiming at? In view of the fact discussed earlier, that the *Schonell* is a severely limited instrument based on notions of mechanical reading, the EBR team did teachers a tremendous disservice by suggesting that they should sharpen their evaluation expertise by improving their ability to predict *Schonell* scores.

It's no coincidence that the *Schonell* was used to support the kinds of statements about teachers and testing made in the EBR report. The test was selected over other tests 'on the grounds that all teachers had access to it' (p. 91). And so we come full circle. I began by raising questions about the *Schonell's* widespread use in schools, but that is only the beginning of the cycle:

1 Despite strong opposition *Schonell* is used in most primary schools, mainly for pragmatic reasons;
2 Because of its wide availability, the test is used by a research project which equates *Schonell* scores with 'reading ability' and compares them with teachers' assessments;
3 Teachers are found to be frequently erratic at predicting *Schonell* scores unless they have other scores to hand;
4 Teachers are therefore advised to use the *Schonell* more often because of its regulating influence on their judgement;
5 And this advice is easily implemented, since the *Schonell* is already widely available to teachers.

This to me is the real danger of the *Schonell* and tests like it. It is not so much that it is out of date, nor that it only measures the mechanics of reading, nor that it has little diagnostic value. The real danger is that the test's very quickness, cheapness and familiarity lure us into the trap of accepting its results as measures of 'real reading', making it easy to draw conclusions which indict teachers and perpetuate the need for more testing. And what is the notion of 'real reading' conveyed to young readers by teachers who are encouraged by a national research project to emulate the *Schonell Graded Word Reading Test* in their classroom assessment practices?

NOTES

1. This refers to a major survey of teachers' attitudes and practices with respect to standardised testing which constitutes one part of the Evaluation of Testing in Schools Project. Other work includes a study of the Assessment of Performance Unit (DES) and a study of LEA testing programmes which is reported elsewhere in this issue of *Primary Education Review*.

REFERENCES

Bullock, Sir Alan (1975) *A Language for Life*. London: HMSO.

Burt, C. (1954) *The Burt (Rearranged) Word Reading Test*. London: University of London Press.

Pumfrey, P. D. (1976) *Measuring Reading Abilities: Concepts, Sources and Applications*. London: Hodder and Stoughton.

Schonell, F. (1945) *The Psychology and Teaching of Reading*. London: Oliver and Boyd.

Southgate, V., Arnold, H. and Johnson, S. (1981) *Extending Beginning Reading*. London: Heinemann Educational Books, for the Schools Council.

3.5 | THE PRIMARY LANGUAGE RECORD

MYRA BARRS, SUE ELLIS, HILARY HESTER AND ANNE THOMAS

HOW IT WORKS

This new ILEA Primary Language Record is designed with certain principles in mind:

THE INVOLVEMENT OF PARENTS

A discussion with the child's parent(s) is the first section of the record form. This section gives parents and teachers the opportunity to meet early in the school year in order to share information and discuss a child's language and literacy development at home and at school. There is also space, in Part C, for parents to comment on the completed record, and to sign the form to indicate that they have read it.

THE INVOLVEMENT OF CHILDREN

There are two sections on the record for language/literacy conferences with the child (in the Autumn and Summer Terms). These conferences are intended to provide an opportunity for children to be actively involved in the evaluation of their own progress and the planning of their work.

The involvement of all teachers who teach the child

The record is designed to allow all teachers who teach the child to be involved in compiling a full picture of the child's progress and to ensure that the special insights of bilingual development/community language teachers, support teachers and head teachers are incorporated.

The involvement of children with special educational needs

It is hoped that the approach to language development in the record will be as relevant to teachers in special schools as to those in mainstream schools, and that the observation-based methods of assessment in the record will help teachers of children with special educational needs.

The importance of recording children's progress in the other community languages they know as well as in English

The record offers positive support for the gathering of information about language and literacy developments in languages other than English. This handbook offers a number of ideas as to how such information may be gathered, with the help of bilingual colleagues, or through sensitive observation and questioning. This is an area of rapid development, and many schools will be looking for ways of logging bilingual children's progress in more than one language. It is hoped that the approaches suggested here will be useful to them.

The importance of recording developments across the curriculum in all major language modes

Regular record-keeping is recognised as being an important part of teaching but most official records only ask for brief summative end-of-year statements. The new ILEA Primary Language Record is accompanied by an optional observation and sample sheet, which allows teachers to make regular, detailed observations of language and literacy development. These observations provide information that teachers can draw on in completing the record.

Developments in language and literacy do not take place in isolation from one another. This record provides a basis for making connections between different aspects of development in all the major language modes – talking and listening, reading, and writing – and for observing children using language for learning across the whole curriculum.

THE IMPORTANCE OF A CLEAR FRAMEWORK FOR EVALUATING PROGRESS IN LANGUAGE

The new record offers a coherent view of what constitutes progress and development in language. It encourages teachers to identify children's strengths and note growth points, to regard errors as information, and to analyse patterns of error in a constructive way. It will be particularly helpful to teachers who are interested in informal methods of assessment, based on observation and on teacher judgement.

THE RECORDS 'PACKAGE'

The whole Primary Language Record 'package' consists of:
a) the main record – the Primary Language Record – which is an official ILEA record and can replace the language section on the existing yellow record, and
b) an optional observation and sample sheet in four parts, which is intended to help teachers in completing the main record. This observation and sample sheet is a flexible document which can be incorporated into existing record systems and used at teachers' own discretion.

THE PRIMARY LANGUAGE RECORD

The language record is designed to be completed at several points in the school year, and not just at the end of the year. In this way it is hoped that it will inform the *teaching* that goes on during the year, and not become merely an administrative record. It should also provide a good basis for discussing a child's progress with parents. Completed records will be passed on throughout the child's primary school career, and into the secondary school, forming a cumulative language profile.

The Record is divided into three parts:

Part A   to be completed during the Autumn Term
Part B   to be completed during the Spring Term
Part C   to be completed during the Summer Term (by the Summer half term for 4th year junior children).

At whatever point in the year a child enters school it will be helpful if as much as possible of the record can be filled in, even if some has to remain incomplete.

These timings will obviously vary for some children – for instance, children in the nursery, or those entering school at times of the year other than the beginning of the Autumn Term.

Children in nursery schools or classes may of course be entering the nursery at any point in the school year, and the timings suggested on the record may not therefore be appropriate for them. In these circumstances teachers will obviously need to adapt the suggested timings, and complete as much of the record as seems appropriate, considering the extent of a child's experience in school. However it should always prove valuable to complete part A in a child's first term in the nursery, as the kind of information parents and children can provide about pre-school experiences will help teachers with their planning. Nursery teachers may find that, for children who have four or five terms in the nursery, they need only complete one main record, though they may wish to make fuller use of the observation and sample sheet.

The same considerations will apply to all children entering school at other times of the year than in September, for whatever reason (e.g. family movement, sickness, children in temporary accommodation, children who have had to wait for a place in school). In all cases it will be useful to complete as much of the record as is appropriate, and particularly Part A.

Part A consists of:

1 boxed information of an administrative nature and
2 spaces where the discussion with parents (A1) and the first language/literacy conference with the child (A2) are to be recorded.

Part B 'The Child as a Language User' has sections on:

- Talking and listening (B1)
- Reading (B2), and
- Writing (B3).

Teachers completing Part B may want to draw on the detailed information that they have gained from the observation and sample sheet and/or from their own records. The completed Part B should give a full and balanced picture of the child as a language user.

Each section ends with a space where teachers can record:

1 the experiences and teaching that have helped or would help the child's development in a particular aspect of language, and
2 the outcomes of any discussions that have taken place between the class teacher and the head teacher or the child's parent(s), about the child's development in this aspect of language.

Where there is reason for concern about a child's progress or if in any way it is exceptional, it will be useful to arrange such a discussion and record what has been decided.

Part C is designed to allow the information contained in Part B to be added to, so that the account of the child's language progress is as up-to-date as possible. It also provides an opportunity for parents to comment on the record, if they wish to, and for a second language/literacy conference with the child.

OBSERVATION AND SAMPLES (Primary Language Record)

The observation and sample sheet (white form) is a teacher's informal record which complements the Primary Language Record and can be incorporated into a school's own recording systems on an optional basis. The detailed information provided by the observation and sample sheet should be of considerable value to teachers in completing the main Primary Language Record.

The observation and sample sheet is in four parts:

1 Talking and listening: diary of observations
2 Reading and writing: diary of observations
3 Reading samples
4 Writing samples.

There is therefore space to record significant developments in language and literacy in an open diary format, and to analyse in depth particular examples of a child's reading and writing.

Like the sections on 'Talking and listening' and 'Writing', the section on 'Reading' is to be completed in the Spring Term. It is intended to give teachers an opportunity to record observations and analyses of a child's progress and development as a reader. Information can be gathered from previous records, the teacher's own records, knowledge of the child's reading experiences outside school, the child's view of her/himself as a reader and the teacher's detailed observations noted in the observation and sample sheet.

Additional pieces of information can be recorded in Part C during the Summer Term.

READING AND LANGUAGE DEVELOPMENT

Reading cannot be examined in total isolation from talking, listening and writing, so it is important to consider each child in the context of her/his language and learning experiences. Furthermore many children will be learning to talk, read and/or write in a second or even third language and it is crucial that their learning in more than one language is supported, developed and understood as valuable and enriching.

B2 Reading

Please comment on the child's progress and development as a reader in English and/or other community languages: the stage at which the child is operating (refer to the reading scales on pp....); the range, quantity and variety of reading in all areas of the curriculum: the child's pleasure and involvement in story and reading, alone or with others; the range of strategies used when reading and the child's ability to reflect critically on what is read.

At the beginning of the year C. was reluctant to move away from a small number of books which she read accurately. Since she has gained confidence as a reader C. is tackling more demanding print. She is a Beginner reader/Non-fluent reader on the reading scale 1. C. is developing quite a number of known words in her reading. She is also developing strategies – picture/meaning/context cues and she can also use some initial sounds and her one-to-one correspondence is good. The range of books she is happy to read has increased dramatically since she has become more sure of herself. C. enjoys listening to stories and being read to.

What experiences and teaching have helped/would help development in this area? Record outcomes of any discussion with head teacher, other staff, or parents.

Encourage her to continue choosing a wide range of books that will stretch her.
Encourage her knowledge of initial sounds.

Reception class – girl. *Languages*: **English**
This example shows clearly how the wording of this section and the accompanying notes in the handbook have helped the teacher to structure her comments. She has found a way of talking about C's growing competence as a reader in clear and cogent terms which will be of value to other members of staff and to C's parents.

The view of reading adopted in the record is one which acknowledges the fact that learning to read has much in common with learning to talk. A child's capacity for learning language will be one of the greatest assets in learning to read. Bilingual children will have demonstrated already their language learning powers, and how they use what they know about one language to learn another. They process and reprocess the language they hear, speculate, check, confirm or reject – continually refining their understanding of the less familiar language in the light of new information.

Over the last twenty years or so there have been several fundamental developments in our understanding of what is involved in learning to read. It may be helpful to review some of the changes that have taken place in thinking about the subject in order to see how the psycholinguistic approach to reading, implicit in the record, has evolved.

B2 Reading
Please comment on the child's progress and development as a reader in English and/or other community languages: the stage at which the child is operating (refer to the reading scales on pp...); the range, quantity and variety of reading in all areas of the curriculum: the child's pleasure and involvement in story and reading, alone or with others; the range of strategies used when reading and the child's ability to reflect critically on what is read.

A. is becoming far more confident in tackling known and some unknown texts. He is progressing towards being a 'moderately fluent' reader and is making steady progress. He is developing strategies such as checking guesses, initial sounds, picture cues, and is beginning to read in phrases. Although still below the class average, A. is highly motivated and shows a sound interest and pleasure in reading. He attempts a wide variety of books in terms of subject matter and complexity

What experiences and teaching have helped/would help development in this area? Record outcomes of any discussion with head teacher, other staff, or parents.

- Access to reading material that is within his capability to tackle alone to really boost his confidence and increase his motivation.
- He needs lots of opportunity to share reading with an adult and more interesting and challenging reading material.
- A. needs opportunities to discuss / explore books.

Middle Infants – boy. *Languages*: **English**
There is a strong feeling that although A is still at the early stages of reading his involvement and enthusiasm for a wide range of books are likely to be key factors in his further development. The teacher has made some very helpful recommendations about ways of supporting the child's progress: developing his autonomy as a reader on the one hand, while at the same time, increasing the opportunities he has for reading and discussing with other children and adults.

TEACHING AND LEARNING TO READ: A HISTORICAL PERSPECTIVE

In the early part of this century many psychologists concentrated almost exclusively on studying reading as a perceptual process (decoding print). It was not until the middle of the century that linguists began to suggest that there were other elements to consider in the learning-to-read process. So in reading research there was a movement away from a narrow concentration on the visual characteristics of individual words towards using children's knowledge and experience of oral language as a powerful basis for literacy learning. The language-experience approach, as it eventually became known, stressed the importance of using children's first-hand experiences and natural interests as motivating forces in helping them to acquire and develop reading and writing skills. Children's descriptions of particular experiences were written down and became reading resources. As children became more confident they were expected to copy their own dictated sentences. In 1970 *Breakthrough to Literacy* was published in this country as part of a Schools Council project; it drew on language-experience approaches and translated them into a systematic programme.

PSYCHOLINGUISTICS AND READING

In North America in the 1960s and 1970s psycholinguistic research focused on bringing together all that was now known about how children acquired language in order to consider how they learned to read. Kenneth Goodman and colleagues came to refer to the learning-to-read process as a psycholinguistic guessing game: research findings demonstrated so clearly the way in which even beginning readers brought all their linguistic knowledge and experience of life to the task of processing text. Thus the 'errors' children make as they read aloud became more favourably known as miscues; miscue analysis, the study of oral reading behaviour, emerged as a nucleus for a whole new way of thinking about what was involved in learning to read.

Frank Smith argued that as children learn to talk by talking so they learn to read by reading. The teacher's task was to make reading easier. He further proposed that learning to read was not made easy by breaking down the process into a series of component parts nor by presenting children with contrived or over-simplified texts. To develop increasing control over any new learning process the learner had to take on the whole activity and make sense of it. In *Reading*, he suggested that there were two basic needs for apprentice readers: 'the availability of interesting material that makes sense to the learner and an understanding and more experienced reader as a guide'.

Psycholinguists articulated the ways in which the reader draws upon the cue systems already available in written language in order to make sense of texts by using all the available cues. These are:

1 semantic cues (meaning cues)
   - using knowledge and experience of stories and of written texts to predict events, phrases and words and above all to make the text make sense;
2 syntactic cues (language cues)
   - drawing on knowledge and experience of patterns in oral and written language to predict text;
3 grapho-phonic cues (print cues)
   - using knowledge and experience of relationships between sounds and symbols to read particular words.

Obviously the reader applies a combination of strategies in order to read and the process is a cycle of predicting, sampling, confirming, and correcting as Constance Weaver shows in this diagram from *Psycholinguistics and Reading*:

LANGUAGE
CUES

READING STRATEGIES

	Predict	Sample	Confirm/ Correct
Syntactic			
Semantic			
Grapho-phonic			

This research and in particular the work and thinking of the advocates of language-experience approaches, and of psycholinguists like Kenneth Goodman, was brought to the attention of a wide audience in the Bullock Report published in 1975. The Report was also important in setting reading in the context of language and learning so that it was no longer envisaged as an isolated skill.

HOME AND SCHOOL

In the 1980s one of the most important developments in the field of reading has been the growing emphasis placed on home-school links, on children's knowledge of literacy before schooling, and on contributions that all parents make to their children's development as readers.

We are now more aware of the broad knowledge of literacy that children acquire before coming to school. Contrary to what used to be thought, it is now known that the language of all children, except those with severe language learning difficulties, is an adequate basis for literacy learning.

The research programme which produced convincing evidence for this was the Bristol Language Development Research Project, which studied a group of children from infancy and into primary school. Gordon Wells, the director of the project, also sought to discover whether there were any particular pre-school activities/experiences that contributed to children's educational achievement at primary school level. The results were clear-cut: *listening to stories* was significantly associated with children's development as readers and writers:

> Stories read aloud and discussed in a way which encourages reflection upon their own experience and imaginative exploration of the world created through the language of the text are probably the best way of helping young children to begin to develop these abilities (Gordon Wells (1985) *Language, Learning and Education*).

LEARNING TO READ

As a result of these research findings, we are now in a better position to consider how children learn to read and the kinds of classroom environments that support this learning.

A child learns to talk in the company of others; it is an interactive process where meanings are explored, shared and developed. So it is with reading. In the early stages when an adult (or older child) reads to the child it is normal for the child to ask questions or make comments about the pictures, the print and the nature of the text itself. Through this kind of talk, the conversations that naturally surround shared reading and the sharing of books, children come to know more about what is involved in being a reader.

To be literate means many things and children are growing up in a world where there are ever-increasing demands made upon them in the field of literacy. Children have to learn what to read and what not to read depending on individual needs and interests. In this technological age, at home and in the world outside home and school, print abounds; it serves many purposes, often of a purely functional nature, for example signs in the supermarket, the bus timetable, television advertisements. So children come to school with some knowledge and understanding of print and very often in more than one language. But as Margaret Meek said in *Learning to Read* (1982):

> literacy doesn't begin and end in the official sphere of social contracts ... Good readers are more than successful print-scanners and retrievers of factual information. They find in books the depth and breadth of human experience.

So it is essential that we invite children to be members of literate communities in the fullest sense.

THE ROLE OF TEXTS IN LEARNING TO READ

It seems clear that texts have a key role to play in a child's development as a reader. Books that make up a child's repertoire of known texts should be books that are worth returning to again and again. Stories and rhymes that stem from oral and literate traditions are arguably the most powerful source of texts for apprentice readers.

Children will have their own favourites but it is remarkable how often certain texts (e.g. *Rosie's Walk, Where the Wild Things Are, Bringing the Rain to Kapiti Plain, Mr. Gumpy's Outing, The Very Hungry Caterpillar, Bears in the Night*) are mentioned as being particularly popular with young readers. Books like this share:

- a strong story
- a lively, rhythmical text
- powerful, imaginative content
- memorable language
- interesting illustrations, that complement the text
- humour
- language that is not contrived or unnatural (as it sometimes is in published reading schemes).

Bilingual children can expect to find in schools an increasing number of memorable stories, such as those mentioned above, published in dual language editions, and stories published in a number of community/home languages. The importance of including a wide selection of quality books from a variety of cultural settings and in a variety of languages cannot be over-emphasised. This wide selection of books will offer valuable support to bilingual children in learning to read in more than one language and in widening all children's experiences of other people's linguistic and literary heritages.

As well as commercially published texts, children's own texts play a powerful role in developing reading ability. These texts may be dictated and scribed by another child or member of staff or may be written by children themselves. The written texts (in English and/or other community languages) can be accompanied by illustrations or designs and made into books. Subsequently these books become part of the classroom's reading resources offering a wide range of reading experience for all children.

READING ALOUD TO CHILDREN AND LEARNING TO READ

It seems that reading aloud to children is of the utmost importance in supporting their development as readers.

A child who is learning to read and who is read to frequently builds up a repertoire of known texts which s/he wants to return to again and again. On each occasion and over time the child plays a more active role in the reading. S/he is familiar with the story-line, with the tune on the page and has a natural inclination to predict; so s/he becomes the story-teller and re-enacts the text. It is the familiarisation that helps a child develop a growing awareness of what is involved in being able to do it for her/himself.

Similarly a more experienced reader will gain much pleasure and learn a great deal from being read to. S/he will develop an understanding of different genres and different styles, will come to know and enjoy an increasing number of writers and will experience certain books that otherwise s/he might never encounter.

Growing in confidence

With continued support – being read to, by teachers and other experienced readers in and out of school, discussing texts, being invited to read familiar phrases – a child develops an understanding that it is the print that carries the message: s/he becomes more aware of the significant features of print itself. Over time and with experience – the experience of reading familiar texts – the child's confidence and competence grow. S/he plays an increasingly autonomous role, understanding the interaction of picture and text; taking risks with print by making informed guesses based on semantic, syntactic and grapho-phonic information and using a number of strategies that s/he is developing to try out hypotheses and to confirm or reject them as new knowledge is added to the old.

Over a period the child's reading strategies and the language cues of print begin to mesh and the child takes on more and more of the reading for her/himself, bringing to the activity all s/he knows and can do to make the text meaningful.

Moving into silent reading

Some time in the primary school, often in the infant department, most children move from reading aloud to reading silently. The transition period is an important one where, in the initial stages, a child sub-vocalises the words reading at the same pace as if s/he were reading aloud. With experience and maturity, the words become 'thoughts in the head' and the rate of reading increases. During this time a child still needs support and guidance. S/he also needs time to browse and to engage in silent reading for sustained periods of time.

The difficulty with silent reading from a teacher's standpoint is that it is naturally a private process so teachers have to find ways of working with children that support their development. Group discussion is often a good way of extending the understanding and experiences of books that have been read silently, as are opportunities to explore stories, for instance, through drama. In order that children can feel confident about themselves as readers, their tentative as well as their carefully considered responses to texts should be valued and encouraged. As they experience a greater variety of books and reading material across all areas of the curriculum they will need support in coming to realise that different texts demand different styles of reading.

AN EXPERIENCED READER

As the child becomes more fluent and experienced across the wide range of reading demands that exist in the primary classroom s/he will be willing to take on more extended and more challenging texts. Illustrations become less crucial in supporting understanding, although this is not to underestimate the power and vitality of picture books for older children. With encouragement, the child will become more critical of what s/he reads, and what writers have to say. S/he will become more able to question and/or admire aspects of content, form and function. S/he will come to realise that there exist in some texts elements of prejudice and will be able to recognise and criticise texts or illustrations that are biased. Developing readers will also be extending their understanding of texts by detecting elements like ambiguity or irony.

DEVELOPMENT IN READING AND THE READING SCALES

There are, therefore, generalisations that can be made about what constitutes growth and development in reading. It is important to think of development in reading as development along a continuum; in their growth as readers children initially move from *dependence to independence*.

To begin with, learners depend on an adult or more experienced reader to read the text aloud to them. But as their knowledge of texts and of written language(s) grows, they gradually become more confident about tackling, in the first instance, familiar texts, and then unfamiliar ones for themselves.

BECOMING A READER: READING SCALE 1

The diagram that follows shows in more detail aspects of a child's move along the *dependence–independence* continuum. The scale was devised in the first instance to help teachers of children in the top infant age range log individual development using this reading scale with a set of operational definitions to support their decisions. The scale can however be used as a base for thinking about children's progress across a wider age range; it offers some helpful ways of describing what a child is able to do, with increasing ease, on the road to becoming a fluent reader. This scale can also be used to identify children whose reading development is causing some concern. If a child at the top of the infant school is described as a beginner reader or a non-fluent reader on this scale, s/he may require particular support and help.

DEPENDENCE

Beginner reader 1	Does not have enough successful strategies for tackling print independently. Relies on having another person read the text aloud. May still be unaware that text carries meaning.
Non-fluent reader 2	Tackling known and predictable texts with growing confidence but still needing support with new and unfamiliar ones. Growing ability to predict meanings, and developing strategies to check predictions against other cues such as the illustrations and the print itself.
Moderately fluent reader 3	Well launched on reading but still needing to return to a familiar range of texts. At the same time beginning to explore new kinds of texts independently. Beginning to read silently.
Fluent reader 4	A capable reader who now approaches familiar texts with confidence but still needs support with unfamiliar materials. Beginning to draw inferences from books and stories read independently. Chooses to read silently.
Exceptionally fluent reader 5	An avid and independent reader, who is making choices from a wide range of material. Able to appreciate nuances and subtleties in text.

INDEPENDENCE

Table 6 *Becoming a reader: reading scale 1*

USING THE READING SCALE – TOP INFANTS AND FIRST-YEAR JUNIORS

As part of an assessment procedure it is proposed that in the Spring Term of the top infant and first-year junior age groups each child's development is recorded using this reading scale and noted in section B2 of the Primary Language Record, for example: 'Moderately fluent reader (date)'. Subsequent information on a child's development as a reader can be recorded in Part C in the Summer Term.

Teachers will appreciate that this scale is particularly useful for top infants and first-year juniors but it may also be helpful in considering the reading of children in the general age range of 6 to 8. There may also be individual cases where it is appropriate for an older child who is not yet reading independently.

BILINGUAL DEVELOPMENT AND THE READING SCALE

Many bilingual children will be becoming readers in more than one language. Bilingual development/community language teachers will be able to provide a great deal of feedback about literacy in first languages and discuss with the class teachers strategies that each child is developing on the way to becoming biliterate. In schools where there is no support for particular bilingual children, class teachers can observe and listen to children reading aloud in other languages and discover a great deal about them as readers (see Appendix C: Informal Assessment). This kind of information can be recorded in B2.

Some bilingual children will be more competent as readers in their first language, others not. Whichever is the case it is valuable, where possible, for teachers who share the child's language or who have the help of bilingual development/community language teachers to log children's development in both languages. The reading scales can obviously be useful here. So, for instance, a child whose first language is Turkish may be a *fluent reader* in Turkish, but because of little experience of reading in English might be described as a *non-fluent reader* in English. It will be important in assessing a child's reading in English, to note also how long s/he has been learning English.

ADAPTING THE SCALE

There will be times when a teacher feels that for one reason or another the definitions do not adequately describe what a child can do as a reader. It is reasonable to expect that there will be other signs that are indicative of development and it is important that these signs are noted in B2. Furthermore there will be instances when a child seems to be moving between one set of definitions and another; it is also relevant to record this information, for example: Beginner reader/Non-fluent reader. After the age of eight the scale will probably become less useful as a reliable guide for logging and describing reading development. For older and experienced readers, therefore, a second scale has been developed, which focuses, in greater detail, on the qualitative aspects of children's developing experiences in reading across the curriculum areas.

EXPERIENCE AS A READER ACROSS THE CURRICULUM: READING SCALE 2

The first reading scale is concerned with a reader's journey from dependence to independence; it is a *fluency scale*. The second reading scale focuses on a child's increasing involvement with a diverse range and variety of reading materials; it is *a scale of experience*.

The diagram that follows illustrates in some detail elements of a child's developing experience as a reader. In the junior school years children engage with a much greater selection of books and texts – fiction and non-fiction books, and computers. ... It is crucial that they are supported in their endeavours to take on the multi-faceted reading demands of a junior school curriculum. So in assessing second, third and fourth year children's progress and development as readers, we need to consider that in addition to a growing ability to be able to read silently, fluently and with ease, there is a widening of reading horizons where the notions of range and variety play an increasingly important part in children's interactions with texts.

INEXPERIENCED

Inexperienced reader 1	Experience as a reader has been limited. Generally chooses to read very easy and familiar texts where illustrations play an important part. Has difficulty with any unfamiliar material and yet may be able to read own dictated texts confidently. Needs a great deal of support with the reading demands of the classroom. Over-dependent on one strategy when reading aloud: often reads word by word. Rarely chooses to read for pleasure.
Less experienced reader 2	Developing fluency as a reader and reading certain kinds of material with confidence. Usually chooses short books with simple narrative shapes and with illustrations and may read these silently; often re-reads favourite books. Reading for pleasure often includes comics and magazines. Needs help with the reading demands of the classroom and especially with using reference and information books.

Moderately experienced reader 3	A confident reader who feels at home with books. Generally reads silently and is developing stamina as a reader. Is able to read for longer periods and cope with more demanding texts, including children's novels. Willing to reflect on reading and often uses reading in own learning. Selects books independently and can use information books and materials for straightforward reference purposes, but still needs help with unfamiliar material, particularly non-narrative prose.
Experienced reader 4	A self-motivated, confident and experienced reader who may be pursuing particular interests through reading. Capable of tackling some demanding texts and can cope well with the reading of the curriculum. Reads thoughtfully and appreciates shades of meaning. Capable of locating and drawing on a variety of sources in order to research a topic independently.
Exceptionally experienced reader 5	An enthusiastic and reflective reader who has strong established tastes in fiction and/or non-fiction. Enjoys pursuing own reading interests independently. Can handle a wide range and variety of texts, including some adult material. Recognises that different kinds of texts require different styles of reading. Able to evaluate evidence drawn from a variety of information sources. Is developing critical awareness as a reader.

EXPERIENCED

Table 7 *Experience as a reader across the curriculum: reading scale 2*

As their ability and experience increase, children become more skilful at knowing what to read and what not to read: in other words they are more discerning and experienced as readers and realise that different texts require different reading approaches. The *scale of experience* is therefore intended to help teachers note the quality of a child's experiences as a reader, and not merely the amount they have read.

USING THE SCALE OF EXPERIENCE – SECOND, THIRD AND FOURTH YEAR JUNIORS

As part of an assessment procedure it is proposed that in the Spring Term of the second, third and fourth year junior age groups each child's development is recorded using this reading scale and noted in Part B2 of the Primary Language Record, for example: Moderately experienced reader (date). Subsequent information on a child's development as a reader can be recorded in Part C in the Summer Term.

Teachers will probably find that this scale is particularly useful for children of nine, ten and eleven years of age although there may be cases where this is not so; occasionally it will be helpful when considering a seven or eight year-old's progress.

Many bilingual children will be developing as readers in more than one language. Some will be more competent in English than in their community language, others not. Whichever is the case, and as was suggested for the younger age range, it is helpful to chart children's development in both languages where possible.

For more detail on charting reading development in more than one language see the previous section.

If there are occasions when the teacher feels that for one reason or another the definitions do not adequately describe what a child is able to do as a reader then it will be valuable if s/he records any relevant observations in B2. In addition s/he may think that a child fits between one set of descriptions and another, in which case s/he may like to record the information like this: Experienced reader/Exceptionally experienced reader (date).

SOME EXPLANATIONS OF TERMS USED IN THE 'READING' SECTION

'... stage at which the child is operating ...'

It is hoped that the two reading scales will help teachers to identify the stage at which a child is operating as s/he becomes a more independent and experienced reader. The descriptions will enable teachers to identify a reader's strengths, and to pinpoint the areas where support is needed. More detailed analysis can be obtained from sampling the child's reading using a running record, making a miscue analysis or through informal assessment (see observation and sample sheet).

... the range, quality and variety of reading in all areas of the curriculum ...

In school and at home children read for a variety of purposes. Many aspects of the curriculum will involve reading. Over a period of time a child may be reading different kinds of fiction, poems, comics/magazines, newspapers, and jokes, as well as instructions for making something, explanations of a mathematical problem or concept, reports on scientific topics, computer programs and information/text-books.

Children may not read equally across the range but at different times will need to read more in one area than another, as well as developing preferences and special interests within the range.

... pleasure and involvement in story and reading, alone or with others ...

If children are to develop as readers there must be personal involvement in reading. The pleasures of reading often begin as shared pleasures and arise from reading with an adult. When a child experiences the emotional satisfaction of involvement in story, s/he is likely to want to read more. Even when children are reading quite independently, the satisfactions they find in books can be increased by being shared with other readers. When there is time and space for this kind of sharing in the classroom, and as children encounter a widening variety of books, the range of their personal reading choices will grow.

... range of strategies used when reading ...

Observation of a child reading silently will reveal some of the ways in which s/he approaches the task, and it is possible to identify some strategies being used. When the child reads aloud other strategies may be revealed. The teacher needs to notice:

- whether the child uses illustration (initially to help retell the story, later to check guesses),
- whether the child makes use of the context to help work out the meaning; does what s/he reads make sense?
- whether the child reads in meaningful 'chunks', or word by word,
- whether the child uses the structure of language to help work out the meaning,
- whether the child uses knowledge about books and written language to help work out meaning,
- whether the child uses knowledge of what words/letters look or sound like to help work out unknown words,
- whether s/he makes a good guess at unknown words or waits to be told,
- whether s/he is using several strategies to get meaning from the text or has a heavy dependence on one strategy (e.g. phonic analysis),

B2 Reading
Please comment on the child's progress and development as a reader in English and/or other community languages: the stage at which the child is operating (refer to the reading scales on pp....); the range, quantity and variety of reading in all areas of the curriculum: the child's pleasure and involvement in story and reading, alone or with others; the range of strategies used when reading and the child's ability to reflect critically on what is read. Ay. is a fluent reader in English and Bengali and one of the more able readers in the 2nd year. She seeks meaning from the texts she reads and grasps understanding from sentences read or by reading on. she uses graphophonic cues with unknown words, self corrects and is able to retain newly introduced vocabulary. She stumbles on longer words, nominally longer verbs (e.g. polishing, managing) and as she continues to read so enthusiastically she will combat this difficulty. Ay is much more critical about books this term and selects with more interest. She is more confident now in reading aloud and enjoys reading to her friends and in assembly. Ay. is also reading silently more often. when she reads in Bengali she translates readily.

What experiences and teaching have helped/would help development in this area? Record outcomes of any discussion with head teacher, other staff, or parents.

Continue to offer a range of interesting books with humerous storylines and with understandable developments in text. Also develops reference book skills (index, glossary, information retrieval.)

2nd year junior – girl. *Languages:* **Sylheti, Bengali, English**
There is a great deal of information here about Ay's growing competence as a reader, reading in English and Bengali. The teacher recognises the importance of supporting the child's literacy development in both languages, knowing that development in one will support development in the other. There are significant references to the wide range of strategies Ay uses when reading aloud, her growing ability to read between the lines and her increasing preference for silent reading.

- whether the child self-corrects, and seems to be monitoring her/his own reading.

The reading samples will help to identify the strategies a child uses when reading.

... ability to reflect critically on what is read ...

Children need to talk about books in order to clarify their ideas, to relate reading to experience and to reflect on what they have read. This is the real meaning of comprehension. They need to understand that different readers may respond differently to the same book, and that books may be biased, inaccurate or inadequate.

The greater the child's experience of reading a wide variety of texts, the better s/he will be able to evaluate what is read and to make informed choices.

part four
AFTER SCHOOL

INTRODUCTION

In all parts of the United Kingdom, curricular and assessment reform proposals for students between 14 and 19 years of age often become controversial. In England and Wales, GCSE was launched after several 'false dawns' and watered down. Alternatives to the 'A' level regime do exist – more schools now adopt the International Baccalaureate for example – yet it is the vocational and training fields, where students of the same age prepare for jobs and careers under assessment regimes, that would have been unrecognisable a decade ago.

The intervention of the Manpower Services Commission (now the Training Agency) introduced a major commitment to training for specific *competences*. Administratively, the National Council for Vocational Qualifications seeks to unite and make coherent different accreditation systems.

In Chapter 4.1, John Burke and Gilbert Jessup argue that the central issue in assessing competence is the conformity of the judgement of a learning outcome with established performance criteria. As such, the *validity* of the assessment is paramount.

Jenny Shackleton describes the introduction of the National Vocational Qualification system (NVQs) at Wirral Metropolitan College. She also outlines the establishment of a five-year plan for the institution based on 'flexibility', 'employment' and 'learning support'. Her descriptions illustrate how assessment 'regimes' can nurture or inhibit learning strategies.

ASSESSMENT IN NVQs: DISENTANGLING VALIDITY 4.1 FROM RELIABILITY IN NVQs

JOHN BURKE AND GILBERT JESSUP

INTRODUCTION

National Vocational Qualifications (NVQs) are essentially concerned with the assessment of competence. The key feature of such assessments is that they take place against predetermined standards. Assessment is therefore firmly grounded in a criterion–referenced system where the standards are explicit and made available not only to the assessors but also, significantly, to the assessees. In such a system, validity (does the assessment measure what we intend to measure?) becomes the central focus of concern. Reliability (essentially a matter of consistency between different assessments) is relegated to a side-line issue. This is a somewhat provocative statement as 'reliability and validity' are usually linked in a seemingly indissoluble embrace like Tweedledum and Tweedledee in most texts which deal with assessment. They are usually considered vital as criteria for determining the *adequacy* of an examination or assessment; we shall argue that *because NVQs are assessed by reference to explicit standards which constitute an external reference point* the adequacy of the assessment should be judged primarily (if not exclusively) in terms of its validity, i.e. the extent to which the assessment process engages and assesses against these externally derived standards.

To understand why this should be, we must examine the process of assessment in an NVQ. And in order to do that we must briefly examine some of the essential concepts which underlie the NVQ model.

UNDERLYING CONCEPTS IN THE NVQ MODEL OF ASSESSMENT

An NVQ is a statement of competence. That statement is supported by a number of individual assessments which take place as the qualification is acquired, incrementally. Each NVQ may be broken down into its constituent parts: *Units of Competence, Elements of Competence* and associated *Performance Criteria*. Figure 3 [see overleaf] illustrates their relationship.

UNITS OF COMPETENCE

A *unit of competence* represents a relatively discrete area of competence which is recognised as having value in employment. It is defined by the National Council for Vocational Qualifications (NCVQ) as:

> [A] coherent group of elements of competence and associated performance criteria which form a discrete activity or sub-area of competence which have meaning and independent value in the area of employment to which the NVQ relates. It will normally embrace a combination of aspects of employment-related activities, together with associated skills and under-pinning knowledge and understanding. It may also be a generic unit (NCVQ, 1988i, 2.41, p. 5.).

Once it has been fully assessed, it can be accredited towards a complete *statement of competence*, a cluster of units, which is a freestanding qualification for an individual, an 'NVQ'.

Each individual NVQ is assigned a place within an overall, national *NVQ framework* which will provide a coherent system of vocational qualifications issued by the many different awarding bodies whose examinations have been accredited or 'kite-marked' by the NCVQ. A sophisticated database has been devised so that employers, potential NVQ candidates, trainers and lecturers can access the framework. Initially, this framework was limited to four levels, spanning the most basic qualifications up to those at approximately 'higher national' level. In 1989, the NCVQ's remit was extended to cover, potentially, all vocational qualifications including degrees and professional awards. Participation by professional bodies is entirely voluntary, but exploratory talks and negotiations are already underway with a number of different professions (cf. Jessup, 1989).

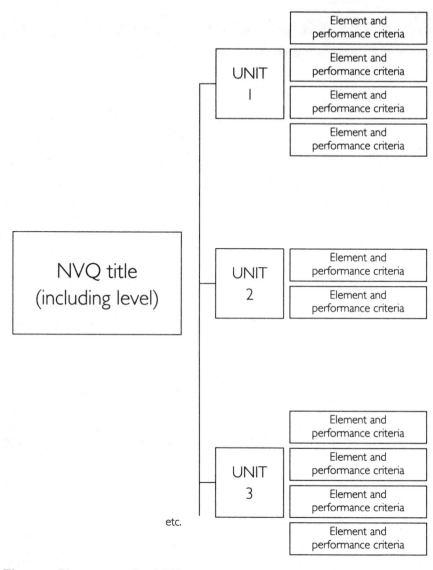

Figure 3 *The structure of an NVQ*

ELEMENTS OF COMPETENCE AND THEIR ASSOCIATED PERFORMANCE CRITERIA

An *element of competence* is a smaller area of competence (than the unit of competence). The assessment process focuses on each element which is assessed separately. A coherent cluster of elements, which may vary in number (four to six would be common) are grouped together to form a unit. In contrast to individual units, elements by themselves would not have negotiable, recognised value as competences in employment; they are smaller, assessable competences which contribute to the formation of more complex and individually recognised, discrete competences known as units.

Associated *performance criteria* are always linked to their respective elements of competence. They are the 'yard-sticks', the criteria against which performance in each element may be assessed. Great care has to be taken when formulating performance criteria to ensure they are unambiguous and transparently clear, as these performance criteria provide the *standards* against which performance is judged. In particular, the NCVQ (NCVQ, 1988ii, pp. 3–4) stresses that the problems experienced by ethnic minorities, issues relating to gender, possible discrimination on the grounds of religion and the special needs of people with disability or learning difficulties should be borne in mind. In addition, the NCVQ clearly defines a commitment to freedom of access as a criterion for the accreditation of any award as an NVQ.

STANDARDS

The concept of standards needs to be understood in the technical sense as applied to NVQs. The NCVQ (1987, p. 5) defines it as follows:

1.1.2 *Employment led standards of competence* are agreed and recognised levels of vocational competence – skills, knowledge, understanding and ability in application – needed to perform a task, a job or a range of jobs normally in a specified group of occupations, sector of industry or commerce, or profession.

The Training Agency (1988ii, p. 4) elaborates:

Standards for vocational education and training, and future qualifications, must be based on a broad view of competence. They should include all activities contributing to effective performance in all aspects of:

1 performance of individual tasks;
2 management of different tasks;
3 dealing with unusual occurrences;
4 responding to the demands of the work environment.

The concept is very much to do with agreed and recognised levels of performance. These agreements relate to competent performance in employment, they are national agreements and they are recognised within the occupational sector to which they relate. Embodied in this concept is the ability to transfer skills and knowledge to new situations within the occupational area. It encompasses organisation and planning of work, innovation and coping with non-routine activities. A measure of this agreement is that the standards are employ*ment* related, not employ*er* related. They represent a consensus agreed by and supported by all sides of industry concerned (cf. TUC, 1988; CBI, 1989; FEU, 1989; CITB, 1988; NRTC, 1988). These agreements are occupational standards.

Stuart (1989, p. 11) comments:

> Occupational standards are the expression of competence in reality. They describe what competence means in a particular occupational area and do so in a manner which allows an individual's competence to be assessed.

Standards, then, in the NVQ model are not something the individual strives to attain as a quality; rather, they are a benchmark against which performance may be assessed. Mitchell (1989, p. 55) emphasises that the concept of standards in assessment should be recognised as an external reference point to an individual, a description of what an individual would have to do in demonstrating competence. She compares the concept of standards with the sociological construct of 'work role' in order to stress that a standard is not a characteristic or a trait of a particular individual; it is an expectation of required performance. (See also: Mansfield and Mathews, 1985; Mitchell and Mansfield, 1988; and Mansfield, 1989.)

If we take an actual example of a statement of competence we can see how the units, elements and performance criteria fit together Figure 4 (see p. 195).

The NVQ Model of Assessment

We are now in a position to look at the NVQ Assessment Model. Basically, this involves the collection or assembling of evidence which may be judged in terms of each element of competence set against its associated performance criteria. The model distinguishes three categories of evidence: performance evidence, supplementary evidence and evidence from prior achievements (Figure 5 – see p. 196).

Validity and Reliability

The process of assessment in an NVQ is revealed as a judgement of evidence against explicit performance criteria for each element of competence under

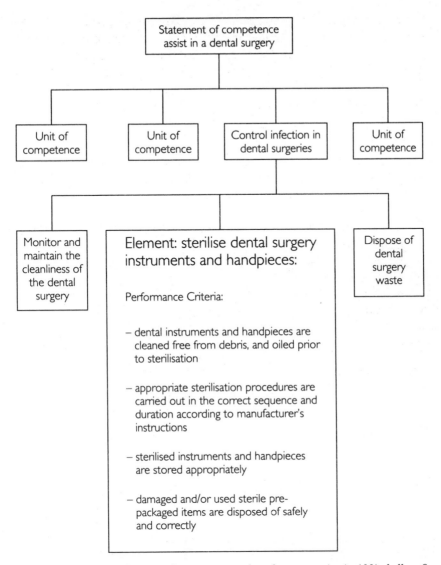

Figure 4 *Standards – elements of competence and performance criteria (Mitchell, 1989, p. 57)*

consideration. Explicit guidance is given by both the National Council for Vocational Qualifications and the Training Agency on the scope and kind of evidence which may be considered. Likewise, the format for expressing elements and criteria and the process whereby standards are derived are explicitly laid out. Under these circumstances, the key question is: *Is the judgement made in conformity with the performance criteria?* If the answer is 'yes', the assessment is valid.

It could be argued that any such system inherently lacks perfect reliability: even if compliance with the criteria *theoretically* confers validity on the assessment, *in practice* judgements made by the same assessor may differ when

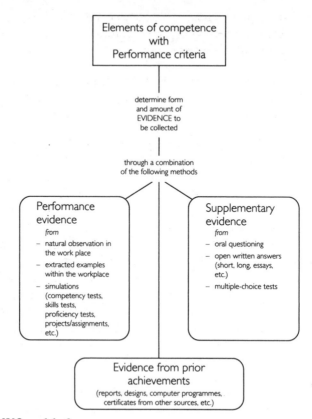

Figure 5 *NVQ model of assessment*

presented with the same evidence on different occasions. Or it might be pointed out that the judgements of different assessors of the same performance may differ, even if the criteria are precisely stated. The simple answer must be that no system is infallible and there will always be a possible margin of error. But the way to deal with this is to try to maximise validity, for as Oppenheim (1966, p. 70) observes: 'if you find that a system has excellent validity, it must also be reliable'. On the other hand, as Jessup (1989) points out, to try to maximise reliability might actually reduce validity:

If I faithfully observe the performance criteria and make a valid assessment of an individual's competence and you do not, a comparison between us would indicate that the assessment is unreliable. The solution to this problem, and I suggest to all similar problems, is to check whether the assessments conform to the requirements in the elements of competence and their performance criteria, i.e check the validity. In all circumstances assessments, should be checked against the external criterion and not with each other. If two assessments are both valid they will naturally be comparable and thus reliable, but this is incidental.

He goes on to say that this issue is of further importance because different assessors in different contexts may draw on different sources of evidence in making their assessment of the same element:

> It is difficult to see in what sense their judgements might be consistent and reliable in such circumstances. What is important is that they both obtain sufficient relevant evidence to attest to competence in respect of the element.

Reliability is vital in any norm-referenced system because by definition it is concerned with comparing one individual with another (Child, 1973, 1981, p. 228ff, stresses the importance of reliability by invoking a third criterion, 'comparability', a subset of reliability). Indeed, in many norm-referenced systems of assessment – especially in education – the chief function of the assessment appears to centre on differentiation, selection or rank ordering. In many cases the objectives of the assessment beyond the differentiation of individuals is far from clear. In a criterion-referenced assessment the intention is very different: the object is to assess individual attainment or achievement, not to make comparisons (although, of course, the results may be used for any purpose). Once external, explicit criteria have been established, the over-riding concern must be the extent to which an assessment instrument or method does in fact measure what it is designed to measure – an issue of validity. In the NVQ model of assessment, the 'statement of competence' provides an external reference point for assessment. The adequacy of this statement (does it exemplify what is required?) is bound up in the question of standards which need to be constantly reviewed; if we may assume these standards are indeed valid, the essential question of validity centres on comparing the judgements made on the evidence of competence collected against the performance criteria associated with each element, and *not* between different assessors or assessments. In these circumstances, reliability is not an issue.

REFERENCES

CBI (1989) *Towards a Skills Revolution*. London: CBI.

Child, D. (1973, 1981) *Psychology and the Teacher*. London: Holt, Rinehart and Winston.

CITB (1988) *Competence in Construction* pamphlet from Construction Industry Training Board. King's Lynn: CITB.

FEU (1988) *National Vocational Qualifications: Initial Criteria and Guidelines for Staff Development*. London: Further Education Unit.

Jessup, G. (1989i) 'The emerging model of vocational education and training', in J. Burke (ed.) *Competency Based Education and Training*. London: Falmer.

Jessup, G. (1989ii) Unpublished internal note, NCVQ.

Mansfield, B. (1989) 'Competence and standards', in J. Burke (ed.) *Competency Based Education and Training*. London: Falmer.

Mansfield, B. and Mathews, D. (1985) *Job Competence*. FESC: Coombe Lodge.

Mitchell, L. (1989) 'The definition of standards and their assessment', in J. Burke (ed.) *Competency Based Education and Training*. London: Falmer.

Mitchell, L. and Mansfield, B. (1988) *Identifying and Assessing Underpinning Knowledge*, draft TAG note. Wakefield: Barbara Shelborn Developments.

NCVQ (1987) *The National Vocational Framework*. London: National Council for Vocational Qualifications.

NCVQ (1988i) *Access and Equal Opportunities in Relation to National Vocational Qualifications*. London: NCVQ.

NCVQ (1988ii) *The NVQ Criteria and Related Guidance*. London: NCVQ.

NRTC (1988) *New National Qualifications (NVQs) in Retailing*, pamphlet from National Retail Council. London: NRTC.

Stuart, D. (1989) 'The concept of occupational competence', in *Competence and Assessment*, Issue 8, Spring 1989.

Training Agency (1989) *Developing Standards by Reference to Function*, TAG Note 2. Sheffield: Training Agency.

TUC (1988) *A TUC Guide to National Vocational Qualifications*. London: Trades Union Congress.

4.2 | AN ACHIEVEMENT-LED COLLEGE

JENNY SHACKLETON

INTRODUCTION

During the last year the Wirral Metropolitan College has been preparing for the numerous changes facing further education by organising itself behind an approach which it has come to call achievement-led institutional development. Due to the interests stimulated by this activity, this chapter has been prepared setting out its main features.

ACHIEVEMENT-LED INSTITUTIONAL DEVELOPMENT

A RATIONALE FOR A NEW APPROACH

Despite the commitment and hard work which has gone into college and curriculum development during the last two decades, the results are mixed. There is much good practice, but this may still be vulnerable to changes in funding and staff. FE is still the part of the education system which is least attended to from outside, and least thought through from inside. The plethora of smaller initiatives in further education over the last decade have demonstrated that things can be done differently for small numbers of people, and rounded a few hard edges. However, they have so far failed to deliver their key objectives: increased participation; a more informed and qualified public; greater personal, corporate and public investment in, and support for, learners, education and training.

By and large it is still the case that syllabuses and lecturers constitute the conceptual centre and starting point for colleges; and that students are secondary. The student is still normally required to adjust him or herself to an established curriculum. Whatever the individual lecturer's disposition, a college's organisation and structure tends to make this so. Too strong a focus on the teaching role can make the learning process a matter of covering the syllabus; narrow efficiency targets can turn negotiation with students into covert persuasion or pressure.

Nevertheless, the various changes now underway, and the context in which they are occurring, provides a window of opportunity for reviving and developing FE on an exciting new basis. From having operated as a largely once-for-all terminal service within a restrictive array of qualifications, FE now has the possibility of becoming the essential intermediate component of an open education and training system based on unit credit transfer for individuals and institutional honesty.

Education and training is not value-free, and a mature institution is one that is capable of working through and articulating its values and purposes. Given its greater autonomy and lack of shelter in the future, and the requirement to contribute to and win support within its locality, a college has to set out clearly what it stands for and is responsible for. And whatever else it may be there for, a college has as a prime purpose the development of individuals and the certification of achievement. Therefore all of its values and purposes are bound to stem from, and interact with, the learner and his or her achievement.

It is accepted wisdom that everything a college does can be regarded as the curriculum, since everything will have a bearing upon teaching and learning. Achievement-led institutional development takes a similarly holistic view by regarding everything that an institution does as having a bearing upon individual achievement. However, it then goes on to suggest that the curriculum is itself so tied into courses, teachers and teaching, that it should for the present be replaced as the central tenet and starting point by the real thing: individual development and achievement. Thus we arrive at achievement-led institutional development.

Being a strategy, achievement-led institutional development embodies most of what we as a college are thinking and moving towards. As a new mental set it is inherently reforming or corrective in nature. It therefore seeks to dispense with the industrial conservatism which may affect formal and informal relations within a college; with separate and different agreements and conduct for various groups of staff and students; with the teacher as proxy and spokesperson for the learner; and with teaching as proxy for learning. It recognises that a college as an entity may be less mature than its students and staff as individuals, and may as a result limit and condition its and their behaviour, to the detriment of personal development and achievement.

A COLLEGE MISSION

The challenge to be responsive to disconnected external pressures can only be handled effectively by a college which has an understanding of its environment, its purposes and its characteristics. This can be worked through and established by the production of a mission statement, which is by its nature a normative statement.

Personal achievement is the core of this college's mission statement. The document states:

1 Personal achievement is every individual's right, and the College should organise itself behind this right.
2 The establishment of personal achievement is a powerful aid to learning and motivation; it should be seen primarily in these terms, within a framework of standards.
3 The physical, mental and psychological involvement of learners with their own development and achievement, and that of their peers, should be adopted as an organising principle for the College.
4 Personal achievement should constitute the core mission of the College. To encourage the College to be self-critical about its ability and preparedness to support personal growth, positive appraisal measures should be introduced and developed for learning, teaching and learner support.

In keeping with the belief that everything a college does has a bearing upon personal achievement, our mission incorporates five associated and supportive themes:

1 learner involvement and empowerment,
2 institutional appraisal and self-scrutiny,
3 needs analysis and responsiveness,
4 human resource development,
5 reflective management.

These come together in the mission statement to express an organisation with consistent principles and approaches throughout.

CURRICULUM OR LEARNING SUPPORT

The mission statement and the position it takes regarding the curriculum have an inevitable impact upon the next stage of strategic planning, which would normally be curriculum policy and principles. Currently the widely accepted curriculum principles include access, progression, autonomy, relevance, breadth, balance, differentiation, coherence. Their meaning has been defined through their operation in schools and colleges, and their existence is often much more real to lecturers, teachers and managers, than to the students.

For achievement-led institutional development, the curriculum has to be redefined in terms which can be directly recognised by the learner, and engaged with directly by him or her without mediation or interpretation. Ideally the learner should be as self-directed within a college as he or she would expect to be elsewhere, and as entitled to receive a range of developmental and certification services according to his or her needs, aspirations and circumstances. This approach when taken forward into actual services significantly expands and diversifies the college offering, making its developmental and certification services the collective responsibility of the whole college in a direct and thoroughly practical sense.

This means that coherence is a matter for the student to determine, and not the lecturer or institution. Coherence emerges through the relationship formed between the student and the various services provided for him or her, rather than in the mind of the provider. Coherence can occur when the institution responds to individual need and circumstances within a progressive system of credits. It is not necessarily the same as curriculum continuity.

Therefore a new set of 'learning (curriculum) principles' has been developed for the Wirral Metropolitan College, the headings for which are as follows:

recurrence
advocacy
flexibility
empowerment
personal achievement
visibility
learning support.

Once defined further, these give rise to a series of objectives for college development. As an example, 'personal achievement' has been defined by the following objectives:

1 The motivating effect of personal achievement should be optimised.
2 Programmes should recognise and build upon the learner's prior achievements.
3 Under-prepared learners should have the means of acquiring the essential preliminary achievements for entry to courses and programmes without delay, and where possible as part of course entry.
4 Assessment and reviews of progress should be incorporated in all learners' programmes.
5 The learner should have in his or her keeping an action plan showing, among other things, achievement targets and achievements gained.
6 Assessment should at all times be visible to and understood by the learner.
7 Supplementary and reinforcement learning should be available to assist learners.

8 Learners should be able to test their progress and achievements on demand.

From these, required action and targets can be established, and their attainment monitored.

ACTION PLANS AND IMPLEMENTATION

By embracing the concepts, values and principles of achievement-led institutional development, a college has a means of evaluating and responding to the various national and international developments associated with assessment and certification. By standing behind the student rather than any of his or her proxies a college is able to regard courses and classes as one delivery option among many, and to avoid a psychological dependency upon current ways of doing things. Of course this does not mean that changing is straightforward; most of the parts for the new approach have yet to be assembled and organised into a delivery system. Nevertheless, a strongly communicated vision of comprehensive arrangements to generate and optimise personal achievement enables a college to revitalise its talent and resources and step out of its old skin. For most colleges, change cannot wait until the values and principles underlying them have been thoroughly worked through and subscribed to. An interactive and reciprocal process is needed, which involves rapid practical activity alongside and integrated with the refinement of ideas and communication.

In this College during the last year we have tried to move forward by:

1 reviewing the College's structure and as a result significantly reducing its lateral and vertical internal divisions;
2 developing a fuller internal career structure for support staff, who in increasing numbers provide educational services to individual learners;
3 introducing a five-year action plan for the College which also provides the basis for the TVEI extension programme (in the College from 1989);
4 acquiring external funding to reflect, comment and report upon the changes, but not to shoulder the changes, which are being carried through as a priority for the College's substantive budget.

A development team of senior and key colleagues reviews and steers developments, undertakes the most complex activities, sustains networks with other organisations and helps to embed the changes through the staff development programme.

The College five-year action plan gives an impression of the most concrete and practical steps now being planned and undertaken:

1 To create a College which is strikingly ahead of its current image and activity.
2 To plan and implement an admissions service.
3 To plan and introduce a range of student support services including counselling, study centres, careers centres and work placement units.
4 To plan, introduce and evaluate a universally available core curriculum framework which includes continuing experience and achievement in communication, mathematics, information technology and science.
5 To plan and introduce individual learning programmes for all major vocational routes, based upon learning centres.
6 To plan, introduce and evaluate assessment on demand for the core, individual and open learning programmes, and a selection of vocational competences.
7 To design and introduce a summative assessment and certification service which links with the range of current qualifications on offer, and those which will emerge through NCVQ and SEAC.
8 To plan and introduce an exit and transfer service.
9 To develop the College's marketing practices to include family and weekend learning, summer schools, and assessment and placement services for employers.
10 To exchange and disseminate information and experience for the benefit of the College, its users and clients, and the service generally.

This chapter stems from a wish to communicate and share ideas and practice, not because this college is particularly special or advanced, but because everyone benefits from exchanging and networking.

THE LINK WITH NVQs AND EXTERNALLY SPONSORED INITIATIVES

Achievement-led institutional development facilitates the delivery of NVQs by distinguishing assessment and certification from courses and teaching. This does not, however, mean that the process of delivery is ignored. The achievement-led approach is equally intended to facilitate the educational objectives expressed by the National Curriculum. Guiding principles include:

1 the power of assessment as a learning tool;
2 the desirability of introducing a modular curriculum as a means of stretching achievement in all directions;
3 the importance of designing learning and achievement for long-term economic, social and cultural goals.

This means that the College is seeking to introduce NVQs as a new certific-ation system, rather than as a set of qualifications. Therefore we are much more concerned to relate to NCVQ's long-term aims than to the present characteristics of individual awarding bodies and conditional awards. The College has therefore prioritised the following tasks for the next 12 months:

1 the establishment of a collegiate admissions service with standard features in respect of information, diagnostic assessment, advice and record raising;
2 the introduction of NROVA for all full-time and as many part-time students as possible, and incorporating a formative record-system for TVEI purposes;
3 the establishment of individual learning workshops for an educational core comprising communication, mathematics, IT and science and technology;
4 the identification of core requirements and achievements within vocational courses;
5 the organisation of courses into vocational, generic/core, and integrating components;
6 the establishment of College centres for study, support and assessment.

These tasks are being monitored and supported by externally funded projects. The arrival of TVEI Extension within the collège from September 1989 is facilitating these changes in a striking manner.

Index